Cake My Day!

Cake My Day!

eye-popping designs for simple, stunning, fanciful, and funny cakes

Karen Tack and Alan Richardson

A Rux Martin Book
Houghton Mifflin Harcourt
Boston New York 2015

For information about permission to reproduce selections from this book, write
to Permissions, Houghton Mifflin Harcourt Publishing Company,
215 Park Avenue South, New York, New York 10003.

www.hmhco.com

Library of Congress Cataloging-in-Publication Data
Tack, Karen
Cake my day / Karen Tack and Alan Richardson.
pages cm
Includes index.
ISBN 978-0-544-26369-7 (pbk); 978-0-544-26376-5 (ebk)
1. Cake. I. Richardson, Alan, 1956- II. Title.
TX771.T3145 2015
641.86'53—dc23
2014023047

Book design by Elizabeth Van Itallie
Illustrations by Sandy Ploy
Author photos by Jorge Madrigal

Printed in the United States of America
DOW 10 9 8 7 6 5 4 3 2 1
4500519801

Whether a cake artist or just a casual baker, you are our inspiration.

acknowledgments

It has been an amazing journey creating our four decorating books, and this time out, we are especially proud to be A Rux Martin Book. We have been lucky to have worked with Rux on all four books and have a wonderful recipe for working together: We give her confection, and she gives us class.

We feel bad for authors who can't call their agents close friends. Martha Kaplan does both jobs exceedingly well, and we love her for it. After all these years working together, we probably don't need to call her to confer on every minute detail, but we think she might miss the drama.

At times it seems Larry Frascella is the ringmaster of our show. He raises a flag when a creation falls short, applauds us when we hit the mark, and then writes about it three times a week on our blog (you may recognize him as the Cupcake Historian at hellocupcakebook.com). Thanks to Larry, this show is still on the road.

Ellie Ritt has been with us in the kitchen for more years than we would like to mention. She keeps our batter mixed, our candy organized, and our spirits high. (She also reminds us when it's time to stop and eat lunch, and we love that!)

Michaela Sullivan has held our hands through the art direction of four books now. We love her patience with our process and her enthusiasm for our designs (nothing encourages us more than hearing which of our projects she has recently made and how they turned out).

Susan Dickinson, our eagle-eyed copy editor, once claimed that reading our manuscript was like training for the brain. After two books with us, Susan must be a genius. Thanks also to Jessica Sherman for her astute editing and ace typist Jacinta Monniere for turning our scribble into typed words. Everyone needs a Laney Everson on their team. She is the person who dotted every i and crossed every t to make sure we had put all the parts in place . . . bet she's good at the Sunday puzzle!

We are so lucky to have Elizabeth Van Itallie once again bringing style and wit to the design of our book. Many authors live in dread of seeing their pages: We dance around like little kids on Christmas morning anxious to see what Elizabeth gave us.

Sandy Ploy first came to us as the Milwaukee Cupcake Queen. She is now not only a friend but also a collaborator. Sandy's wonderful cake illustrations help us create all those "aha!" moments in the book.

Cakes are bigger than cupcakes in so many ways, including organization. Sue Caruso cracked the whip in the kitchen and made our lives a breeze.

Our interns Manuela Rincon and Sandy Arana are now masters at tinting frosting, baking cakes, rolling candy, testing recipes, and listening to our same bad jokes with a smile every time. We couldn't have had better assistants.

Aunt Hank doesn't know it, but her 1960s-era, mostly knit, polyester fabrics with wild prints lend panache to our photos every time we use them. They were well hidden in the attic; now they are in our prop closet.

Deb Donahue is the other fashionista in our lives, offering us fabrics, plates, cake stands, and a joke whenever we need it.

Erik and Liam Tack have grown up to be our best test audience. If they give a cake the thumbs-up, we know it turned out well.

Joan McCoy is the gift that keeps on giving. She never lets any of our cakes go to waste, taking slices to her friends (along with copies of our books). She told two friends, and they told two friends, and so on. She may just be Mom to us, but for our books, she has been a one-woman marketing machine.

We have to give a big thanks to the publicity, sales, and marketing team at our publisher, Houghton Mifflin Harcourt. Everyone on the team has been incredibly supportive of our books over the years, and without their talent and skills, there wouldn't be a *Cake My Day!* We are your fans.

We also want to recognize our partners in the cake and candy world. The folks at Duncan Hines, SweetWorks, OXO, McCormick, Reynolds, Ziploc, Sara Lee, the National Confectioners Association, and so many more have been incredibly generous with products and support over the years. We appreciate it.

contents

introduction

We have always believed that more is more, and when it comes to decorating, what could be better than having more canvas to fill? That means more candy, more snacks, and more decorating fun.

In our books *Hello, Cupcake!*, *What's New, Cupcake?*, and *Cupcakes, Cookies & Pie, Oh, My!* we use candy and snacks from the grocery aisle to create ingeniously simple cupcakes. And we do it without resorting to fancy decorating tools. In *Cake My Day!* we use the same ideas to create one-of-a-kind cakes. At first glance, you may ask, "Is that really a cake?" But on the second look, you'll say, "Hey, I can do that!"

Not only do cakes have the advantage of scale, but they can be baked in all sorts of containers. A round pan can create a rainbow cake or a chic handbag cake, and with a few simple cuts, you can transform a round cake into a barnyard rooster cake or even a classical guitar cake.

We've turned simple rectangular cakes into a retro toaster and a lawn mower. A loaf cake can become a canister vacuum or a pineapple with Pringle leaves, and a jelly-roll cake changes into a stump cake sure to please any woodsman.

Cakes baked in oven-safe bowls work perfectly for the bellies of our plush-toy collection and serve up a tasty ladybug with doughnut-hole spots. Two-cup oven-safe measuring cups make heads for everything from a zebra and a pink poodle to a piñata.

There's also a chapter with fantastic designs made from store-bought frozen pound cake. Because they are so firm, these delicious cakes are just right for decorating. We take them straight from the foil container and turn them into boots for your favorite fashionista, a rocket ship, a baseball bat, a quartet of hooty owls, and a dance-party cake that will make you want to twist and shout.

Cake My Day! has loads of new decorating techniques. "Smashed sugar" fixes all your decorating flaws. "Flavor painting" delivers vibrant color you can't get from regular store-bought food coloring, and you can use an artist's brush to paint intricate details like wood grain. Because we know it's what's on the outside *and* the inside that counts, we show you how to transform cake-mix batter into a cubist cake, a polka-dot cake, a leopard cake, and more. (Throughout the book, recipes labeled "Surprise Inside!" indicate these treatments.)

Now it's time to rattle those pans and shake those pots, because we've baked so much decorating fun into this book that we're pretty sure your family and friends will shout, "Go ahead, *Cake My Day!*"

10-step program to a better cake

1 PLEASE RELEASE ME

- Everyday wax (or parchment) paper makes an easy-release lining for your baking pan.

- Coat the bottom and sides of the pan with vegetable cooking spray.

- For round pans, fold a sheet of wax paper in half. Fold it in half again crosswise. Next, fold the paper on the diagonal by bringing the two folded edges across to the single folded edge to make a wedge shape. Measuring from the tip of the wedge, make a mark equal to half the width of your pan (4 inches for an 8-inch round pan). Cut the open end of the wedge at the mark in a slight curve. Unfold the wax paper, place it in the bottom of the pan, and smooth it flat with your fingers. The cooking spray will hold it in place.

- For loaf, square, and rectangular pans, allow the wax paper to extend beyond the edges of the pan for ease of removal.

- For baking in bowls or measuring cups, simply coat them with the vegetable cooking spray.

2 EVEN IT OUT

- To bake a cake in an even layer, push the batter all the way to the sides of the pan.

- Using an offset spatula makes it easy to move the batter around the pan.

- Leave the batter slightly higher at the sides than in the center to help prevent doming as the cake bakes. Less doming means you'll need to trim less cake when you level it.

- For an even cake layer, make sure the baking pans and the oven racks are level.

- For stability, place small baking containers on a baking sheet for baking.

3

3 LET'S GET BAKED

- Be sure to preheat the oven; 350°F is optimal for most cakes.

- An oven thermometer will help you determine whether your oven is well calibrated. You can adjust the heat as necessary to bake at the proper temperature.

- Any oven can have hot spots. Get to know your oven and how cakes bake in it.

- Bake the cake in the center of the oven. If you are baking more than one cake at a time, place them side by side on the same rack or on separate racks (not one directly above the other).

- If you are baking more than one cake or if your oven has hot spots, carefully rotate the pans midway through the baking time.

- To test whether the cake is done, insert a toothpick or wooden skewer into the center of the cake. It should come out clean; a few stray crumbs are fine.

- If sticky or gummy batter clings to the toothpick, continue baking for a few more minutes and test again.

- Transfer the pan to a wire rack and cool for 10 minutes. Run a small knife around the edge of the pan and remove the cake, invert it onto the rack, and cool completely.

4 ON THE LEVEL

- To cut down on crumbs, place the cake in the freezer for 15 to 20 minutes before leveling.

- Use toothpicks and a ruler as guides to mark a straight edge on the cake and help keep the knife level.

- To cut the cake, use a serrated knife long enough to go all the way through the cake and a gentle sawing motion.

- For more control, try holding the knife in one position while turning the cake. Using a cake stand or lazy Susan makes this easy.

5 GETTING ON BASE

- If you need to transfer or handle a cake while decorating it, it must be on a firm base.

- If you are not using a cake board, you can cut a piece of cardboard to size.

- Use a template or ruler to measure the outline of the bottom of the cake on the cardboard.

- Use a good pair of scissors to cut the cardboard. You want to support the cake right up to the edge but do not want the base to show.

- Wrap the cardboard in foil.

- Use a big, wide spatula to transfer the cake to the cardboard base. A flimsy spatula is a disaster waiting to happen.

6 A CUT ABOVE

- Use a row of toothpicks as a guide when making a straight cut.

- Find the center of the cake using a ruler. To avoid mistakes, always measure twice before cutting.

- Use a long, serrated knife for long cuts.

- To make an even cut when cutting through the cake, be sure to keep the knife straight.

- Use a gentle sawing motion to prevent tearing or smashing the cake.

- Use a small knife with finer teeth, like a steak knife, to bevel the edges of the cake. Hold the knife at a 45-degree angle while cutting.

7 GENERAL ASSEMBLY

- Turn the bottom side up to make a flat, even surface for frosting and decorating, with fewer crumbs.

- Use frosting as glue to hold cakes together. Spread the frosting as evenly as possible.

- If the cake sags or has an uneven side, use the frosting to fill and level between the layers.

- Lightly press the top of each cake as you go to sandwich the layers together and make sure the frosting adheres to both sides.

- Use plastic drinking straws to stabilize layered cakes. Gently insert the straws through the cake layers, then cut the straws flush with the surface.

- After assembling, place the cake in the freezer to chill for about 30 minutes.

8 GOT CRUMBS?

- The crumb coat is like a primer for paint. It glues down any crumbs so that they don't get in the frosting.

- Fill in any gaps or holes in the cake to make a smooth surface.

- After spreading some frosting on the cake, squeegee it off using an offset spatula, leaving a thin, smooth layer of frosting behind.

- This crumb coat is your chance to smooth over any imperfections and sharpen the edges of the cake.

- After crumb coating, place the cake in the freezer to chill for about 30 minutes.

- If you are not using the cake right away, you can stop at this point. After chilling the cake, wrap it tightly with plastic wrap and freeze it for up to 2 weeks.

9 CHILL OUT

- A chilled cake means cleaner cuts, sharper edges, and a firmer foundation for decorating.

- A chilled cake is easier to transfer and handle. A large cake is more stable if it is kept chilled.

- Frosting stays moist longer when chilled than at room temperature. While decorating, return the cake to the freezer for a few minutes to help keep the frosting soft and sticky.

- Remember, your assembled cake is often higher than its constituent parts. So before you start assembling, make sure you have room in the freezer or refrigerator for the chilling step.

- Many techniques, like flavor painting (see page 45), require well-chilled frosting so that the color stays on the surface of the frosting rather than mixing in.

- Remember that you are placing the cake in the freezer to chill it, not to freeze it to the core. Freezing cake solid and thawing it out several times can break down its structure.

10 ICING ON THE CAKE

- Most projects start with a smooth coat of frosting. For best results, use an offset spatula and a generous amount of frosting. You can always remove excess frosting later.

- To apply the frosting smoothly, push it in one direction in long, overlapping swipes. Clean your spatula between each swipe so that you get clean strokes.

- Make a second pass over the entire cake, using a very light touch, to eliminate any edges or bumps.

- To prevent any remaining frosting from drying, keep it covered with plastic wrap until you are ready to use it.

cosmetic sugary
surface treatments

Depending on how you handle it, adding frosting can give a critter cake a coat of fur or a rocket ship cake its panels of steel. Smashed sugar can lend a lawn mower the look of shiny paint or give a zebra its stripes. Flavor painting can put a vibrant glaze on a pumpkin or detail the knothole in a stump. And adding candies, snacks, or patterns to the batter can make a cake even groovier. The techniques illustrated in this chapter will put a pretty face on your cake and fool your eye in projects throughout the book.

One cake, four surface treatments. *Clockwise from left:* **Forked Frosting, Sprinkle Appliqué, Flavor Painting, and Smashed Sugar.**

ANGORA OMBRÉ CAKE
Surprise Inside!
MAKES 24 SERVINGS

Combining the soft look of angora with the graduated color layers of ombré, this elegant cake is easy to make using regular food coloring and a table fork for the textured frosting. Slice it for a surprise: It has ombré layers on the inside too.

2 recipes Perfect Cake Mix batter (page 289) made with French vanilla cake mix
Neon pink food coloring (McCormick)
2 cans (16 ounces each) plus 1 cup vanilla frosting

1 Preheat the oven to 350°F and prepare three 9-inch round pans (see Please Release Me, page 12). Divide the batter evenly among three bowls (about 3⅓ cups in each). Tint each bowl a different shade of pink by adding 1 drop of the food coloring to one bowl, 3 drops to the second bowl, and 5 drops to the third bowl. Stir the batter in each bowl to mix the color well. (You can add more food coloring to the second and third bowls, as necessary, to create distinct shades of pink.)

2 Spoon each of the colored batters into one of the prepared pans. Spread the batter to the edges and smooth the top (see Even It Out, page 12). Bake until golden brown and a toothpick inserted in the center comes out clean, 35 to 40 minutes.

3 Transfer the cakes to a wire rack and cool for 10 minutes. Invert, remove the pans, and cool completely.

4 Trim the top of each cake level (see On the Level, page 14). Place the darkest-color cake, trimmed side up, on a cardboard cut to fit (see Getting on Base, page 14). Spread ½ cup of the vanilla frosting on top. Place the medium-color cake on top, trimmed side down, and frost the top with ½ cup of the vanilla frosting. Place the lightest-color cake on top, trimmed side down, pressing gently to make the layers even. Spread a thin crumb coating of frosting (see Got Crumbs?, page 16) on the cake, filling any gaps, and smooth. Place the cake in the freezer until set, about 30 minutes.

5 Spoon ½ cup of the remaining vanilla frosting into each of 4 separate bowls. Using the food coloring, tint each bowl of frosting a different shade of pink, from dark to light (the lightest shade needs only a drop or two). Spoon each color into a separate freezer-weight ziplock bag. Press out the excess air and seal the bags.

6 Snip a ¼-inch corner from each bag of frosting. Starting with the darkest frosting, pipe a row of frosting around the base of the cake. Continue adding more rows to reach ¾ inch up the side of the cake. Smooth with an offset spatula. Use a fork to pull the frosting in a downward and outward motion (see Forked Frosting, page 22), in horizontal overlapping rows, to the top of the piped frosting. Repeat the piping and forking around the sides of the cake using the remaining 3 shades of pink frosting, going from darkest to lightest. Spread the remaining vanilla frosting on the top of the cake in an even layer. Add any leftover pink frosting in a 2½-inch circle in the center of the top of the cake. Starting from the outer edge and working in concentric circles, fork the frosting on top of the cake, pulling it out and up.

frosting

Frosting is the simplest way to spruce up a cake. Sometimes all you need to do is spread it smooth. Then there are projects that benefit from a special texture, like furry for a teddy bear or scalloped for the scales on a fish. To master these techniques, spread some frosting on the back of a cake pan, pick a tool, and practice until you get a feeling for how the tool shapes the frosting. You can always scrape the frosting off the pan and reuse it.

FORKED FROSTING

1 Pipe or spread 2 or 3 rows of frosting around the cake, starting at the bottom. Don't pipe more than you can fork in a few minutes or the frosting will start to dry.

2 Use any fork: the closer the tines, the finer the pattern. Starting at the bottom, push the tips of the tines into the frosting and pull down and out, making little spikes.

3 Continue forking the frosting in overlapping rows, working around and up the side of the cake, to create fur texture. Wiping the fork tines clean every so often will produce a prettier pattern.

SPOONED FROSTING

Use any size spoon: small for sharp scoops and large for soft scoops. Push the tip of the spoon into the frosting and pull back and up in overlapping rows to cover the cake. Start at the bottom for the side of the cake and at the outside edge for the top.

TOWELED FROSTING

Use a clean, dry dish towel or paper towel; coarse fabric creates more texture. Give the cake a smooth coat of frosting and let stand until the frosting is dry to the touch, about 30 minutes. Fold the towel and, working with a flat side, press the towel lightly into the frosting and pull it straight off without smearing the frosting. Use light pats of the towel to smooth out any bumps or ridges. If the towel starts to stick, move on to a new area of frosting and let the sticky part dry a bit before toweling.

CLASSIC SWIRLED FROSTING

Use an offset spatula or the back of a spoon. Start by covering the cake with a generous layer of frosting. Then hold the spatula at an angle and press the tip into the frosting. Push it slightly forward and make an S-shape. (The S-shape can be small or large, as desired.) Continue making overlapping S-shapes to cover the entire cake. If there is not enough frosting to push into S-shapes, add more to the cake. If frosting builds up on the spatula, clean it before making a new swirl. After you have covered the cake with swirls, you can alter them to your liking using the tip of the tool. (Work quickly. When the frosting begins to firm up, stop working the frosting, or it will crack.)

ARGYLE CAKE

MAKES 12 SERVINGS

We think argyle is as attractive on cake as it is on socks, and it's as easy as press and play to make. Our Highland design uses shades of green and blue candy for the diamonds and chocolate sticks for the diagonal overlay.

1 recipe Perfect Cake Mix (page 289) made with French vanilla cake mix, baked in a 9-x-13-inch pan for 25 to 30 minutes
1 can (16 ounces) vanilla frosting
½ cup each blue, light blue, neon green, and pearlized green round candy-coated chocolates (Sixlets)
36–40 chocolate-covered mint sticks (Ovation)
35 white pearlized gumballs (SweetWorks)

1 Trim the top of the cake level (see On the Level, page 14). Place the cake, bottom side up, on a cardboard cut to fit (see Getting on Base, page 14) or a serving platter. Spread a thin crumb coating of vanilla frosting (see Got Crumbs?, page 16) on the cake and smooth. Place the cake in the freezer until set, about 30 minutes.

2 Spoon 2 tablespoons of the vanilla frosting into a freezer-weight ziplock bag. Press out the excess air and seal the bag. Spread the remaining vanilla frosting on the chilled cake in an even layer and smooth.

3 Place the cake with a short side facing you. Measure the sides of the cake and place a toothpick at the center of each side. To mark the center of the cake, score a line across the cake from left to right between the toothpicks and another line from top to bottom between the 2 remaining toothpicks. Place 4 same-color chocolate candies in a row at the center of the horizontal cross line, 2 to the left of the vertical line and 2 to the right. Add 3 same-color candies centered above the 4, pressing them against the center row. Add 2 same-color candies above the 3 candies. Finish with 1 same-color candy above the 2. Repeat below the center row to make the diamond in the center of the cake. Add mint sticks to each side of the diamond, trimming to fit and pressing the candies together to keep the diamond tight. Continue adding diamonds in alternating colors, working your way out from the center to the edges (use the photo as a guide for the colors).

4 Snip a small (⅛-inch) corner from the bag with the vanilla frosting. Pipe a dot of frosting on the mint sticks at each point of the diamonds and attach a white gumball.

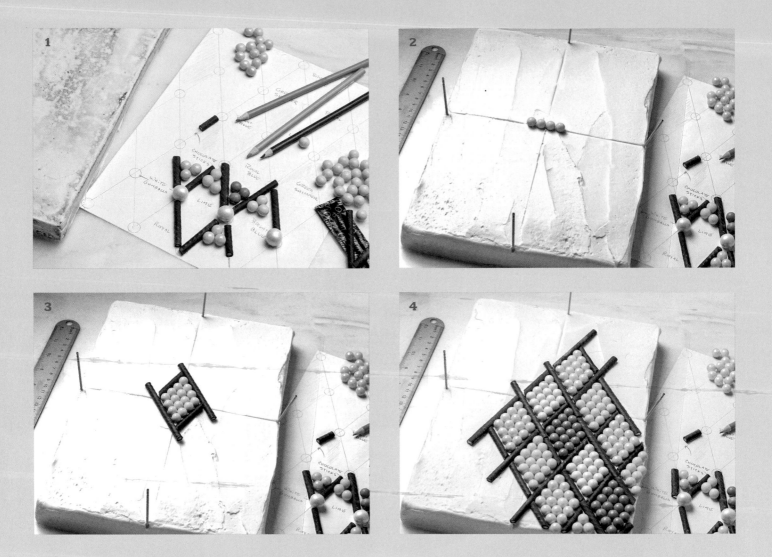

press and play

This technique is as easy as it sounds. Simply press the candy into the frosting. Not every pattern is as ambitious as the Argyle Cake, but no matter the blueprint, these strategies will help you get the most out of your candy designs.

1 Start with a drawing of the design on paper that is the same size as the top of the cake. It's a good idea to plan colors, shapes, and sizes on paper before committing them to the frosting.

2 Cakes are irregular by nature, so it helps to measure and mark the center before starting. Score a line across the center from side to side and one from top to bottom. Use a ruler to make sure the placement is evenly spaced. Because the edges of the cake may be uneven, always start decorating at the center.

3 For the argyle design, make a diamond pattern in the center using one color of the candies (use the cross marks for alignment). Place chocolate sticks around the diamond, trimming them to fit. Be sure to press the candies together to keep the design tight.

4 Add more diamonds to the left and right, working your way to the edges of the cake. Use the cross marks and a ruler from time to time to keep the pattern aligned. After forming each diamond, press the sides to keep the candies tight.

Argyle variation on a chocolate layer cake.

PINWHEEL CAKE
Surprise Inside!
MAKES 24 SERVINGS

This carousel of color is made from an appliqué of sprinkles and candy decors. Worried about staying inside the lines? Wax paper and a small spoon simplify the process.

2 recipes Perfect Cake Mix batter (page 289) made
    with French vanilla cake mix
1 cup rainbow jimmies
2 cans (16 ounces each) plus 1 cup vanilla frosting
½ cup each yellow, red, orange, pink, purple, green,
    blue, and chocolate sprinkles, nonpareils, decors,
    or jimmies (see Sources, page 294)
1 cup white nonpareils (Wilton)
1 cup white jimmies (Wilton)
1 tablespoon chocolate frosting
1 plain doughnut hole (Munchkins)

1 Preheat the oven to 350°F and prepare four 9-inch round pans (see Please Release Me, page 12). Add the rainbow jimmies to the batter and stir well. Divide the batter evenly among the 4 prepared pans. Spread the batter to the edges and smooth the top (see Even It Out, page 12). Bake until golden brown and a toothpick inserted in the center comes out clean, 22 to 25 minutes. Transfer the cakes to a wire rack and cool for 10 minutes. Invert, remove the pans, and cool completely.

2 Trim the top of each cake level (see On the Level, page 14). Place one cake, trimmed side up, on a cardboard cut to fit (see Getting on Base, page 14). Spread ½ cup of the vanilla frosting on top of the cake. Place a second cake on top, trimmed side down, pressing gently on the cake to level. Spread ½ cup of the frosting on top. Repeat the process with a third cake, trimmed side up.

Place the last cake, trimmed side down, on top. Spread a thin crumb coating of frosting (see Got Crumbs?, page 16) on the cake, filling any gaps, and smooth. Place the cake in the freezer until set, about 30 minutes.

3 Cut a 9-inch circle of wax paper. Fold the circle in half, then in half again into quarters. Now fold in half two more times by bringing the straight edges together. Unfold the wax paper and you have 16 equal-size wedges. Using the fold marks as a guide, cut out the wedges. From a separate sheet of wax paper, cut 16 strips, about 1¾ inches x 5 inches.

4 Place the chilled cake on a work surface. Spread the remaining vanilla frosting on the cake in an even layer and smooth. Use a ruler to find the center of the cake and mark with a toothpick. Arrange the wax-paper wedges in a round on top of the cake, pointing toward the center. Press the strips of wax paper around the sides of the cake vertically, lining up each strip with a wedge on top. Press the wax-paper pieces into the frosting to remove any air bubbles. Return the cake to the freezer for 15 minutes to chill.

5 Work with one color of sprinkles at a time (leaving the white sprinkles for last). Peel 1 wax-paper wedge and the side strip below it from the chilled cake. Using a small spoon, add sprinkles to the frosting on the exposed top and side of the cake, gently pressing to secure, to cover completely (see Sprinkle Appliqué, page 31). Brush any excess sprinkles from the cake. Repeat the process on alternate wedges and side strips, using a different color on each set. Take care not to mix the colors in the wedges; remove any stray sprinkles with tweezers. Return the cake to the freezer for 15 minutes to chill before adding the white sprinkles.

6 Remove the remaining wax-paper wedges and side strips and carefully add the white sprinkles (alternating strips of jimmies and non-pareils) on the exposed frosted cake, pressing to secure. Remove any stray sprinkles with tweezers.

7 Place the remaining chocolate sprinkles in a small bowl. Spread the chocolate frosting over the doughnut hole and smooth. Roll the frosted doughnut hole in the sprinkles to cover completely. Place the doughnut hole in the center on top of the cake.

sprinkle appliqué

Candy applied to frosting in a surface pattern can look like a beaded appliqué. And while the results may appear daunting, all you need is a wax-paper mask and a small spoon. Appliqué patterns can be as simple as stars and stripes or as complex as the Mona Lisa in sprinkles. Any small coating can be used, such as jimmies, decors, crushed candy, chopped nuts, sugar, and coconut.

1 Use a ruler to find the center of the cake and mark with a toothpick. Place the wax-paper masks on the cake and press them into the frosting to seal the edges and work out any air bubbles. (For the Pinwheel Cake, you need 16 wedges plus 16 rectangles of wax paper.)

2 Gently remove the mask from the first section to be appliquéd. (For the Pinwheel Cake, remove both the top wedge and the rectangle on the side directly below it.)

3 Using a small spoon, add sprinkles to the exposed frosting on top. Press gently with your fingers to secure the sprinkles in the frosting.

4 Use the spoon and your fingers to apply sprinkles to the side of the cake. A skewer or tweezers are useful for repositioning any stray sprinkles.

5 Remove excess sprinkles from the surrounding masked areas, and brush the surface with a dry pastry brush to remove loose sprinkles.

6 Continue removing the masks one at a time and applying the sprinkles called for in the recipe.

LOVE AND PEACE CAKES

MAKES 12 SERVINGS

Feeling groovy? Then start smashing sugar. While it sounds a bit aggressive, smashed sugar actually creates a very mellow look.

For each cake

Love Cake: 1 recipe Perfect Cake Mix (page 289)
    made with French vanilla cake mix, baked in two
    8-inch square pans for 25 to 30 minutes

or

Peace Cake: 1 recipe Perfect Cake Mix (page 289)
    made with devil's food cake mix, baked in two
    8-inch round pans for 25 to 30 minutes
1 can (16 ounces) plus ½ cup vanilla frosting
Yellow, green, red, neon pink, and neon blue food
    coloring (McCormick)
1 can (16 ounces) dark chocolate frosting
2 cups coarse white decorating sugar (Wilton)
¾ cup assorted round candy-coated chocolates
    (Sixlets; optional)

1 Spoon ¼ cup of the vanilla frosting into each of 4 small bowls for the Love Cake or 5 small bowls for the Peace Cake. Tint each bowl a different color with the food coloring: neon pink, neon blue, bright green (mixing yellow and green), and orange (mixing yellow and red), plus yellow for the Peace Cake. Spoon each color into a separate freezer-weight ziplock bag. Spoon ½ cup untinted vanilla frosting into a freezer-weight ziplock bag. Spoon ½ cup dark chocolate frosting into a freezer-weight ziplock bag. Press out the excess air and seal the bags.

2 Trim the top of each cake level (see On the Level, page 14). Place 1 cake layer, trimmed side up, on a cardboard cut to fit (see Getting on Base, page 14). Spread some of the remaining chocolate frosting on top of the cake. Place the second cake layer, trimmed side down, on top, pressing to level. Spread a thin crumb coating of the remaining chocolate frosting (see Got Crumbs?, page 16) on the sides of the cake, filling any gaps, and smooth. Spread a thin crumb coating of the remaining vanilla frosting on top of the cake and smooth. Place the cake in the freezer until set, about 30 minutes.

3 Line a baking sheet with wax paper. Place the decorating sugar in a large bowl. Place the chilled cake on the cookie sheet. Spread the sides of the cake with the remaining chocolate frosting and smooth. Gently press handfuls of the sugar onto the sides of the frosted cake to cover completely (see Smashed Sugar, page 37). Brush

the excess sugar back into the bowl (if desired, leave the sides unsugared). Using a large spatula, transfer the cake on its cardboard base to a serving platter.

4 For the Love Cake, make a copy of the template and enlarge it to 200 percent to fit the top of your cake. Mark the template design in the frosting using a toothpick to score the outline of the letters. Snip a small (⅛-inch) corner from the bag of chocolate frosting. Pipe a thin line around the edge of the top of the cake. Then pipe a thin line from the center of the top edge to the bottom and another line from the center of the left edge to the right, dividing the top into quarters. Now pipe the outline of the letters that are scored in the frosting. Fill in each letter with one of the 4 tinted frostings.

5 For the Peace Cake, use a toothpick to score a circle in the frosting 1 inch in from the edge of the cake to make a border. Score a 1-inch-wide strip down the center, top to bottom. Then score a 1-inch-wide strip from the center to the 4 o'clock position and another to the 8 o'clock position to create the peace sign. Snip a small (⅛-inch) corner from each bag of frosting. Using the chocolate frosting, pipe around the edge of the cake. Then pipe the scored outline of the peace sign on top of the cake. Fill in the peace sign with irregular spots of the 5 tinted frostings, alternating the colors.

6 For either cake, use the bag of untinted vanilla frosting to pipe frosting in the white areas of the design. Sprinkle the top of the cake with a generous layer of the remaining sugar. Using an offset spatula, gently press the sugar into the frosting to cover completely and level. Use a clean pastry brush to remove the excess sugar from the top of cake and the serving platter (any damaged spots on the cake can be repaired with some frosting and sugared again, if necessary).

7 Optional: Pipe a line of chocolate frosting around the base of the cake and attach the candy-coated chocolates.

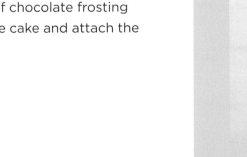

smashed sugar

We are big fans of anything that can hide mistakes and make our cakes look stunning. Smashed sugar is a new favorite because the technique smooths away imperfections, leaving behind a soft, impressionistic design, almost like a watercolor.

1 Give the cake a smooth coating of frosting. Using a ziplock bag, pipe an outline around each area of the design. (For the Love Cake, use the template.)

2 Fill in the outlines with piped tinted frosting. (It could be the same color as the outline or a contrasting color, as we've done.) No need to make it smooth and perfect; the sugar smash will do that.

3 Sprinkle on enough coarse white decorating sugar to cover the design completely. (Do not leave any frosting exposed.)

4 Lightly press the decorating sugar into the frosting using an offset spatula or your fingertips (take care not to smear or press too hard). If any frosting becomes uncovered, add more sugar to cover and continue pressing.

5 Use a dry pastry brush to gently brush the loose sugar from the top of the cake and the serving platter, exposing the layer of sugar that has adhered to the frosting.

6 After brushing, use the offset spatula again to lightly press the entire surface to smooth. (As the sugar is pressed farther into the frosting, the colors will brighten.)

POLYNESIAN FLOWER CAKE

MAKES 12 SERVINGS

Some flowers need regular watering. Ours require flooding! Pipe the outline of a flower on a flat cake, then flood the shape with melted frosting. Gravity (and a little help from a small craft brush) will do the rest.

1 recipe Perfect Cake Mix (page 289) made with yellow cake mix, baked in a 9-x-13-inch pan for 25 to 30 minutes

2 cans (16 ounces each) vanilla frosting

Green, yellow, red, neon blue, neon pink, and neon purple food coloring (McCormick)

3 tablespoons each orange, pink, blue, purple, and yellow plus 1 tablespoon green pearl candies (SweetWorks)

28 yellow banana-shaped hard candies (Runts)

1 cup light green round candy-coated chocolates (Sixlets)

1 Trim the top of the cake level (see On the Level, page 14). Place the cake, trimmed side down, on a cardboard cut to fit (see Getting on Base, page 14). Spread a thin crumb coating of the vanilla frosting (see Got Crumbs?, page 16) on the cake and smooth. Place the cake in the freezer until set, about 30 minutes.

2 Spoon ¼ cup of the vanilla frosting into each of 5 separate small bowls. Tint each frosting a different color with the food coloring: yellow, neon pink, neon blue, neon purple, and orange (mixing red and yellow). Spoon each color of frosting into a separate freezer-weight ziplock bag. Press out the excess air and seal the bags. Tint the remain-

ing vanilla frosting bright green (mixing green and yellow). Spoon ¼ cup of the bright green frosting into a freezer-weight ziplock bag. Press out the excess air and seal the bag.

3 Transfer the chilled cake to a serving platter. Spread the sides and top of the cake with the remaining bright green frosting and smooth, allowing some of the frosting from the sides to come up over the edge.

4 Make a copy of the flower template below and enlarge to 200 percent. Using the template, score overlapping flowers in the frosting with a toothpick, leaving a few areas open to see the green background.

5 Snip a small (⅛-inch) corner from each bag of frosting. Pipe the outline of the flowers, including where they meet the cake edge, in the desired colors. Pipe a green outline around the edge of the cake except where the flower outlines already mark the edge. The piping forms the floodgates to contain the flooding (see page 41).

6 Working with one color of frosting at a time, put the frosting bag in a bowl, keeping the cut tip up to prevent leaking, and microwave, massaging the bag every few seconds, until smooth, about 5 seconds. Carefully squeeze some of the melted frosting inside the same-color outlined areas, using a small craft brush or a toothpick to spread the frosting to fill the outline. Repeat with the remaining frosting colors.

7 Use tweezers to place the same-color pearl candies around the edge of each flower. Place 3 green pearl candies in the center of each flower and arrange 3 to 5 banana-shaped candies in a cluster around them.

8 Press the green candy-coated chocolates around the base of the cake.

pouring and flooding

Poured frosting and flooded frosting are the lazy decorator's answer to creating a flawless coating. Canned frosting is easy to melt, and when poured on cake, it coats smoothly and dries to a silky finish. Add color and pattern to the design by piping an outline with frosting and then flooding the piped area with melted frosting. And, unlike some fancy cake coatings, it tastes great.

FOR A MELTED COATING

1 Place the frosting in a microwavable measuring cup. Microwave the frosting, stopping to stir from the sides and bottom every 5 seconds, until it is evenly melted and has the texture of lightly whipped cream, 10 to 45 seconds total, depending on the amount in the cup; follow the timing in each recipe. Take care not to make it too thin. It is ready to use when a drizzle from a spoon piles up only slightly and then incorporates right back into the frosting in the cup.

2 Place the chilled cake on a wire rack with wax paper underneath. Pour the melted frosting over the cake to cover. Use a spoon to help coat odd shapes and fill in any gaps.

FOR A FLOODED DESIGN

3 Frost the chilled cake and smooth. Using a toothpick, score an outline in the frosting (use a template or draw freehand). Snip a small (⅛-inch) corner from the freezer-weight ziplock bag of frosting called for in the recipe. Pipe outlines (floodgates) around the areas to be flooded.

4 Place the bag of frosting in a microwavable bowl, keeping the cut corner upright to avoid leaking. Melt the frosting as directed in the recipe. Hold the tip of the bag over the area to be flooded and fill the area with melted frosting (take care not to breach the floodgates).

5 Use a small craft brush or a toothpick to push the frosting into the small areas and up to the edges of the piped outline.

6 Continue adding flowers in different colors of melted frosting.

PUMPKIN CAKE
Surprise Inside!
MAKES 24 SERVINGS

Adding red and yellow food coloring and cocoa powder to vodka or vanilla extract creates richly colored glazes that can be layered and detailed to look just like a pumpkin.

2 recipes Perfect Cake Mix (page 289) made with devil's food cake mix, baked in three 8-inch round pans for 30 to 35 minutes
3 cans (16 ounces each) plus 1 cup vanilla frosting
3 tablespoons vodka or vanilla extract
Red and yellow food coloring (McCormick)
1 teaspoon unsweetened cocoa powder
2 mini wafer cones (Joy Kids Cones)

1 Line a cookie sheet with wax paper. Trim the top of 2 of the cakes level (see On the Level, page 14). Transfer all 3 cakes to the cookie sheet and place in the freezer for 30 minutes to chill.

2 Place 1 trimmed cake on a work surface. Insert 2 sets of toothpicks around the side of the cake to mark the cake into 3 equal layers. Using the toothpicks as a guide, cut the cake horizontally into 3 layers with a long serrated knife. Repeat with the other trimmed cake.

3 Place the untrimmed cake on the work surface. Starting from the bottom of the cake, use toothpicks to mark 2 layers the same thickness as the other cut layers (the top layer will be thicker and slightly domed). Cut the layers with the serrated knife, using the toothpicks as a guide. Reserve the domed cake for the top of the pumpkin.

4 Transfer 1 of the cake layers to a cardboard cut to fit (see Getting on Base, page 14). Spread ⅓ cup of the vanilla frosting on top of the cake and smooth. Place another layer on top, pressing on the cake to level, and spread ⅓ cup of the vanilla frosting on top. Repeat with the remaining 6 layers of the same thickness. Place the thicker layer, domed side up, on top to make 9 layers. Do not frost the dome. Place the cake in the freezer until set, about 30 minutes.

5 Place the chilled cake on the work surface. To create the pumpkin shape, use a cookie cutter or a toothpick to score a 2½-inch circle in the center of the top of the cake. Using a small knife or fork, scoop out cake from inside the marked

STEP 5

circle to create a 2½-inch-deep cone shape. Trim 2 inches from both the top and the bottom edges of the cake to round them (see photo, page 42). Spread a thin crumb coating of vanilla frosting (see Got Crumbs?, page 16) on the top and sides of the cake, filling any gaps, and smooth. Return the cake to the freezer to chill, about 15 minutes.

6 Spread the remaining vanilla frosting over the chilled cake in vertical strokes, and smooth. To create the pumpkin ribs, press a wooden skewer against the side of the cake, vertically, making indentations every 1½ inches. Return the cake to the freezer to set, about 30 minutes.

7 Tint 2 tablespoons plus 1 teaspoon of the vodka orange with the red and yellow food coloring. Using a small pastry brush and vertical strokes, paint the entire cake with a coat of the orange vodka mixture (see Flavor Painting, opposite page), smoothing the rib indentations and any frosting flaws as you paint. Darken the remaining orange vodka mixture with additional red food coloring and paint darker strokes, vertically, to create a variegated, glazed skin.

8 Dissolve the cocoa powder in the remaining 2 teaspoons vodka. Use a small craft brush dipped in the cocoa vodka mixture to paint the indentations for the ribs and to shade a few areas on the skin. Dip the tip of a firm pastry brush into the cocoa vodka mixture, hold it near the pumpkin, and run a wooden skewer or fork over the bristles to lightly spritz the cake, dipping again when necessary, to apply a pattern of brown spots.

9 For the stem, brush the sides of the wafer cones with the remaining cocoa vodka mixture. Stack the cones on top of each other. Arrange the stem, open end down, in the center of the cake.

flavor painting

How would Michelangelo decorate a cake? With a paintbrush, of course! A small amount of alcohol is the painting medium, and when it evaporates, it leaves behind a rich glaze of color. Use an alcohol-based extract, such as vanilla or almond, instead, and it becomes flavor painting.

1 Place about 1 tablespoon vodka (or alcohol-based extract) in a small bowl. Add food coloring and stir to blend. More coloring equals richer color.

2 Working on a cake with a smooth coating of well-chilled frosting, use a pastry brush to add a glaze of color. Brush the paint in long, smooth, overlapping strokes.

3 To create an even richer glaze, add more food coloring to the mixture to make it darker and paint a second coat. Smooth out any bumps or ridges in the frosting as you paint. If the frosting becomes too soft, return the cake to the freezer for a few minutes before continuing.

4 Dissolve 1 teaspoon unsweetened cocoa powder in 2 teaspoons vodka. Use a small craft brush to add detailing between the ribs and on the skin of the pumpkin.

5 Using a small amount of the orange vodka mixture, lightly brush the entire surface to blend the cocoa details with the glaze.

6 Dip a pastry brush in the cocoa vodka mixture and use a skewer or a chopstick to add splatter marks to the glaze.

POLKA-DOT CAKE
Surprise Inside!
MAKES 12 SERVINGS

*Don't worry if you're seeing spots on your cake—
they're just doughnut holes! On the outside,
they form a striking pattern, and baked into
the chocolate batter, they make the easiest
polka-dot cake ever.*

1 recipe Perfect Cake Mix batter (page 289) made
   with devil's food cake mix
15 plain doughnut holes (Munchkins)
3 each cinnamon-sugar, powdered sugar, and
   chocolate doughnut holes (Munchkins)
1 can (16 ounces) chocolate frosting

1 Preheat the oven to 350°F and prepare an
8-inch springform pan (see Please Release
Me, page 12). Spoon one third of the batter into
the bottom of the prepared pan and smooth.
Press 7 of the plain doughnut holes into the batter. Spoon half of the remaining batter over the
doughnut holes to cover and smooth. Press 5 more
plain doughnut holes into the batter (reserve the
remaining 3 plain doughnut holes for decoration).
Spoon the remaining batter on top, making sure
that the doughnut holes are completely covered,
and smooth.

2 Bake until the cake is firm and a toothpick
inserted in the center comes out clean, 45 to
50 minutes. Transfer the cake to a wire rack and
cool for 10 minutes. Invert, remove the pan, and
cool completely.

3 Cut all the remaining doughnut holes in half to
make 24 semicircles.

4 Transfer the cooled cake to a serving platter. Spread the chocolate frosting on the
sides and top of the cake and make soft swirls
with an offset spatula or the back of a spoon (see
Spooned Frosting, page 23). Press the halved
doughnut holes, cut side down, into the frosting in
an evenly spaced pattern over the top and sides of
the cake.

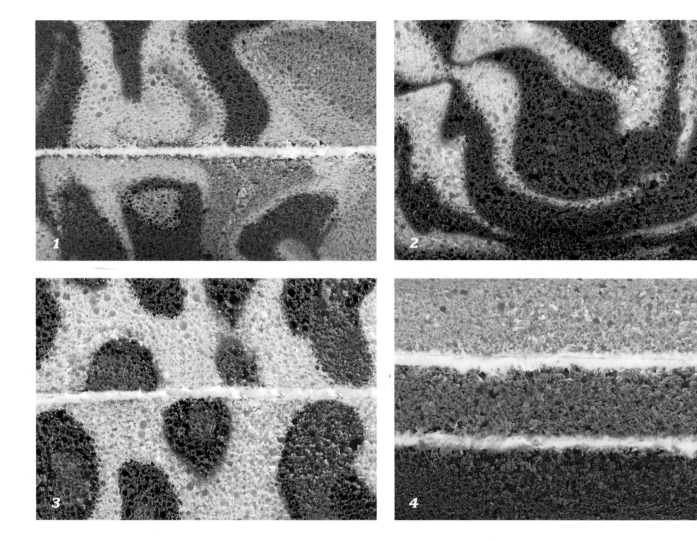

surprise inside!

Decorating a cake on the inside is a bit like gilding the lily, but we love a dessert that says "Wow!" twice.

1 DOLLOPING BATTER

Different-color batters can be added to the baking pan in small dollops. This gives you some control over color and pattern, but the really fun part is that every time you make a dollop cake, the pattern is different. You never know exactly what you're going to get until you slice the cake. For the Rainbow Cake (page 83), we use 5 colors of batter, dolloped in alternating colors, in 2 layers.

2 LAYERING BATTER

To make a striped cake, add the batter to the pan in thin layers, alternating the colors. Gently spread each layer to the edges without stirring the batter. When baked, the layers in this cake fold and twist into fun, striped patterns. Alternating layers of chocolate and French vanilla batter are used to create the stripes for our Zebra Cake (page 192).

3 PIPING DESIGNS

Patterns can be added to batter when it is in the pan. Add a base-color batter to your baking pan, then use a freezer-weight ziplock bag filled with batter in a contrasting color to pipe a pattern. To get the pattern

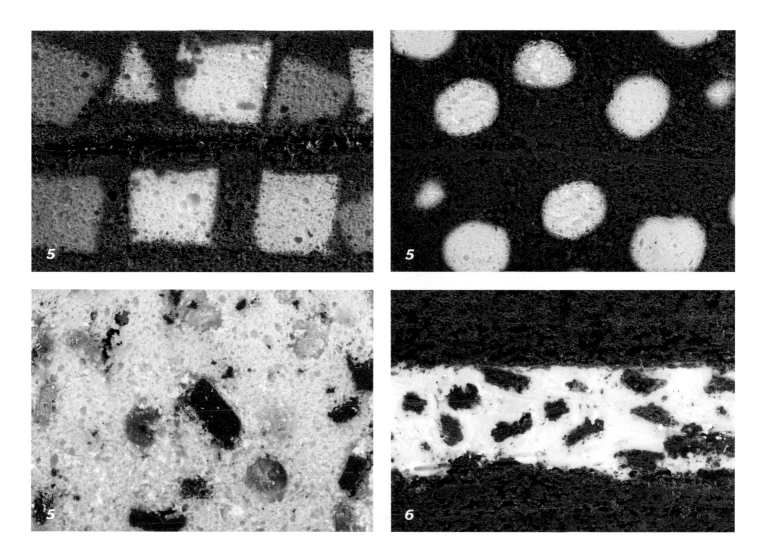

deeper into the cake, push the tip of the piping bag into the batter and inject the pattern. For a Leopard-Skin Purse Cake (page 78), use a yellow-batter base and pipe with chocolate-batter circles in the batter with orange-batter dots at the center.

4 TINTING LAYERS

Batter can be divided and each portion tinted. For clean colors, use a white cake mix, like French vanilla. Colors darken a bit when baked, so make the batter slightly lighter than your desired final color. For an elegant look, tint each layer a different color, like the three pinks we used for our Angora Ombré Cake (page 21).

5 ADDING INGREDIENTS

Tossing candy and snacks into batter adds texture and color. Keep in mind that sugary or whipped candies like jelly beans and marshmallows melt, so don't overdo it. Tinted cake cubes are used inside our "Pop" Cake (page 102). Doughnut holes are added to our Polka-Dot Cake (47), and candy is in our Vacuum Cleaner Cake (page 133).

6 FILLING THE CAKE

Add a surprise between the cake layers. Chunks of Oreos added to the ice-cream layer of the Monstrous Unbaked Alaska (page 87) make the inside as much fun as the outside.

any way you slice it

round cake pans

Circular baking pans may be ordinary, but they are a cut above when it comes to cakes. That's because all it takes is a simple slice or two to create a multitude of shapes. Cut a round cake in half crosswise to form an arc for a rainbow, trim one into shapes for a barnyard full of critters, or sandwich two together to make a goofy goldfish with two quick cuts. Any way you slice it, round cake is fun.

Goat (page 58) made with a combination of vanilla and black-tinted frosting.

BARNYARD MASTER CAKE

Two cake rounds plus five simple cuts equals a barnyard full of animals. We use the same shapes, but move them around to create new creatures. Below are five in our menagerie, but surely there are more in this herd, hidden in the pieces.

1 recipe Perfect Cake Mix (page 289) made with cake mix specified in recipe, 2 cups batter baked in an 8-inch round pan for 23 to 28 minutes and 3 cups batter baked in a 9-inch round pan for 23 to 29 minutes

½ cup vanilla frosting

1 Line a cookie sheet with wax paper. Place the 8-inch cake on a work surface. Cutting on an angle, remove a 1½-inch-thick slice from one edge of the cake. Remove another 1½-inch-thick slice from the other side of the cake, leaving 1½ inches at the narrow end of the cake (see illustration, top right). Remove a 1½-inch-thick slice from the narrow end of the cake for the head support. Cut the 2 long pieces in half crosswise. Transfer the 6 pieces to the cookie sheet and spread a thin crumb coating of frosting (see Got Crumbs?, page 16) over them.

2 Place the 9-inch cake on a cardboard cut to fit. Transfer the cake and the coated pieces to the freezer to chill, about 30 minutes.

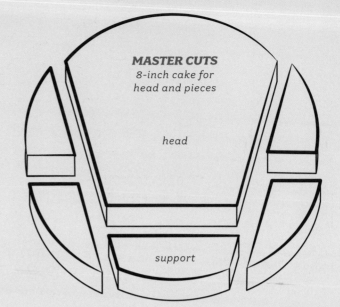

MASTER CUTS
8-inch cake for head and pieces

head

support

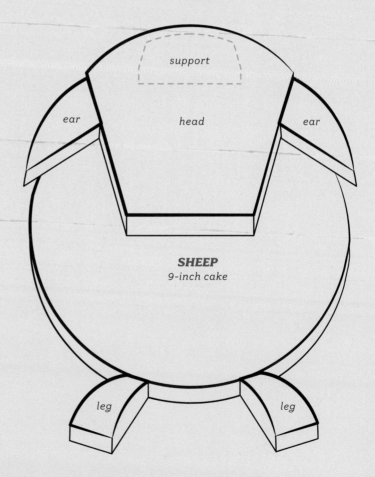

support

ear

head

ear

SHEEP
9-inch cake

leg

leg

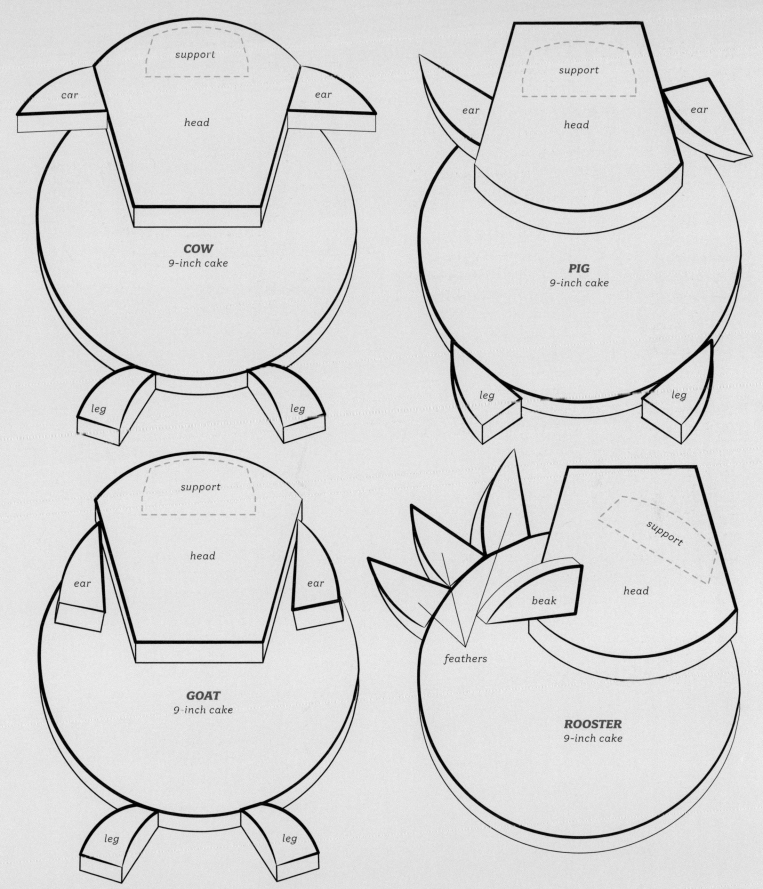

COW
9-inch cake

support

ear

head

ear

leg

leg

PIG
9-inch cake

support

ear

head

ear

leg

leg

GOAT
9-inch cake

support

head

ear

ear

leg

leg

ROOSTER
9-inch cake

support

head

beak

feathers

SHEEP CAKE

MAKES 12 SERVINGS

1 Barnyard Master Cake (page 52) made with
  chocolate cake mix
1 can (16 ounces) vanilla frosting
1 can (16 ounces) dark chocolate frosting
5 cups kettle corn (Smartfood)
2 chocolate flat candy wafers (Necco)
2 mini chocolate-covered mints (Junior Mints)
1 tube (4.25 ounces) black decorating icing
  (Cake Mate)
1 pink fruit chew (Laffy Taffy, Starburst)
2 creme-filled chocolate sandwich cookies (Oreos)

1 Spoon ¼ cup of the vanilla frosting into a freezer-weight ziplock bag. Press out the excess air and seal the bag.

2 Line a cookie sheet with wax paper. Arrange the chilled cut cake pieces on it, using the sheep diagram as a guide (see illustration, page 52). Spread the chocolate frosting over the top and sides of the cake pieces and smooth. Return the pieces to the freezer until ready to assemble.

3 Place the chilled 9-inch cake on a serving platter. Spread the remaining vanilla frosting on the cake to cover. Place the head-support piece on the platter at one edge of the cake.

4 For the legs, trim 1 inch from the pointed end of 2 of the 4 tapered cake pieces. Place the legs on the opposite side of the cake from the head support, rounded side up (see illustration), with the short end flush with the cake. Secure with some chocolate frosting, if necessary. Use a spatula to place the head piece on the cake, wide end at the top and resting on the support. Add the ear pieces on either side of the head, rounded side up, with the wide end flush with the cake, securing with chocolate frosting, if necessary (see illustration).

5 Snip a small (⅛-inch) corner from the bag with the vanilla frosting. Press the kettle corn into the vanilla-frosted cake body to cover completely and add a cluster of kettle corn on top of the sheep's head, using the bag of vanilla frosting to secure, as necessary.

6 Place the chocolate wafers for the eyes. Attach the chocolate mints as the pupils with a dot of vanilla frosting. Pipe a small white highlight on each eye. Using the black decorating icing, pipe a semicircle and a small vertical line to make the nose. For the tongue, flatten the pink fruit chew and shape it into a small teardrop. Press a knife into the center lengthwise to create a crease. Insert the pointed end of the tongue into the bottom side of the head, just below the nose. Attach a chocolate sandwich cookie to the bottom of each leg with a dot of black icing.

COW CAKE

MAKES 12 SERVINGS

1 Barnyard Master Cake (page 52) made with
  chocolate cake mix
1 can (16 ounces) vanilla frosting
6 creme-filled chocolate sandwich cookies (Oreos)
1 anisette toast (Stella D'oro)
6 pink fruit chews (Laffy Taffy, Starburst)
2 pink jelly beans
4 pink licorice pastels (Jelly Belly)
2 white flat candy wafers (Necco)
2 mini chocolate-covered mints (Junior Mints)
1 tube (4.25 ounces) black decorating icing
  (Cake Mate)
2 red licorice laces (Twizzlers Pull 'n' Peel)
1 red candy-coated chocolate (M&M's)
1 large yellow gumdrop (Farley's)

1 Spoon ¼ cup of the vanilla frosting into a freezer-weight ziplock bag. Press out the excess air and seal the bag.

2 Spread some vanilla frosting over the 6 cake pieces and smooth. Return the pieces to the freezer until ready to assemble.

3 For the spots, place 4 of the chocolate sandwich cookies in a freezer-weight ziplock bag; do not seal the bag. Use a rolling pin to crush the cookies in the bag until finely ground.

4 For the horns, use a small serrated knife to cut 2 inches from each end of the anisette toast; discard the center.

5 For the nose and udder, microwave the pink fruit chews for 2 to 3 seconds to soften. Press the fruit chews together and roll out on a work surface to an oval about ⅛ inch thick. Use a small knife or scissors to cut the candy into a 2-x-3-inch oval and a 1½-inch circle. Transfer the pieces to a sheet of wax paper.

6 Place the chilled 9-inch cake on a serving platter. Place the head-support piece on the platter at one edge of the cake. Spread the remaining vanilla frosting over the cake to cover.

7 For the legs, trim 1 inch from the pointed end of 2 of the 4 tapered cake pieces. Place the legs on the opposite side of the cake from the head support, rounded side up (see illustration, page 53), with the short end flush with the cake. Secure with some frosting, if necessary. Use a spatula to place the head piece on the cake, wide end at the top and resting on the support. Add the ear pieces on either side of the head, securing with frosting, if necessary (see illustration). To make the spots, sprinkle the cake with the crushed cookies.

8 Snip a small (⅛-inch) corner from the bag with the vanilla frosting. Place the pink candy oval as the cow's nose. Pipe dots of frosting and attach the pink jelly beans for the nostrils. Insert the pink licorice pastels into the pink candy circle and place on the side of the cake, between the legs, as the udder, securing with frosting, if necessary.

9 Press the cut ends of the anisette cookies into the cake at the top of the head for the horns. Place the white candy wafers for the eyes. Attach the chocolate mints for the pupils with a dot of vanilla frosting. Pipe a small white highlight on each eye. Using the black decorating icing, pipe an eyebrow above each eye. Insert the 2 red licorice laces under the cow's chin as the collar and trim off any excess. For the bell, press the small red candy into the flat end of the gumdrop and arrange on the collar. Attach a chocolate sandwich cookie to the bottom of each leg with a dot of black icing.

GOAT CAKE

MAKES 12 SERVINGS

1 Barnyard Master Cake (page 52) made with yellow
   cake mix
1 can (16 ounces) plus 1 cup vanilla frosting
1 pink and 2 orange flat candy wafers (Necco)
3 anisette toasts (Stella D'oro)
2 mini chocolate-covered mints (Junior Mints)
1 2-inch piece black licorice lace
2 black jelly beans
2 creme-filled chocolate sandwich cookies (Oreos)

1 Spoon ¾ cup of the vanilla frosting into a freezer-weight ziplock bag. Press out the excess air and seal the bag.

2 Spread some vanilla frosting over the 6 cake pieces and smooth. Return the pieces to the freezer until ready to assemble.

3 For the mouth, use a small serrated knife to cut one third from the pink candy wafer. For the horns, cut 1¼ inches from one short end of 2 of the anisette toasts and discard. Insert the pointed end of a 6-inch bamboo skewer about 1 inch into the cut end of each trimmed toast. Cut the remaining anisette toast in half crosswise for the beard.

4 Place the chilled 9-inch cake on a serving platter. Place the head-support piece on the platter at one edge of the cake. For the legs, trim 1 inch from the pointed end of 2 of the 4 tapered cake pieces. Place the legs on the opposite side of the cake from the head support, rounded side up (see illustration, page 53), with the short end flush with the cake. Secure with some frosting, if necessary. Spread the remaining vanilla frosting over the cake to cover, including additional frosting on the legs.

5 To make the goat's hair, start at the bottom of the legs and use a fork to pull the frosting in a downward and outward motion (see Forked Frosting, page 22). Continue forking in one direction in overlapping rows to the top of the cake to cover. Use a spatula to place the head piece on the cake, wide end at the top and resting on the support. Add the ear pieces on either side of the head, rounded side out, with the short end flush with the cake, securing with frosting, if necessary (see illustration, page 53).

6 Snip a ¼-inch corner from the bag with the vanilla frosting. For the beard, sandwich the long, straight sides of the anisette toast halves together, using a dot of frosting to secure, and place the cut sides against the narrow end of the head, flat side down. For the horns, insert the skewer end of each anisette toast into the top of the head, about 2 inches apart. Place the orange wafers for the eyes. Attach the chocolate mints for the pupils with a dot of frosting. Pipe a small white highlight on each eye. Place the licorice lace and the black jelly beans for the nose and cut the pink wafer for the mouth.

7 Starting at the top of the beard, pipe long, wavy lines of frosting to completely cover the toasts. Pipe tufts of wavy frosting in front of the horns. Pipe a wavy line of frosting above each eye for the eyebrows. Attach a chocolate sandwich cookie to the bottom of each leg with a dot of frosting.

PIG CAKE

MAKES 12 SERVINGS

1 Barnyard Master Cake (page 52) made with yellow
   cake mix
1 can (16 ounces) vanilla frosting
Red food coloring (McCormick)
8 creme-filled chocolate sandwich cookies (Oreos)
7 pink fruit chews (Laffy Taffy, Starburst)
2 black jelly beans
2 white flat candy wafers (Necco)
2 mini chocolate-covered mints (Junior Mints)
3 1-inch pieces black licorice lace
2 tablespoons chocolate syrup (Hershey's)

1 Spoon 2 tablespoons of the vanilla frosting into a freezer-weight ziplock bag. Press out the excess air and seal the bag. Tint the remaining vanilla frosting pink with the food coloring. Spoon 2 tablespoons of the pink frosting into a freezer-weight ziplock bag. Press out the excess air and seal the bag.

2 Line a cookie sheet with wax paper. Arrange the chilled cut cake pieces on it, using the pig diagram as a guide (see illustration, page 53). Spread the pink frosting on the top and sides of the 6 cake pieces and the 9-inch cake and smooth. Return the cakes to the freezer until ready to assemble.

3 For the dirt, place 2 of the chocolate sandwich cookies in a freezer-weight ziplock bag; do not seal the bag. Use a rolling pin to crush the cookies in the bag until finely ground.

4 For the snout, microwave the pink fruit chews for 2 to 3 seconds to soften. Press the fruit chews together and roll out on a work surface to a circle about ⅛ inch thick. Use a small knife or scissors to cut the candy into a 3½-inch

circle. For the tail, gather the scraps and roll them between your hands into a rope about ½ inch thick, tapering it at one end. Curl the rope into a corkscrew about 2 inches long. Transfer the pieces to a sheet of wax paper.

5 Place the 9-inch cake on a serving platter. For the legs, place 2 of the 4 tapered cake pieces on either side of the cake, with the straight side against the cake and the rounded side out (see illustration, page 53). Place the head-support piece on the platter at the top of the cake. Use a spatula to place the head piece on the cake, narrow end at the top and resting on the support. Snip a small (⅛-inch) corner from the bags with the vanilla and pink frostings. Attach 2 chocolate sandwich cookies together with a dot of vanilla frosting. Repeat to make 2 stacks. Arrange the cookie stacks near the top edge of the cake, on either side of the head, for the ear supports. For the ears, position the 2 remaining tapered cake pieces on either side of the head (see photo, opposite), resting on the cookie supports, and secure with vanilla frosting.

6 Place the pink candy circle as the pig's snout. Pipe dots of vanilla frosting on the snout and attach the black jelly beans for the nostrils. Pipe a few tufts of pink frosting on the top of the head. Place the white wafers for the eyes. Attach the chocolate mints for the pupils with a dot of vanilla frosting. Pipe a small white highlight on each eye. Place the black licorice laces as the eyebrows and the mouth. Attach a chocolate sandwich cookie to the bottom of each leg with a dot of vanilla frosting.

7 For the mud, drizzle the chocolate syrup on the pig's belly, legs, and ears. For the dirt, sprinkle with the crushed cookies. Place the pink candy tail against the cake on one side.

ROOSTER CAKE

MAKES 12 SERVINGS

1 Barnyard Master Cake (page 52) made with yellow
   cake mix
1 cup dark chocolate frosting
1 can (16 ounces) vanilla frosting
Yellow and red food coloring (McCormick)
1 can (16 ounces) chocolate frosting
3 red fruit slices
1 thin pretzel stick (Bachman)
6 yellow banana-shaped hard candies (Runts)
6 orange circus peanuts
2 white flat candy wafers (Necco)
2 mini chocolate-covered mints (Junior Mints)
1 small brown candy-coated chocolate (M&M's Minis)

1 Spoon the dark chocolate frosting into a freezer-weight ziplock bag. Spoon 1 tablespoon of the vanilla frosting into a freezer-weight ziplock bag. Press out the excess air and seal the bags. Tint ¼ cup of the remaining vanilla frosting light yellow with the yellow food coloring. Add 1 tablespoon of the chocolate frosting to the remaining vanilla frosting and tint it burnt orange with the red and yellow food coloring.

2 For the rooster comb and wattle, cut the red fruit slices in half lengthwise to make 6 semicircles; discard one. Insert the pretzel stick into one short end of one of the slices.

3 For the feet and claws, insert a banana-shaped candy about halfway into the end of one of the circus peanuts. Repeat with the remaining banana-shaped candies and circus peanuts. Pinch to taper the opposite end of one of the circus peanuts. Press 2 untapered circus peanuts on either side of the tapered one and pinch the rounded ends together to make a foot. Repeat with the remaining 3 circus peanuts to make another foot. Transfer to a sheet of wax paper.

4 For the beak, line a cookie sheet with wax paper. Arrange one of the tapered cake pieces on it using the rooster diagram as a guide (see illustration, page 53). Spread yellow frosting over the top and sides of the cake piece and smooth. Return the cake piece to the freezer until ready to assemble.

5 Place the chilled 9-inch cake on a serving platter. Place the head-support piece on the platter near the upper right edge of the cake (see illustration, page 53). Spread the cake and the head-support piece with the remaining chocolate frosting. Starting at the bottom of the cake, make the feathers by using the tip of an offset spatula or the back of a small spoon to pull the frosting away from the cake (see Spooned Frosting, page 23). Continue making feathers, working in one direction in curved, slightly overlapping rows, to the top of the cake to cover.

6 Arrange the remaining 3 tapered cake pieces next to the cake along the upper left edge with the rounded side curving downward (see illustration, page 53). Snip a ¼-inch corner from the bag with the dark chocolate frosting. Pipe vertical lines of frosting on the tail pieces to cover.

7 Spread the burnt orange frosting on the head piece and smooth. Starting at the bottom of the wide end of the head, make feathers by using the tip of an offset spatula or the back of a small spoon to pull the frosting away from the cake. Continue until you have 2 or 3 rows of overlapping feathers on the neck. Use a spatula to place the head piece on the cake, narrow end at the top and resting on the support.

8 Snip a small (⅛-inch) corner from the bag with the vanilla frosting. Place the white wafers for the eyes. Attach the chocolate mints for the pupils with a dot of vanilla frosting. Pipe a small white highlight on each eye.

9 Place the yellow beak below the eyes, rounded side to the top. Place the small brown candy as the nostril. Insert the pretzel end of the red fruit slice into the top of the head. Arrange 2 more slices on either side, facing the same direction, to make the comb. Press the remaining 2 fruit slices into the frosting under the beak, facing the same direction, for the wattle. Position the feet at the lower left edge of the cake.

CHEESE CAKE

MAKES 24 SERVINGS

We are so European that we've turned cheese into dessert. Swiss, Gouda, and Brie get an all-American treatment using caramels, flavor painting, and a dusting of confectioners' sugar.

2 recipes Perfect Cake Mix (page 289) made with yellow cake mix, baked in three 9-inch round pans for 35 to 40 minutes
2 cans (16 ounces each) plus 1 cup vanilla frosting
Yellow and red food coloring (McCormick)
2 tablespoons dark chocolate frosting
1 (5-inch) piece red fruit leather (Fruit by the Foot)
56 soft caramels (Kraft)
2 tablespoons vodka or vanilla extract
2 teaspoons unsweetened cocoa powder
¼ cup confectioners' sugar
Plain butter cookies (LU)

1 Tint 1 cup of the vanilla frosting light yellow with the yellow food coloring. Tint 3 tablespoons of the yellow frosting darker yellow and spoon it into a freezer-weight ziplock bag. Spoon 2 tablespoons of the vanilla frosting into a freezer-weight ziplock bag. Spoon the dark chocolate frosting into a freezer-weight ziplock bag. Press out the excess air and seal the bags.

2 Line a cookie sheet with wax paper. Place 1 cake on a work surface, bottom side up. Spread some vanilla frosting on top. Place another cake on top, bottom side down, pressing it into the frosting to secure. For the Gouda cheese shape, use a small serrated knife to trim ¾ inch from the top and bottom edges of the cake, to round them. Discard the trimmings. Transfer the cake to a cardboard cut to fit.

3 For the Swiss cheese, trim the top of the remaining cake level (see On the Level, page 14). Cut the cake in half to make 2 semicircles. Spread some vanilla frosting on the trimmed top of 1 cake. Place the other cake, trimmed side down, on top to make a 2-layer semicircle, pressing down to secure. Cut the cake in half again to make 2 quarter wedges. Spread some vanilla frosting on top of 1 wedge and place the other wedge on top to make a 4-layer wedge of cake, pressing to secure. Remove a 1½-inch wedge and set aside to use for the Brie. Place the remaining large wedge on its side on a piece of cardboard cut to fit. Spread a thin crumb coating of vanilla frosting (see Got Crumbs?, page 16) on the cakes, filling any gaps, and smooth. Place the cakes in the freezer until set, about 30 minutes.

4 Place the reserved 1½-inch cake wedge in a medium bowl and crumble. Mix the crumbs with ⅓ cup of the remaining vanilla frosting until well blended. Shape the cake mixture into a 3½-inch disk with straight sides, similar to a hockey puck (you can use a straight-sided kitchen

container, such as a measuring cup, to assist in making the shape). Place this cake in the freezer until set, about 30 minutes.

5 Spread an even layer of light yellow frosting on the chilled Swiss wedge cake and smooth. Return the wedge to the freezer for 15 minutes to chill the frosting.

6 Cut two ½-x-2½-x-2½-inch triangles from the fruit leather.

7 Microwave 6 of the caramels for 3 seconds to soften. Press the candies together and roll them out on a sheet of wax paper to a 4½-x-5-inch rectangle. In two batches, microwave the remaining 50 caramels for 3 to 5 seconds, stop and rotate to avoid hot spots, and microwave for another 3 to 5 seconds to soften. Press the candies together and roll them out on a sheet of wax paper to a 16-inch circle.

8 Spread an even layer of vanilla frosting on the chilled round Gouda cake. Transfer the caramel circle to the top of the cake. Wrap the caramel over the entire cake, smoothing any ridges and tucking the edges under the cake. Trim away any excess caramel with a small knife. Tint 1 tablespoon of the vodka red with the red food coloring. Using a small pastry brush, lightly paint the caramel with the vodka mixture, moving the brush in one direction (see Flavor Painting, page 45).

9 When the paint is dry, transfer the cake to a sheet of parchment paper on a cheese board. Carefully cut a 2½-inch wedge from the cake using a sharp knife. Transfer the cake slice to a serving plate. Spread the cut sides of the exposed cake with the remaining light yellow frosting and smooth. Insert 3 drinking straws about 1 inch apart

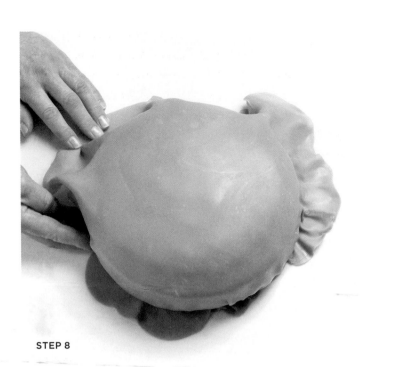

STEP 8

STEP 8

into the top of the Gouda cake and all the way to the bottom. Cut the straws flush with the top of the cake (these will support the Swiss cheese wedge when assembled). Refrigerate the cakes until ready to assemble.

10 For the Swiss cheese wedge, use a melon baller or small spoon and a straw to make random holes in the large, flat side of the chilled wedge. Snip a small (⅛-inch) corner from the bag with the dark yellow frosting and pipe some frosting inside the holes. Spread the frosting in the holes to make it as smooth as possible. Tint 1 teaspoon of the remaining vodka yellow with the yellow food coloring. Paint the 2 small ends of the wedge cake yellow. Press the caramel rectangle along the rounded back of the wedge, coming over the edges of the 2 small ends, and trim, if necessary.

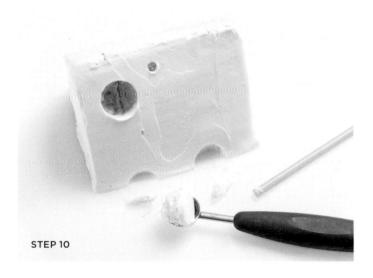

STEP 10

11 Combine the cocoa powder with the remaining 2 teaspoons vodka. Using a small pastry brush, paint the caramel side of the wedge cake to look like the cheese rind. Arrange the 2 fruit leather triangles on one small end of the wedge cake. Snip a very small (⅟₁₆-inch) corner from the bag with the dark chocolate frosting and pipe a dark chocolate squiggle at the base of each triangle and write SWISS on the triangles. Use a large spatula to transfer the wedge of Swiss cheese on its cardboard base to the top of the Gouda cheese, positioning it over the straws for support.

12 For the Brie, coat the chilled cake disk with the confectioners' sugar to make the rind, rubbing away some of the sugar along the edges to show the cake. Cut a small wedge from the cake and discard. Place the cake on the cheese board next to the other cakes. Soften the vanilla frosting in the bag for 3 seconds in the microwave. Massage the bag, snip a small (⅛-inch) corner from the bag, and pipe an oozy line of frosting just under both top cut edges of the Brie rind to look like ripe, runny cheese.

13 Arrange the butter cookies alongside the cake for the crackers to go with the cheese.

BUBBLES THE GOLDFISH CAKE

MAKES 12 SERVINGS

Bubbles may be the first fish cake your kids eat with no complaints. It's hard to believe you can get so much fun out of two round cake layers and frosting shaped with a spoon. Keeping it simple, we roll out circus peanuts for the fins and add candy for the scales.

1 recipe Perfect Cake Mix (page 289) made with
   yellow cake mix, baked in two 8-inch round pans
   for 25 to 30 minutes
1 can (16 ounces) plus ½ cup vanilla frosting
Yellow and red food coloring (McCormick)
12 orange circus peanuts
5 thin pretzel sticks (Bachman)
2 jumbo marshmallows
2 peach jelly rings
18 orange, 8 yellow, and 2 purple chewy sour candy
   disks (Spree)
Large white pearlized gumballs (SweetWorks;
   optional)

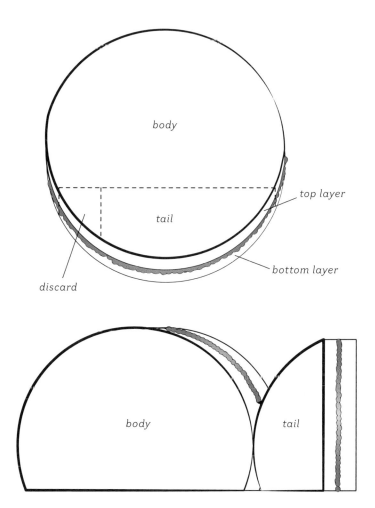

1 Spoon 2 tablespoons of the vanilla frosting into a freezer-weight ziplock bag. Press out the excess air and seal the bag. Tint the remaining frosting bright orange with the yellow and red food coloring.

2 Line a cookie sheet with wax paper. Place 1 cake, bottom side up, on a work surface. Spread some orange frosting on top. Place the other cake on top, bottom side down, pressing to secure. For the tail, trim a 2½-inch piece from one side of the cake. Place the trimmed cake, cut side down, on the cookie sheet. Trim 2 inches from one tapered end of the trimmed piece and discard. Attach the tail to the cake, short cut side down,

rounded side against the large cake, using frosting to secure. Transfer the assembly to a cardboard cut to fit (see Getting on Base, page 14). Spread a thin crumb coating of orange frosting (see Got Crumbs?, page 16) over the cake. Place the cake in the freezer until set, about 30 minutes.

3 For the fins, roll out each circus peanut to a ⅛-inch thickness. Cut each piece into a 1-x-3½-x-3½-inch triangle. Cut the edge of the 1-inch side of each triangle with pinking shears and score the top lengthwise with the back of a small knife. To make the 2 front fins, pinch the pointed end of each of 2 fins around the tip of a separate pretzel stick.

long, parallel strokes in the frosting on the tail cake. Add the yellow and orange candies to some of the scale scoops, spacing them out in clusters all over the body. Arrange the 10 flat fins on the tail cake with the wide, pinked end out, spacing them evenly and pressing them into the frosting to secure.

4 For the eyes, insert a toothpick into one flat side of each marshmallow (it will look like a lollipop). Spoon ½ cup of the orange frosting into a small bowl. Microwave the frosting, stirring every few seconds, until it has the texture of lightly whipped cream, about 7 seconds. Dip each marshmallow, holding it by the toothpick, into the melted frosting to cover completely, allowing the excess to drip back into the bowl. Press the flat side of the marshmallow against the rim of the bowl to remove any excess frosting and transfer to a piece of wax paper, flat side down. Refrigerate to set the frosting, about 30 minutes.

5 For the mouth, press the end of a pretzel stick through one flat side of a peach ring until about ¼ inch comes out the other side. Place another peach ring directly on top, pressing it into the tip of the exposed pretzel stick, just to secure (you don't want to see the pretzel stick).

6 Spread the remaining orange frosting over the chilled cake and smooth. Working forward from the back end of the body cake, not the tail, use the tip of an offset spatula or the back of a small spoon to pull the frosting back and away from the cake to make scoop-shaped scales (see Spooned Frosting, page 23); leave the rounded front part of the cake smooth for the face. Make

7 Snip a small (⅛-inch) corner from the bag with the vanilla frosting. Using a small spatula, carefully remove the marshmallow eyes from the wax paper. Working one at a time, hold the marshmallow by the toothpick and insert a pretzel stick into the flat side that was on the wax paper (it is okay to press the eye from the front, since it will be frosted; take care not to press the sides). Attach the eyes side by side at the top of the face, inserting the pretzel ends into the cake and securing with some vanilla frosting. Carefully remove the toothpicks. Pipe a circle of vanilla frosting on each eye and place a purple candy in the center for the pupil. Insert the pretzel end of the peach ring mouth under the eyes. Insert the pretzel end of a front fin on each side of the cake, pushing it into the frosting to secure. Scatter the white gumballs on the serving platter as bubbles, if desired.

GUITAR CAKE

MAKES 14 SERVINGS

The sound of guitar cake is music to our ears. We use flavor painting to give the body warm tones, string the guitar with frosted spaghetti to get a perfect pitch, and add a Nutty Bar neck that hits all the right notes.

1 recipe Perfect Cake Mix (page 289) made with devil's food cake mix, 3 cups batter baked in a 9-inch round pan for 23 to 29 minutes and 2 cups batter baked in an 8-inch round pan for 23 to 29 minutes

1 can (16 ounces) plus 1 cup vanilla frosting

½ cup dark chocolate frosting

1 whole chocolate graham cracker

3 thin honey wheat sticks (Pringles Stix) or long thin pretzel sticks (Bachman)

1 purple and 6 yellow spice drops

6 violet licorice pastels (Jelly Belly)

49 chocolate chews (Tootsie Rolls)

2 teaspoons vodka or vanilla extract

Yellow food coloring (McCormick)

1 teaspoon unsweetened cocoa powder

1 chocolate-covered wafer bar (Kit Kat)

2 boxes (12 ounces each) chocolate-covered peanut butter wafer cookies (Little Debbie Nutty Bars)

7 violet large flat sprinkles (Wilton)

6 strands uncooked spaghetti

6 purple pearl candies (SweetWorks)

1 Trim the top of each cake level (see On the Level, page 14). Invert an 8-inch cake pan and place it over the edge of the 9-inch cake, overlapping by 1½ inches. Score the cake along the curve using a toothpick (see illustration, center right). Following the scored mark, cut a semicircular piece from the cake using a small knife and discard. Snug the 8-inch cake into the semicircular cut of the large cake to make a figure-eight shape.

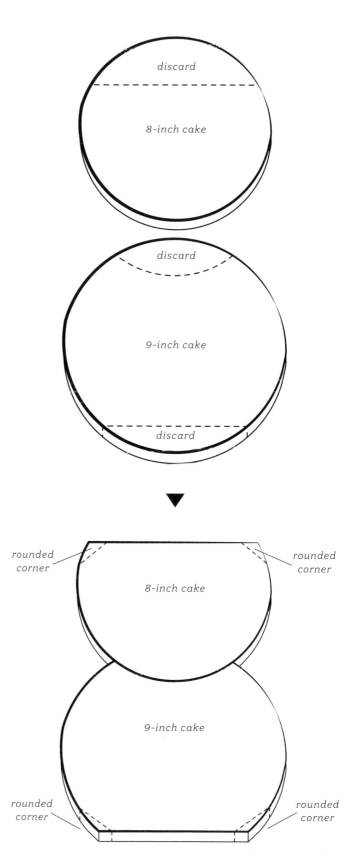

Trim 2 inches from the edge of the small cake at the top of the figure eight and 1 inch from the edge of the large cake at the bottom of the figure eight and discard. Trim the corners of the 2 cuts to round them and give the cakes a continuous curve. Transfer the assembled cake, bottom side up, to a cardboard cut to fit (see Getting on Base, page 14). Spread a thin crumb coating of vanilla frosting (see Got Crumbs?, page 16) on the cake and smooth. Place the cake in the freezer until set, about 30 minutes.

2 Spoon 3 tablespoons of the vanilla frosting into each of two freezer-weight ziplock bags. Tint 2 tablespoons of the vanilla frosting light brown with 1 teaspoon of the dark chocolate frosting. Spoon the light brown frosting into a freezer-weight ziplock bag. Spoon the remaining dark chocolate frosting into a freezer-weight ziplock bag. Press out the excess air and seal the bags.

3 Line a cookie sheet with wax paper. As you make the parts, transfer them to the cookie sheet. For the headstock, use a small serrated knife to cut the graham cracker in half crosswise. Remove a long, narrow triangle (¼ inch) from each short side of one graham cracker piece. Cut the wheat sticks into 4-inch lengths. Press the round end of a yellow spice drop on each end of each wheat stick to make the tuners. Trim the tip off one end of each licorice pastel for the tuning pegs.

4 Spread the remaining vanilla frosting over the chilled cake, filling any gaps and making the top as smooth as possible. Return the cake to the freezer for 30 minutes to chill the frosting.

5 For the pickguard, microwave 5 of the chocolate chews for 3 seconds to soften. Press the chews together and roll out on a sheet of wax paper to a 2½-x-5-inch rectangle. Trim the candy to a 2½-x-4¼-inch rectangle with rounded corners. Use a 4-inch cookie cutter or the rim of a glass to remove a semicircle from one corner (this is for the opening of the sound hole). For the pick, cut a triangle with 1-inch sides and rounded corners from the scraps.

6 To make the sides of the guitar, microwave 22 of the chocolate chews for 3 to 5 seconds to soften. Press the chews together and roll out on a sheet of wax paper to a rectangular band 2¾ inches wide and about 21 inches long. Repeat with the remaining 22 chews to make a second band. Use a ruler to measure the height of the cake assembly. Trim the edges of each candy band to straighten and trim the width to be slightly smaller than the height of the cake (the candy should not come up over the cake edge).

7 Tint the vodka yellow with the food coloring. Use a small pastry brush to paint the vodka mixture, lengthwise and in one direction, on top of the chilled cake (see Flavor Painting, page 45). Add some of the cocoa powder to the mixture and continue painting (see photo, opposite page), shadowing in areas to show the wood grain. Return the cake to the freezer for 15 minutes.

8 To make the sound hole, use a 2¾-inch round cookie cutter or the rim of a glass to score a mark 3 inches in from the top of the small cake and an equal distance from both sides. Use a knife to remove the cake circle, cutting about ¾ inch deep (take care not to get crumbs on the cake or to mark the cut edge of the frosting). Use the rim of a 4-inch glass to score a mark around the edge of the hole.

STEP 7

STEP 9

STEP 12

STEP 13

9 Starting at the bottom of the guitar, gently press a chocolate band into the side of the cake, wrapping it around the cake and pressing to smooth and even (see photo, above). Continue with the second band, starting flush with the end of the first band, to wrap the side of the cake completely, trimming the end to fit flush with the starting piece.

10 Place the pickguard on the cake to the right of the sound hole, with the curved edge against the scored mark. Add the chocolate wafer bar, crosswise, as the bridge, about 3 inches down from the sound hole.

11 Snip a very small (¹⁄₁₆-inch) corner from the bag with the dark chocolate frosting. Pipe a line of frosting around the top of the entire cake, ¼ inch from the outer edge, and on the score mark around the sound hole.

12 To create a support for the neck, stack 2 or 3 cookies (depending on the cake height) up to the level of the cake. Using the dark chocolate frosting for glue, secure the cookies together (see photo, above). Repeat to make a second stack. Place the stacks side by side, oriented as needed for the height, on the serving platter at the top of the guitar. Repeat this process to extend the support 2 cookie lengths from the guitar. Pipe a generous line of dark chocolate frosting on top of the entire support. To assemble the neck, place 2 half cookies, flat sides down and long sides together, at the top edge of the cake, cut ends lined up with the edge. Continue with the neck assembly by placing 2 whole cookies, side by side, flat sides down, against the ends of the 2 half cookies, on top of the support, pressing them into the frosting to secure. Repeat with 2 more cookies to complete the neck.

13 To create a support for the headstock, cut 2 of the remaining cookies in half crosswise. Sandwich the long sides together in a stack, 2 cookies wide and 2 cookies high, and secure with some dark chocolate frosting. Place them on the serving platter, flat side down, 1 inch from the end of the neck support, with short ends facing the neck support (see photo, previous page). Pipe some frosting on top of the cookies and place the 3 wheat stick tuners, crosswise, on top. Pipe more frosting on the wheat sticks and attach the graham cracker headstock, with the narrow end touching the guitar neck.

14 Put the frosting bag with the remaining dark chocolate frosting in a bowl, keeping the cut tip up to prevent leaking, and microwave, massaging the bag, until softened. Carefully pipe the melted frosting into the sound hole on top of the cake, just to cover the bottom of the hole.

15 Snip a very small (1/16-inch) corner from the bag with the light brown frosting and from one of the vanilla frosting bags. For the frets, pipe lines of light brown frosting, crosswise, down the neck of the guitar, starting about 1 inch from

the headstock and spacing them slightly closer together as you go. Place the flat sprinkles in between the fret lines.

16 For the strings, measure the distance from the bridge (Kit Kat) to the start of the neck cookies and cut the spaghetti pieces slightly longer. Pipe 6 dots of vanilla frosting across the bridge.

17 To coat the spaghetti, line a cookie sheet with wax paper. Microwave the remaining bag of vanilla frosting for 5 seconds. Massage the bag to smooth any lumps. Snip a small (1/8-inch) corner from the bag and pipe a pool of frosting on the wax paper. Coat the pieces of spaghetti by dragging them through the frosting and let set for 5 minutes. Press one end of each coated spaghetti piece into a dot of frosting on the bridge and balance the other end on the neck cookie. Using the unmelted bag of vanilla frosting, start at the end of each spaghetti piece and pipe a continuous line of frosting along the neck, ending with a dot of frosting on the graham cracker headstock (note that the 2 outside strings are the shortest and the 2 inner strings are the longest).

18 For the tuning pegs, press the cut ends of the 6 licorice pastels into the frosting dots on the graham cracker. Add the 6 pearl candies to the dots of frosting on the bridge. With a knife, remove the rounded tip of the purple spice drop and discard. Press the cut end of the remaining piece against the bottom side of the guitar as the end pin. Place the chocolate chew pick on the platter alongside the guitar.

LEOPARD-SKIN PURSE CAKE
Surprise Inside!
MAKES 12 SERVINGS

A leopard can't change its spots, but any cool cat can pipe dots of orange frosting surrounded by chocolate circles and then smash them with sugar. The surprise is that you can pipe leopard spots in the batter too!

1 recipe Perfect Cake Mix batter (page 289) made with yellow cake mix
Yellow and red food coloring (McCormick)
1 tablespoon unsweetened cocoa powder
1 can (16 ounces) plus 1 cup vanilla frosting
¾ cup dark chocolate frosting
27 chocolate chews (Tootsie Rolls)
2 thin pretzel sticks (Bachman)
1 large yellow pearlized gumball (SweetWorks)
1½ cups coarse white decorating sugar (Wilton)
4 yellow pearlized round candy-coated chocolates (Sixlets)

1 Preheat the oven to 350°F and prepare two 8-inch round pans (see Please Release Me, page 12). Spoon ½ cup of the batter into each of 2 small bowls. Tint one bowl orange with 15 drops yellow and 9 drops red food coloring. Tint the other bowl brown with the cocoa powder. Spoon each colored batter into a separate freezer-weight ziplock bag. Press out the excess air and seal the bags.

2 Snip a small (⅛-inch) corner from each bag of tinted batter. Starting with the brown batter, pipe several ½- to ¾-inch-wide misshapen circles into the bottom of each of the two prepared pans. Pipe a small dot of the orange batter on top of each of the brown circles. Being careful

not to disturb the spots, spoon one quarter of the remaining vanilla batter into each pan. Gently spread the batter to the edges and smooth the top. Make a second layer of brown and orange spots in each pan (see photos, above) and spoon half of the remaining vanilla batter into each pan. Spread the batter to the edges and smooth. Make a few spots on top with the remaining brown and orange batter.

3 Bake until golden brown and a toothpick inserted in the center comes out clean, 30 to 35 minutes. Transfer the cakes to a wire rack and cool for 10 minutes. Invert, remove the pans, and cool completely.

4 Place 1 cake, bottom side up, on a work surface. Spread some vanilla frosting on top. Place the other cake on top, bottom side down. For the purse shape, cut 1½ inches from one side of the assembled cake. Cut ½ inch from the opposite side. Discard the trimmed pieces. Place the cake, large cut side down, on a cardboard cut to fit (see Getting on Base, page 14). Spread a thin crumb coating of vanilla frosting (see Got Crumbs?, page 16) on the cake, filling any gaps, and smooth. Place the cake in the freezer until set, about 30 minutes.

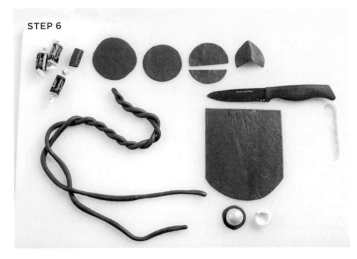

STEP 6

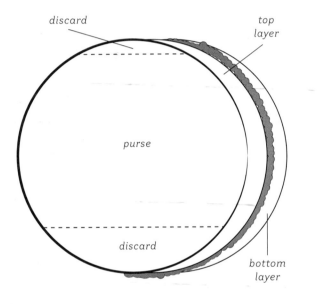

discard

top layer

purse

discard

bottom layer

5 Spoon the dark chocolate frosting into a freezer-weight ziplock bag. Tint ¼ cup of the remaining vanilla frosting orange with the red and yellow food coloring. Spoon the orange frosting into a freezer-weight ziplock bag. Press out the excess air and seal the bags. Tint the remaining vanilla frosting pale yellow with the yellow food coloring and cover with plastic wrap until ready to use.

6 To make the leather pieces, line a cookie sheet with wax paper. As you make the parts, transfer them to the cookie sheet. For the front flap, microwave 8 chocolate chews for 3 seconds to soften. Press the chews together and roll them

out on a sheet of wax paper to a 5-x-6-inch rectangle. Trim the 2 long sides and 1 short side to straighten. Round the remaining short side to create the front flap of the purse. For the corner details, microwave 5 chocolate chews to soften. Working on 1 chew at a time, roll out on a sheet of wax paper to a 2-inch circle. Cut a 1¾-inch circle from 4 of the flattened chews. Trim ¼ inch from one side of each circle for the corners. Cut a 1¼-inch circle from the remaining flattened chew for the front clasp. For the strap, microwave 7 chocolate chews for 3 to 5 seconds to soften. Press the chews together and roll with your hands into a 20-inch-long rope, about ¼ inch thick. Repeat with the remaining 7 chews. Twist the 2 ropes together. Pinch the ropes together at each end and insert the tip of a pretzel stick, perpendicular to the length of the rope, into each end.

7 For the clasp, use a serrated knife and a sawing motion to cut the gumball in half; discard one half. Moisten the cut side of the gumball with a dot of water and press it against the clasp chew.

8 Place the decorating sugar in a large bowl. Spread the yellow frosting over the chilled cake and smooth. Snip a small (⅛-inch) corner

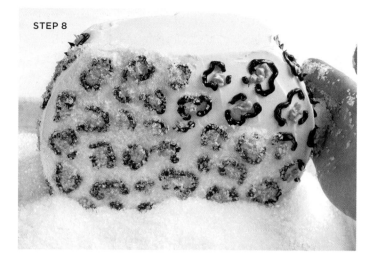

from the bags with the dark chocolate and orange frostings. Pipe thin, curved, wavy lines and irregular open circles of dark chocolate frosting all over the cake. Pipe irregular spots (no more than ¼ to ½ inch in diameter; they get bigger when smashed) of the orange frosting within the curved dark chocolate lines. Gently press handfuls of the sugar all over the frosted cake to cover completely (see Smashed Sugar, page 37). Brush any excess sugar from the cake using a pastry brush. Use the back of a spatula to gently press the sugar into the frosting and make it smooth. Transfer the cake to a serving platter.

9 Using some of the dark chocolate frosting, attach the chocolate-chew flap to the top of the cake, allowing the rounded edge to hang over the front of the cake. Pipe a dot of frosting against the center of the rounded edge and press the gumball clasp into the frosting to secure. Bend the 4 trimmed corner chews in half along the straight edge. Using some frosting, attach one corner chew to each corner of the cake, with the straight edge against the platter.

10 Squeeze the remaining dark chocolate frosting into the other corner of the ziplock bag. Tape the cut corner to seal. Snip a very small (1/16-inch) corner from the bag. For the stitching, pipe small dashes, a scant ¼ inch long, around the edges of the front flap and the clasp. For the corner pieces, pipe dashes along the curved edge and down the center, where the piece bends around the corner.

11 Just before serving, insert the pretzel ends of the strap into the top of the cake, one on each side of the front flap. Pipe a dot of dark chocolate frosting on each side of both strap ends and add a yellow pearl candy to each dot.

RAINBOW CAKE
Surprise Inside!
MAKE 12 SERVINGS

You'll be over the rainbow when you see how colorful rows of candy can transform a simple round cake—and the inside has even more rainbow colors!

1 recipe Perfect Cake Mix batter (page 289) made with French vanilla cake mix
Yellow, green, red, neon blue, and neon pink food coloring (McCormick)
1 can (16 ounces) vanilla frosting
½ cup each light blue, light green, yellow, orange, and red hard candy stars (SweetWorks)
1 cup mini marshmallows

1 Preheat the oven to 350°F and prepare a 9-inch round 2-inch deep pan (see Please Release Me, page 12). Divide the batter evenly among 5 separate bowls (about 1 cup batter per bowl). Tint 1 bowl orange (mixing yellow and red), 1 bowl acid green (mixing yellow and green), 1 bowl yellow, 1 bowl neon pink, and 1 bowl neon blue. Spoon each colored batter into a separate freezer-weight ziplock bag. Press out the excess air and seal the bags.

2 Snip a ¼-inch corner from the bags with the batter. Pipe 1½- to 2-inch dots of batter, about 3 spots of each color, on the bottom of the prepared pan (see photo, following page). Repeat, layering the batter as evenly as possible in the pan, until all the batter has been used. Tap the pan lightly on the work surface to level.

3 Bake until golden brown and a toothpick inserted in the center comes out clean, 40 to 45 minutes. Transfer the cake to a wire rack and

STEP 2

STEP 2

STEP 2

cool for 10 minutes. Invert, remove the pan, and cool completely.

4 Spoon 3 tablespoons of the vanilla frosting into a freezer-weight ziplock bag. Press out the excess air and seal the bag.

5 Cut the cake in half crosswise to make 2 semi-circular cakes. Sandwich the 2 bottom sides of the semicircles together, using some vanilla frosting to secure. Spread a thin crumb coating of vanilla frosting (see Got Crumbs?, page 16) on the cake, filling any gaps and smooth. Transfer the cake to a cardboard cut to fit (see Getting on Base, page 14), cut side down. Place in the freezer to chill, about 30 minutes.

6 Transfer the chilled cake to a serving platter. Spread the remaining vanilla frosting over the cake and smooth. Use the tip of an offset spatula or the back of a small spoon to make soft swirls on the front and back of the cake (see Classic Swirled Frosting, page 23).

7 Working quickly, press the star candies, very close together, into the frosting in rows of 2 like colors, following the curve of the cake and starting with the light blue, then green, yellow, orange, and red (see photo, opposite page). If the frosting begins to dry, snip a small (⅛-inch) corner from the bag with the vanilla frosting and use dots of frosting to attach the candies.

8 Pipe some dots of frosting on the mini marsh-mallows. Attach clusters of marshmallows together to form clouds. Arrange the clouds at each end of the rainbow.

MONSTROUS UNBAKED ALASKA
Surprise Inside!
MAKES 16 SERVINGS

He may be a monster, but a little warmth could melt his cold, cold ice cream heart! This tasty twist on baked Alaska has seven-minute frosting for fur and a surprise layer of ice cream and Oreo cookie chunks hidden inside.

1 recipe Perfect Cake Mix (page 289) made with devil's food cake mix, baked in two 8-inch round pans for 25 to 30 minutes
2 pints vanilla ice cream
10 creme-filled chocolate sandwich cookies (Oreos), coarsely chopped
3 tablespoons purple decorating sugar (Wilton)
10 purple spice drops
1 marshmallow
8 sticks blue gum (Winterfresh)
½ cup chocolate frosting
1 recipe Cooked Frosting (page 291)
2 mini chocolate-covered mints (Junior Mints)
10 blue banana-shaped hard candies (SweetWorks)
2 teaspoons blue decorating sugar (Cake Mate)

1 Soften the ice cream for 10 minutes at room temperature. Line the bottom and sides of an 8-inch round pan with plastic wrap. Combine the softened ice cream with the chopped chocolate sandwich cookies in a large bowl. Spoon the ice cream mixture into the prepared pan, cover with plastic wrap, and press to make level. Return to the freezer until set, at least 1 hour.

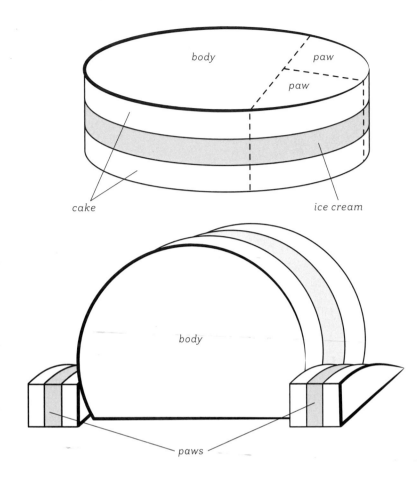

cake

body   paw

paw

ice cream

body

paws

STEP 3

2 Line a cookie sheet with wax paper. Place 1 cake, bottom side up, on a work surface. Unwrap the ice cream and arrange it on top of the cake. Place the remaining cake, bottom side down, on top of the ice cream and press lightly to secure. Cut 2 inches from one edge of the cake assembly (see illustration). Cut the 2-inch section in half crosswise for the paws. Transfer the large cake piece, cut side down, to the cookie sheet. Arrange the 2 small cake pieces, long cut sides down, short cut sides forward, on either side of the cake. Return to the freezer until set, at least 2 hours.

3 Line a cookie sheet with wax paper. As you make the parts, transfer them to the cookie sheet. For the eyes, sprinkle a work surface with some of the purple decorating sugar. Press the purple spice drops together and roll them out, adding more purple sugar to prevent sticking, to an oval about 4 x 7 inches. Slice ¼ inch from each flat side of the marshmallow; discard the center. For the teeth, use scissors to cut each stick of gum in half crosswise. Cut each half to make triangles of various shapes and sizes.

4 Transfer the chilled cake to a serving platter. Spread the chocolate frosting on the front of the cake and smooth (the front of the cake has the short cut sides of the paws facing forward). Attach the purple candy oval horizontally to the top third of the front of the cake. For the mouth, use a toothpick to score a 2½-x-6-inch oval, horizontally, in the chocolate frosting on the lower third of the cake. Return the cake to the freezer.

5 Divide the cooked frosting between 2 freezer-weight ziplock bags. Press out the excess air and seal the bags.

6 Snip a ½-inch corner from the bags with the cooked frosting. Starting along the bottom edge of the cake below the mouth, pipe frosting spikes, using a squeeze, stop, and pull motion, and continue all around the mouth. Continue piping rows very close together, avoiding the purple candy oval, over the rest of the cake, including the two small paw cakes. Finish the fur by piping a row of peaks around the purple candy oval, leaving a figure-eight-shaped mask for the eyes.

7 Use a dot of frosting to attach the marshmallow pieces for the eyes. Add a dot of frosting and attach the chocolate-covered mints for the pupils. Insert the gum triangles for the teeth around the mouth opening. Add 5 blue banana-shaped candies, curved side up, to the front of each small paw cake for the claws. Sprinkle the cake with the blue sugar. Return the cake to the freezer until ready to serve.

everyday pan cakes
rectangle, loaf, and jelly-roll cakes

Open your corner cabinet and pull out these everyday pans, because in our world, more shapes equal more fun. Your loaf pan is waiting to create a retro vacuum cleaner with cookies for the hose. Your jelly-roll pan is perfect for baking a thin cake to roll into a stump. And that 9-x-13-inch pan? That's for the house that Jack built. Everyday shapes make extraordinary cakes!

SPEC HOUSE MASTER CAKE

DIY alert: These makeovers start with one blueprint, but you can customize the design. The basic house is shaped from two cakes, and add-ons, like siding, shingles, doors, windows, and chimney, make it your own. Resale potential is high!

2 recipes Perfect Cake Mix (page 289) made with cake mix specified in recipe, baked in two 9-x-13-inch pans for 25 to 30 minutes
1 can (16 ounces) plus ½ cup vanilla frosting

1 Trim the top of each cake level (see On the Level, page 14). Line a cookie sheet with wax paper. Place 1 cake, trimmed side up, on a work surface. Spread ¾ cup of the vanilla frosting on top. Place the other cake on top, trimmed side down, pressing it into the frosting. Cut the stacked cakes in half crosswise. Spread the top of one stack with ½ cup of the vanilla frosting. Place the other stack on top. Spread a thin crumb coating of vanilla frosting (see Got Crumbs?, page 16) on the cake, filling any gaps, and smooth. Transfer the cake assembly to the cookie sheet. Place the cake in the freezer for 30 minutes to chill.

2 Insert 2 rows of toothpicks lengthwise along the top center of the cake, spacing the rows 3 inches apart. Insert a line of toothpicks lengthwise along each long side of the cake, 1½ inches from the top edge. Using the toothpicks as a guide, hold a long serrated knife at an angle and cut through the cake on each side. Place each trimmed piece lengthwise on top of the cake, frosted side to frosted side, to create the roofline (see illustration, right). Using the side row of toothpicks as a guide, bevel the cake on both sides, cutting on an angle from the toothpicks to ½ inch in at the base. Discard the trimmings unless instructed otherwise. Remove the toothpicks and transfer the cake to a cardboard cut to fit (see Getting on Base, page 14). Spread a thin crumb coating of frosting on the cake and smooth. Push 4 drinking straws through the stack of cakes, along the center of the roof, for support. Cut the straws flush with the top of the cake. Place the cake in the freezer until set, about 30 minutes.

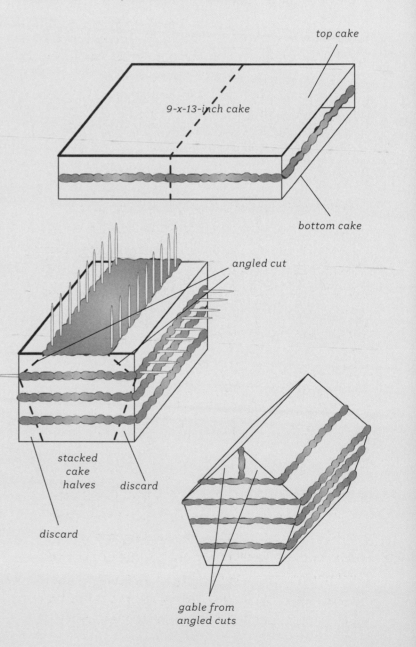

top cake

9-x-13-inch cake

bottom cake

angled cut

stacked cake halves

discard

discard

gable from angled cuts

THE HOUSE THAT JACK BUILT CAKE

MAKES 24 SERVINGS

1 Spec House Master Cake (page 92) made with yellow
  cake mix (reserve cake trimmings)
1 can (16 ounces) plus 1 cup vanilla frosting
½ cup dark chocolate frosting
Yellow and green food coloring (McCormick)
8 pink sugar wafers
5 blue licorice twists (Rainbow Twizzlers)
2 creme-filled chocolate sandwich cookies (Oreos)
1 tablespoon vodka or lemon extract (McCormick)
2 teaspoons unsweetened cocoa powder
52 dark-chocolate-covered thin cookies (Bahlsen
  Afrika)
2 small blue candy-coated chocolates (M&M's Minis)
12 mini orange fruit chews (Starburst Minis)
1 cup sweetened flaked coconut, chopped

1 Spoon ¼ cup of the vanilla frosting and all of the dark chocolate frosting into separate freezer-weight ziplock bags. Press out the excess air and seal the bags. Spoon ½ cup of the vanilla frosting into a small bowl and cover with plastic wrap. Tint the remaining vanilla frosting yellow with the food coloring.

2 Place the chilled cake on a serving platter. Spread the yellow frosting over the cake. Make the sides of the cake as smooth as possible. Return the cake to the freezer for 15 minutes to chill the frosting.

3 Line a cookie sheet with wax paper. As the parts are made, transfer them to the cookie sheet. Snip a small (⅛-inch) corner from the bag with the vanilla frosting. For the doors and chimney, pipe a line of frosting along one long edge of 4 of the sugar wafers and press each one against the long edge of one of the remaining

4 sugar wafers to make a double width. Pipe some vanilla frosting on top of one of the pairs of wafers and press another pair on top to make a double thickness for the chimney. Use a small serrated knife to taper each long side of the chimney and the 2 doors. For the door frames, cut 1 of the blue licorice twists in half lengthwise and cut the licorice into pieces to outline the 2 wafer doors.

4 To make the windows, remove a cookie side from each of the chocolate sandwich cookies and keep the side with the creme filling. Snip a small (⅛-inch) corner from the bag with the dark chocolate frosting. Pipe lines across the creme sides of the cookies for the windowpanes. Pipe a line of frosting around the edge of the creme.

5 Tint the vodka with the yellow food coloring (see Flavor Painting, page 45). Use a 1-inch pastry brush to paint the vodka mixture in horizontal strokes across all 4 sides of the chilled cake (not the roof). Continue brushing to smooth any ridges in the frosting. Add the cocoa powder to the remaining vodka mixture. Using a small craft brush, paint thin horizontal lines and dots around the cake for the wood grain and knotholes.

6 For the roof, cut 4 of the chocolate-covered cookies in half crosswise. Press a row of the whole cookies, close together, along the bottom edge of the roof on both sides, allowing them to overhang the edge by ½ inch. Add another row of cookies, starting and ending with a half cookie and overlapping the previous row by about ½ inch, using some of the dark chocolate frosting to secure the cookies. Repeat to make 2 more rows of cookies. Add a final row of whole cookies to form the peak of the roof.

7 Remove 1 of the chocolate-covered cookies from the roof and insert the narrow end of the pink wafer chimney into the frosting. Trim the cookie, if necessary, to fit next to the chimney, securing it with some dark chocolate frosting.

8 On the front of the cake, pipe a line of vanilla frosting just below the shingles for the gable. Press a blue licorice twist into the frosting, trimming to fit. Pipe a dot of frosting near the peak and attach a cookie window. Repeat to attach a gable and window on the back of the cake.

9 Attach a pink wafer door to the front and back of the cake using a dot of the vanilla frosting. Press on the trimmed blue licorice pieces for the door frames. Pipe a dot of vanilla frosting on each door and place a blue candy for the doorknob. Add 6 orange candies to make a path in front of each door.

10 To make the bushes, crumble the reserved cake trimmings into a medium bowl. Add the reserved ½ cup vanilla frosting to the crumbs and stir well. Shape the mixture into small cake balls, ranging from ¾ inch to 1½ inches in diameter. Place the cake balls in the freezer for 30 minutes to chill. Place the coconut, 1 teaspoon warm water, and several drops of green and yellow food col-

oring in a ziplock bag. Seal the bag and shake vigorously until the coconut is evenly tinted grass green. Just before serving, roll the chilled cake balls in the tinted coconut to coat. Arrange the cake balls around the house as bushes, stacking some for taller shrubs.

CANDYLAND HOUSE CAKE

MAKES 24 SERVINGS

1 Spec House Master Cake (page 92) made with
    yellow cake mix
1 can (16 ounces) plus 1 cup vanilla frosting
Yellow food coloring (McCormick)
½ cup chocolate frosting
8 large pink sugar wafers (Diana Pic-nic)
32 mini yellow fruit chews (Starburst Minis)
120 small pink pearl candies (SweetWorks)
72 small light green pearl candies (SweetWorks)
2 yellow heart candies
12 sticks light green gum (Doublemint)
2 pink and 4 light green lollipops
13 flat candy wafers (Necco)
28 flat brown sugar cookies (Lotus Biscoff)
90 mini vanilla wafers (Mini Nilla)
4 pastel twisted marshmallow sticks (Marpoles)
16 yellow banana-shaped hard candies (Runts)
1 tablespoon confetti decors (Cake Mate)
3 each white and yellow large spice drops
36 mini pink fruit chews (Starburst Minis)
10 chocolate-covered almonds
16 white meringue cookies

1 Tint ½ cup of the vanilla frosting yellow with the food coloring. Spoon the yellow frosting and ½ cup of the vanilla frosting into separate freezer-weight ziplock bags. Press out the excess air and seal the bags. Add the chocolate frosting to the remaining vanilla frosting to tint it light brown, stirring well to blend. Spoon ½ cup of the light brown frosting into a freezer-weight ziplock bag. Press out the excess air and seal the bag. Cover the remaining frosting with plastic wrap to prevent drying.

2 Line a cookie sheet with wax paper. As the parts are made, transfer them to the cookie sheet. To make the windows, use a small serrated knife to cut 2 pink wafer cookies into 1½-inch squares and 4 wafers into 1½-x-3-inch rectangles. For the doors, cut the remaining 2 wafers into 2-x-3½-inch rectangles and round the corners of one short side of each wafer.

3 Snip a small (⅛-inch) corner from the bag with the vanilla frosting. Pipe 6 windowpanes on each of the 4 rectangular wafers and 4 panes on each of the 2 square wafers. Attach a yellow fruit chew with a dot of vanilla frosting for each pane. Pipe a line of vanilla frosting around the edge of each cookie door and press pink pearl candies, close together, into the frosting. Add a green pearl candy to each door with a dot of frosting for the doorknob and a yellow heart close to the top of the door.

4 Cut the sticks of gum crosswise into twelve 1½-inch pieces for the shutters. Reserve the small ends of gum to be used for the path in front of the doors.

5 Pipe a spiral of vanilla frosting on one side of each lollipop.

6 Place the chilled cake on a serving platter. Spread the remaining light brown frosting over the cake. Make the sides of the cake as smooth as possible. Press the cookie windows and doors into the frosting to secure (see photos, next page). Pipe a line of vanilla frosting along the top edge of each of the larger windows. Attach a pink flat candy wafer near the roof peak on the front and back of the house as small windows. Use tweezers to outline these windows with green pearl candies. Press a row of green pearl candies along the top edge of each of the square windows.

7 Snip a small (⅛-inch) corner from the bag with the light brown frosting. Working on one side of the roof at a time, press a row of the brown sugar cookies, close together, short sides pointing down, along the bottom edge of the roof, allowing them to overhang the edge by ¾ inch. Add another row of cookies, overlapping the first row by about 1 inch, using some of the light brown frosting to secure. Add 4 rows of mini vanilla wafers, close together and overlapping like fish scales, to cover the rest of the cake roof.

8 Trim the marshmallow twists to fit lengthwise at each corner of the house, pressing into the frosting to secure.

9 Arrange 8 of the banana-shaped candies as the swag under the roofline on the front of the house. Pipe dots of vanilla frosting at each end and where the yellow candies meet and add a pink pearl candy. Repeat on the back of the house, using the remaining 8 banana-shaped candies.

10 Pipe 3 dots of vanilla frosting, aligned vertically, on each cookie in the bottom row of cookie shingles. Add a pink pearl candy to each dot. Pipe 2 dots of frosting on the cookies in the next row and add a green pearl candy to each dot.

11 Press a green gum shutter into the frosting on each side of the 6 windows. Pipe a decorative line of vanilla frosting along the edge of each shutter, where it abuts the window, to secure.

12 Microwave the yellow frosting for 3 seconds, massaging the bag, just to soften. Snip a ¼-inch corner from the bag and pipe wavy lines along the top edge of the roof. Use an offset spatula to spread the frosting over part of the top 2 rows of shingles, maintaining a wavy edge. Sprinkle the frosting with the confetti decors. Stand the remaining 11 flat candy wafers in a row along the peak of the roof, pressing them into the frosting to secure.

13 Cut a thin slice from the flat side of the 6 large spice drops and discard. Arrange the spice drops, sticky side down, on the serving platter close to the house. Press the stick end of a lollipop into each spice drop. Scatter the pink fruit chews and the chocolate-covered almonds around the house. Arrange the meringue cookies around the house. Place the reserved gum pieces in front of each of the cookie doors as a path.

HAUNTED HOUSE CAKE

MAKES 24 SERVINGS

1 Spec House Master Cake (page 92) made with devil's food cake mix

2 cans (16 ounces each) dark chocolate frosting

Black food coloring (McCormick)

¼ cup vanilla frosting

2 tablespoons yellow decorating sugar (Cake Mate)

11 double-stuffed creme-filled chocolate sandwich cookies (Double Stuf Oreos)

½ cup black decorating sugar (Wilton)

3 waffle cones (Joy, Keebler)

2 whole chocolate graham crackers

20 small orange pearl candies (SweetWorks)

3 cups candy corn (Jelly Belly)

1 cup black round candy-coated chocolates (Sixlets)

¼ cup dark cocoa candy melting wafers (Wilton)

½ cup chocolate cookie crumbs (from about 5 Oreos)

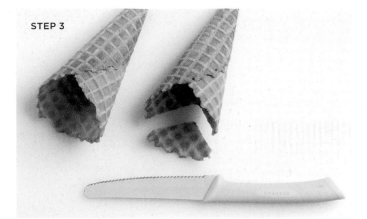

STEP 3

1 Tint ¼ cup of the dark chocolate frosting black with the food coloring. Spoon the black frosting and the vanilla frosting into separate freezer-weight ziplock bags. Press out the excess air and seal the bags. Spoon ½ cup of the dark chocolate frosting into a freezer-weight ziplock bag. Press out the excess air and seal the bag.

2 Line a cookie sheet with wax paper. As the parts are made, transfer them to the cookie sheet. For the windows, place the yellow sugar in a shallow bowl. Remove a cookie side from 4 of the chocolate sandwich cookies (reserve the 4 cookie sides for the shutters). Press the creme sides of the 4 cookies into the yellow sugar to coat the creme. For the roof shingles, separate the remaining 7 chocolate sandwich cookies. Scrape off and discard the creme filling and cut the cookie sides in half with a small serrated knife to make 28 semicircles.

3 Place the black sugar in a medium bowl. Using a small serrated knife, trim the wide end of one waffle cone on opposite sides to create an opening so that the cone can straddle the roof peak (see photo, above). Spread some of the dark chocolate frosting along the length of the cone, moving in one direction, and smooth. Holding the frosted cone over the bowl, sprinkle with the black sugar to coat. Frost and sugar the remaining 2 cones.

4 For the irregular-shaped double doors, use a small serrated knife to trim a 1-inch triangle from one of the narrow sides of each graham cracker. Cut a ¾-inch triangle from one of the long sides. Cut the graham crackers in half lengthwise to create 2 double doors.

5 Place the chilled cake on a serving platter. Spread the remaining dark chocolate frosting over the cake, making the sides of the cake as smooth as possible.

6 Snip a small (⅛-inch) corner from each of the 3 bags of frosting. To make the spiderwebs, pipe vanilla frosting in several concentric semicircles along the edges of the cake (not on the roof). Lightly drag a toothpick through the vanilla frosting in lines radiating out from the center of each web.

7 For the doors, press a set of graham cracker double doors on the front and back of the house. Pipe a line of black frosting around the outer edge of each door. For the doorknobs, pipe 2 dots of vanilla frosting on each cookie door and attach orange pearl candies.

8 Press the trimmed cone onto the center of the roof, straddling the peak. Press the other 2 cones into the frosting on each side of the roof, positioning them so that the cones sit upright, to form spires.

9 Working on one side of the roof at a time, press 5 cookie semicircles, cut side up, into the frosting close together along the bottom edge of the roof, allowing them to overhang the roof by ½ inch. Above this row, add a row of candy corn on its side, pointed side up, slightly overlapping the cookies. Continue adding rows of the candy corn, slightly overlapping the previous row, leaving the top 1 inch of the roof plain (use some of the dark chocolate frosting, as needed, to attach the candies).

10 Press a row of cookie semicircles close together, cut side up, along the top of each side of the roof, trimming to fit as needed. Cap the ridge of the roof with cookie semicircles, securing with some of the dark chocolate frosting. Use the frosting to attach a row of candy corn, pointed end up, along the ridge.

11 Attach the black round candies around the base of the spires with some of the black frosting.

12 For the shuttered windows, pipe 2 crossed lines of black frosting on each of the 4 yellow-sugared cookies to make the windowpanes. Cut the 4 reserved cookie sides in half to make 8 semicircles. Place the candy melts in a freezer-weight ziplock bag; do not seal the bag. Microwave for 10 seconds to soften, massage the candy in the bag, return to the microwave, and repeat the process until smooth. Press out the excess air and seal the bag. Snip a small (⅛-inch) corner from the bag. Pipe dots of the melted candy on either side of 1 window cookie and attach the cut sides of 2 of the cookie semicircles as the shutters. Repeat with the remaining 3 window cookies and refrigerate until the candy sets, about 5 minutes.

13 Pipe melted candy on the back of the chilled windows and attach 2 windows to each side of the roof, holding the window in place until the candy sets, about 1 minute.

14 Pipe a dot of melted candy on top of each spire and add a black round candy to the top and a ring of orange pearl candies below.

15 Sprinkle the platter with the chocolate cookie crumbs.

"POP" CAKE
Surprise Inside!
MAKES 24 SERVINGS

Make your cake pop like comic-book art from the 1960s! The brightly colored melted-jelly design and the cubist-cake interior make this a real art statement!

1 recipe Perfect Cake Mix batter (page 289) made with French vanilla cake mix
Yellow, neon pink, neon blue, black, and red food coloring (McCormick)
1 recipe Perfect Cake Mix batter (page 289) made with devil's food cake mix
1 can (16 ounces) dark chocolate frosting
1 can (16 ounces) vanilla frosting
2 cups apple jelly

1 Preheat the oven to 350°F and prepare three 8-inch round pans (see Please Release Me, page 12). Divide the French vanilla batter evenly among 3 bowls. Tint 1 bowl bright yellow, 1 bowl neon pink, and 1 bowl neon blue. Stir the batter in each bowl to mix the color well.

2 Spoon 1 color of batter into each of the 3 prepared pans. Spread the batter to the edges and smooth the tops. Bake until golden brown and a toothpick inserted in the center comes out clean, 18 to 20 minutes.

3 Transfer the cakes to a wire rack and cool for 10 minutes. Invert, remove the pans, and cool completely. Transfer the cakes to the freezer to chill, about 30 minutes.

STEP 4

STEP 6

STEP 6

4 Line a cookie sheet with wax paper. Trim each chilled cake into a square by removing the browned, curved edges (see photo, page 102). Cut the cakes into 1-inch cubes and transfer to the cookie sheet. Transfer the cake cubes to the freezer and chill until ready to use.

5 Preheat the oven to 350°F and prepare a 9-x-13-inch pan.

6 Spoon half of the devil's food cake batter into the prepared pan. Spread the batter to the edges of the pan and smooth. Arrange the chilled cake cubes in alternating colors on top, pressing slightly into the batter (see photos, page 102).

Spoon the remaining chocolate batter over the cubes to cover. Spread the batter to the edges and smooth the top.

7 Bake until a toothpick inserted in the center comes out clean, 35 to 45 minutes. Transfer the cake to a wire rack and cool for 10 minutes. Invert, remove the pan, and cool completely.

8 Trim the top of the cake level (see On the Level, page 14). Place the cake, trimmed side down, on a cardboard cut to fit (see Getting on Base, page 14). Spread a thin crumb coating of the dark chocolate frosting (see Got Crumbs?, page 16) on the sides of the cake and a thin crumb coating of vanilla frosting on top and smooth. Place the cake in the freezer until set, about 30 minutes.

9 Tint ¾ cup of the dark chocolate frosting black with the black food coloring. Spoon the black frosting into a freezer-weight ziplock bag. Press out the excess air and seal the bag. Spread the remaining vanilla frosting on top of the chilled cake and make it as smooth as possible. Spread

the remaining dark chocolate frosting around the sides of the cake and smooth. Transfer the cake to the freezer to chill, about 30 minutes.

10 Make a copy of the template on the opposite page and enlarge it 200 percent. Place the chilled cake on a serving platter. Using a toothpick, score the template design in the frosting on top of the cake (see Jelly Painting, page 107).

11 Spoon ½ cup apple jelly into each of 3 microwavable bowls. Tint 1 red with the food coloring, 1 bright yellow, and 1 light neon blue. Divide the remaining ½ cup apple jelly between 2 microwavable bowls, leaving 1 bowl plain and tinting the other dark yellow.

12 Snip a small (⅛-inch) corner from the bag with the black frosting. Following the score marks, pipe the outline of the shapes on top of the cake (the details will be piped on later).

13 Working with one color of jelly at a time, microwave the jelly in its bowl, stirring every 5 seconds, until smooth, about 20 seconds. If the melted jelly still has lumps, press the jelly through a fine-mesh strainer to smooth. Spoon the melted jelly into a freezer-weight ziplock bag. Press out the excess air and seal the bag. Snip a very small (⅟₁₆-inch) corner from the bag. Carefully squeeze some of the melted jelly inside the out-lined areas to be filled (see the photos, opposite page, for color references), using a toothpick or a small craft brush to push the jelly into the small areas. Repeat the process with the remaining jel-lies. Refrigerate the cake to set the jelly, about 15 minutes.

14 Pipe the remaining details, dots, lines, and solid areas, including the exclamation point, with the black frosting.

jelly painting

Painting with jelly is similar to flooding with frosting (see Pouring and Flooding, page 41), except you use apple jelly in place of the frosting. When the tinted jelly firms up, it leaves behind a colorful coating like stained glass.

1 Frost the top of the cake and smooth. Make a copy of the template and enlarge it to fit the top of your cake.

2 Cut the template down to the first set of shapes and use a toothpick to score the outline into the frosting. Cut the template down in successive stages to reveal each set of shapes and continue to score the outline of the shapes into the frosting using a toothpick.

3 Snip a small (⅛-inch) corner from a freezer-weight ziplock bag of frosting. Pipe an outline all around the edge of the cake (this creates the dam for the melted jelly).

4 Tint the apple jelly to the desired color in a small microwavable bowl. Microwave the jelly following the recipe directions. Press the melted jelly through a fine-mesh strainer to remove any lumps, if necessary.

5 Spoon the melted jelly into a freezer-weight ziplock bag. Press out the excess air and seal the bag. Snip a very small (¹⁄₁₆-inch) corner from the bag. Squeeze the jelly inside the outlined area, taking care not to overfill.

6 Use a small craft brush or a toothpick to ease the jelly up to the piped outline and into the small areas of the design.

FLOWER POWER CAKE

MAKES 12 SERVINGS

This cake starts blooming when smashed sugar is pressed into the colorful frosted design.

1 recipe Perfect Cake Mix (page 289) made with yellow cake mix, baked in a 9-x-13-inch pan for 25 to 30 minutes
1 can (16 ounces) plus 1 cup vanilla frosting
Red, yellow, and green food coloring (McCormick)
2 cups coarse white decorating sugar (Wilton)
33–36 small green pearl candies (SweetWorks)

1 Trim the top of the cake level (see On the Level, page 14). Cut the cake in half crosswise to make 2 smaller rectangular cakes. Place 1 cake on a cardboard cut to fit, trimmed side up. Spread some vanilla frosting on top of the cake. Place the other cake on top, trimmed side down, pressing it into the frosting. Spread a thin crumb coating of frosting over the cake, filling in any gaps, and smooth (see Got Crumbs, page 16). Place the cake in the freezer until set, about 30 minutes.

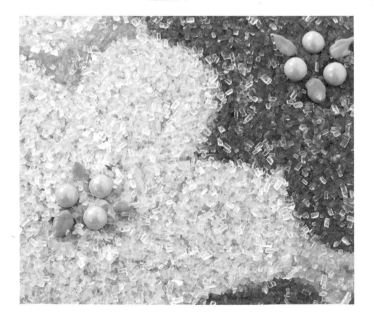

2 Divide the remaining vanilla frosting evenly among 4 bowls. Tint each bowl a different color with the food coloring: pink (with the red), orange (with the red and yellow), yellow, and bright green (with the yellow and green). Spoon each color into a separate freezer-weight ziplock bag. Press out the excess air and seal the bags.

3 Line a cookie sheet with wax paper. Place the decorating sugar in a large bowl. Place the chilled cake on the cookie sheet. Make a copy of the template (page 39) and enlarge it to 200 percent. Using a toothpick, follow the template to score overlapping flower shapes in the frosting all over the cake. Snip a small (⅛-inch) corner from the 4 bags with the tinted frostings. Working on one side of the cake at a time, pipe the outline of each flower with the desired color of frosting—pink, yellow, or orange. Fill in the outlines with the frosting. Pipe the open areas with the green frosting.

4 Gently press handfuls of the sugar into the frosted side of the cake to cover (see Smashed Sugar, page 37). Brush any excess sugar from the cake. Pipe another side of the cake, fill in the outlines, and press on the sugar. Continue until all 4 sides and the top of the cake are completely covered.

5 Using an offset spatula, gently press the sugar into the frosting to smooth. Transfer the cake to a serving platter.

6 Press 3 green pearl candies into the center of each of the sugared flowers. Pipe 3 dots of green frosting near the candies, pulling up and away as you release the bag to form a tiny point.

TOASTER CAKE

MAKES 12 SERVINGS

May we propose a toast? Here's to how easy it is to turn a single cake into a retro appliance. The vintage look comes from poured frosting for the red enamel and chocolate cookies for the Bakelite handles.

1 recipe Perfect Cake Mix (page 289) made with yellow cake mix, baked in a 9-x-13-inch pan for 25 to 30 minutes
3 plain doughnuts (Entenmann's)
2 cans (16 ounces each) vanilla frosting
½ cup dark chocolate frosting
Red paste food coloring (Wilton)
4 chocolate-covered mint cookies (Keebler Grasshopper)
2 black licorice laces
5 large black spice drops
2 white mint gum rectangles (Chiclets, Orbit White)
1 black gumdrop (Crows)
1 small red pearl candy (SweetWorks)
1 tube (4.25 ounces) black decorating icing (Cake Mate)
1 white flat candy wafer (Necco)
9 fudge-covered creme wafers (Keebler Fudge Sticks)
2 thin pretzel sticks (Bachman)
½ teaspoon green decorating sugar (Cake Mate)
1 stick white gum (Extra)

1 For the bagels, preheat the broiler. Cut the doughnuts in half horizontally. Place the pieces, cut side up, on a cookie sheet. Toast the doughnuts under the broiler until just golden brown around the edges.

2 Place the cake on a work surface, bottom side up, and cut it in half crosswise to make 2 smaller rectangular cakes. Spread some vanilla frosting on the bottom side of 1 cake and place the other cake on top, bottom side down and cut edges adjacent to each other, pressing it into the frosting. Place the cake, cut side down, on a cardboard cut to fit (see Getting on Base, page 14). Use a serrated knife to round the corners of the top of the cake. Spread a thin crumb coating of vanilla frosting (see Got Crumbs?, page 16) on the cake, filling in any gaps, and smooth. Place the cake in the freezer until set, about 30 minutes.

3 Spoon the dark chocolate frosting into a freezer-weight ziplock bag. Press out the excess air and seal the bag. Spoon ⅓ cup of the vanilla frosting into a small dish and cover with plastic wrap. Place the remaining vanilla frosting in a glass measuring cup and tint it red with the paste food coloring. Cover with plastic wrap to prevent drying.

4 Line a cookie sheet with wax paper. As the parts are made, transfer them to the cookie sheet. For the lever handles, cut ½ inch from one edge of each of the 4 chocolate mint cookies. Snip a small (⅛-inch) corner from the bag with the dark chocolate frosting. Pipe a dot of frosting on the flat side of 1 cookie and press another cookie on top, flat sides together, with the trimmed edges lining up. Repeat with the remaining 2 cookies.

5 For the electric cord, twist the licorice laces together to make a double strand. Insert one end of the laces into the round end of 1 black spice drop. With a small knife, cut 2 slits parallel to each other on the flat end of the spice drop. Insert the small end of a white gum rectangle into each slit.

STEP 7   STEP 8   STEP 8

6 For the controls, cut a ⅛-inch slice from the flat end of the black gumdrop. Press the red pearl candy into the cut side of the slice for the button. Pipe lines of black decorating icing on the white flat candy and attach the cut side of the black gumdrop as the dial.

7 Line a cookie sheet with wax paper and place a wire rack on top. Place the chilled cake on the wire rack. Microwave the red frosting in the glass measuring cup, stirring every 5 seconds, until it has the texture of lightly whipped cream, about 25 seconds. Pour the melted frosting over the cake to cover completely, allowing the excess to drip onto the cookie sheet. Place the cake in the refrigerator to set the frosting, about 30 minutes.

8 Use a large spatula to transfer the cake to a serving platter. For the toaster openings, use toothpicks to mark 2 side-by-side ¾-x-4-inch rectangles on top of the cake. Use a small knife to remove about 1 inch of cake along the length of each rectangle.

9 Pipe a line around the base of the cake with the dark chocolate frosting. Press the fudge-covered wafers into the frosting, trimming as necessary to fit.

10 Starting about midway up from the base of the cake and centered from side to side, pipe a vertical 2-inch line of dark chocolate frosting on both short sides of the cake. Press the cut edge of the chocolate mint cookies into the cake, crosswise, as the lever handles. Insert a thin pretzel stick into the cake under the cookie for support.

11 Press the black gumdrop candies on one long side of the cake as the button and the dial. Insert the licorice end of the electric cord near the bottom of one end of the cake. For the toasted bagels, pipe a dot of dark chocolate frosting on one edge of 2 of the doughnut slices. Insert the frosted edge into the toaster openings, standing upright.

12 Sprinkle the top of the reserved vanilla frosting in the small dish with the green sugar for the cream cheese.

13 To make the knife, cut the stick of gum into a long peanut shape. Trim ⅛ inch from each flat side of the remaining 4 black spice drops and discard the trimmings. Press the cut sides together to make 2 balls. Trim one rounded side of each ball and press the cut sides together to make the handle. With a small knife, cut a slit in one rounded end of the handle and insert the stick of gum as the blade of the knife. Serve with the 4 extra toasted doughnut slices.

PRINCESS AND THE PEA CAKE

Surprise Inside!

MAKES 24 SERVINGS

Test your inner princess with a bed made from seven cake mattresses and a candy pea. The vodka-painted sheets and puffy caramel duvet hide a surprise inside: Each mattress layer is tinted to match the sheets.

2 recipes Perfect Cake Mix batter (page 289) made with French vanilla cake mix

Yellow, red, neon blue, and green food coloring (McCormick)

3 cans (16 ounces each) vanilla frosting

½ cup white candy melting wafers (Wilton)

14 creme-filled vanilla sandwich cookies (Golden Oreos)

2 plain 9½-inch bread sticks (Stella D'oro)

2 large green gumballs (SweetWorks)

1 whole graham cracker

1 tablespoon yellow decorating sugar (Cake Mate)

20 soft caramels (Kraft)

3 tablespoons vodka or orange or lemon extract (McCormick)

1 green round hard candy (Runts) plus (optional) 70 green round hard candies for serving

1 tablespoon small orange pearl candies (SweetWorks)

2 marshmallows

Whipped cream for serving (optional)

1 Preheat the oven to 350°F and prepare four 9-x-13-inch pans (see Please Release Me, page 12). Divide the batter evenly among 4 bowls. Tint each bowl a different color with the food coloring: orange (with the yellow and red), yellow, neon blue, and lime green (with the yellow and green). Stir the batter in each bowl to mix the colors well.

2 Spoon each color of batter into one of the prepared pans. Spread the batter to the edges and smooth the top. Bake until golden and a toothpick inserted in the center comes out clean, 15 to 17 minutes. Transfer the cakes to a wire rack and cool for 10 minutes. Invert, remove the pans, and cool completely.

3 Spoon 1 cup of the vanilla frosting into a freezer-weight ziplock bag and ½ cup of the frosting into a second freezer-weight ziplock bag. Press out the excess air and seal the bags.

4 Line several cookie sheets with wax paper. Trim the top of each cake level (see On the Level, page 14). Cut each cake in half crosswise to make eight 9-x-6½-inch rectangular cakes. Spread a thin crumb coating of frosting (see Got Crumbs?, page 16) on the cakes, filling in any gaps, and smooth. Place the cakes on the prepared cookie sheets and transfer them to the freezer until set, about 30 minutes.

5 Spread the remaining vanilla frosting on the chilled cakes and smooth. Return the cakes to the freezer to chill the frosting, about 30 minutes.

6 As the parts are made, transfer them to one of the cookie sheets. Place the white candy melts in a ziplock bag; do not seal the bag. Microwave for 10 seconds to soften. Massage the candy in the bag, return to the microwave, and repeat the process until the candy is smooth. Press out the excess air and seal the bag.

7 For the mattress supports, place 7 of the vanilla sandwich cookies on one of the cookie sheets. Snip a small (⅛-inch) corner from the bag of melted candy and pipe some on top of each cookie. Place a second cookie directly on top of

the melted candy on each cookie, pressing to secure, to make 7 supports.

8 For the bedposts, use a small serrated knife to remove one rounded end from each bread stick. Pipe a small amount of the melted candy on the trimmed end and attach a green gumball. Place in the refrigerator until set, about 5 minutes.

9 For the headboard, place the graham cracker on a work surface. Use a small serrated knife to cut a 5-inch-wide semicircle from the graham cracker. Spread some melted candy on one side of the graham cracker and sprinkle with the yellow decorating sugar to cover. Refrigerate until set, 5 minutes.

10 For the duvet, soften the caramels in the microwave for 3 to 4 seconds. Press the caramels together and roll out on a piece of wax paper to an 8-inch square. Use a small knife or scissors to make a wavy edge around the caramel square.

11 Remove one of the yellow cakes from the freezer. Cut the cake into two 2-x-2½-inch rectangles for the pillows and six 1½-inch squares for the puffy duvet. Discard the scraps. Return the pieces to the freezer.

12 Remove 2 orange cakes from the freezer; place 1 cake on a cardboard cut to fit. Spoon 2 teaspoons of the vodka into a small bowl and tint orange with the yellow and red food coloring. Use a small pastry brush to paint the sides and just over the top edge of the 2 cakes (see Flavor Painting, page 45). Snip a ¼-inch corner from the bag with the 1 cup vanilla frosting. Pipe a line of frosting on top along each long side of the cake, about 1½ inches in from the edge. Return the 2 cakes to the freezer. Repeat the process with 6 teaspoons of the vodka, the food coloring, and the remaining 5 cakes, matching colors, piping lines of frosting on top, and returning the cakes to the freezer.

13 Arrange the 7 cookie mattress supports on a serving platter, 1 stack for each corner of the bed and 3 stacks across the center. Pipe a dot of vanilla frosting on top of each stack. Using a large spatula, transfer the orange cake from the cardboard to rest on top of the cookie supports. Adjust the cookie stacks as needed to support the cake. Place 1 green round candy on the edge of one long side of the cake for the pea in the mattress.

14 Transfer a blue cake directly on top of the orange cake, making sure that the green candy stays exposed. Transfer an orange cake directly on top of the blue cake. Repeat the process with the remaining green, yellow, blue, and green cakes (see photo, opposite page).

15 Push a drinking straw through the stack of cakes in each corner for extra support, trimming the straws flush with the cake. Pipe a mound of vanilla frosting on top of the 2 pillow cake pieces and smooth. Place the pillows, side by side, at one short end of the cake. Top the uppermost green cake layer with the six 1½-inch cake squares, spacing them about ½ inch apart.

16 For the sheet patterns, snip a very small (¹⁄₁₆-inch) corner from the bag with the ½ cup vanilla frosting. Pipe dots, lines, or Xs on the sides of the cake layers. Place the graham cracker headboard at the back of the pillows, with the sugared side facing the bed, securing with some vanilla frosting. Pipe a line of vanilla frosting along the top edge of the headboard and add a row of orange pearl candies. Pipe a decorative fringe along the outer edge of each pillow.

17 To make the duvet, cut the marshmallows in half lengthwise. Arrange the pieces, evenly spaced, in a row along one side of the caramel square, about 2 inches in from the edge. To make the turndown, fold that edge of the caramel over the marshmallows to cover. Place the caramel duvet on top of the cake, marshmallow end against the edge of the pillows, gently pressing the caramel to mold it to the 6 cake squares.

18 Place the remaining I teaspoon vodka in a small bowl and tint it orange with the red and yellow food coloring. Lightly brush the top of the caramel with the orange vodka paint to tint it orange. When the paint is dry, pipe a decorative border along the turndown edge with the vanilla frosting and pipe rows of stitching to outline the cake squares. Pipe several small lines radiating out from the point where the rows of stitching intersect and add an orange pearl candy to the center of each.

19 For the bedposts, pipe vanilla frosting on one side of the bottom half of each bread stick and press one into the cake on each side of the headboard.

20 If you like, add a dollop of whipped cream and several round green candies to each serving.

LITTLE CLIPPER LAWN MOWER CAKE

MAKES 12 SERVINGS

On Dad's big day, remind him about how much you need him . . . to mow the grass! Little Clipper is coated in red sugar and has chocolate-covered doughnuts and a bread-stick handle to propel it through even the thickest coconut grass.

1 recipe **Perfect Cake Mix (page 289)** made with yellow cake mix, baked in a 9-x-13-inch pan for 25 to 30 minutes

1 can (16 ounces) vanilla frosting

Red, black, green, and yellow food coloring (McCormick)

1 cup dark chocolate frosting

2 cups sweetened flaked coconut

12 double-stuffed creme-filled chocolate sandwich cookies (Double Stuf Oreos)

¼ cup white chocolate chips

4 plain 9½-inch bread sticks (Stella D'oro)

2 thin pretzel sticks (Bachman)

1 large black spice drop

1 whole chocolate graham cracker

5 chocolate-covered doughnuts (Entenmann's)

1½ cups red decorating sugar (Cake Mate)

1 can (1.5 ounces) silver food decorating spray (Wilton)

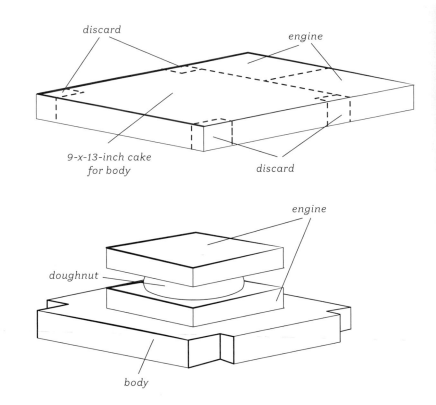

discard

engine

9-x-13-inch cake for body

discard

engine

doughnut

body

1 Line a cookie sheet with wax paper. Trim the top of the cake level (see On the Level, page 14). Place the cake, bottom side up, on a work surface. Cut a 4-inch-wide piece of cake from one short side of the cake. Cut the 4-inch-wide piece into two 4-inch squares. To make the wheel insets, remove a ¾-x-2-inch piece from each corner of the 9-inch square cake and discard; these rectangular cut-outs should all be oriented in the same direction on the cake (see illustration). Place the 3 trimmed cake pieces on cardboards cut to fit (see Getting on Base, page 14) and transfer to the cookie sheet. Place the cakes in the freezer to chill for 30 minutes.

2 Spoon 3 tablespoons of the vanilla frosting into a freezer-weight ziplock bag. Press out the excess air and seal the bag. Tint the remaining vanilla frosting red with the food coloring (don't worry if it isn't a true red; the red sugar will intensify the color). Cover the frosting with plastic wrap until ready to use. Tint the dark chocolate frosting black with the food coloring. Spoon ¼ cup of the black frosting into a freezer-weight ziplock bag. Press out the excess air and seal the bag.

3 Place the coconut, 1 teaspoon warm water, and several drops of green and yellow food coloring in a freezer-weight ziplock bag. Seal the bag and shake vigorously until the coconut is evenly tinted grass green.

CLIPPER

4 Cut 1 of the chocolate sandwich cookies in half crosswise with a small serrated knife to make the pull-cord handle; discard one half. Remove a cookie side from 4 of the remaining sandwich cookies; reserve the creme sides for the wheel covers and the cookie sides for the gas cap.

5 Line a cookie sheet with wax paper. Place the white chocolate chips in a freezer-weight ziplock bag; do not seal the bag. Microwave for 10 seconds to soften. Massage the chips in the bag, return to the microwave, and repeat the process until the candy is smooth. Press out the excess air and seal the bag.

6 For the lawn mower handle, snip a small (⅛-inch) corner from the bag with the melted white chocolate. Place 2 of the bread sticks on the cookie sheet, parallel to each other and slightly less than a bread-stick length apart. Pipe some of the melted chocolate near the top of each bread stick. Place another bread stick, crosswise, on top, pressing the ends into the melted chocolate. Cut the remaining bread stick into two 3½-inch pieces and reserve for the handle supports. For the pull cord handle, place the sandwich cookie half on the cookie sheet. Pipe some melted chocolate on

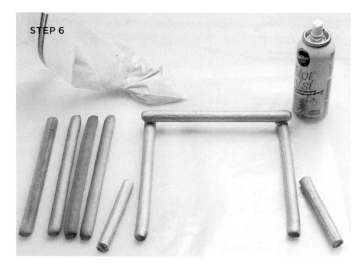

STEP 6

top and place the end of a pretzel stick into the chocolate to coat, allowing the pretzel to overhang from the rounded side. For the gas cap, pipe a dot of melted chocolate on top of one of the 4 whole cookie sides and place another cookie side on top. Repeat the process to make a stack of 4 cookie sides. Refrigerate until the candy is set, about 5 minutes.

7 Press the tip of a pretzel stick into the flat side of the black spice drop.

8 For the nameplate, place the graham cracker on a work surface and cut a 1-inch-wide piece, crosswise, with a serrated knife. Snip a small (⅛-inch) corner from the bag with the vanilla frosting and pipe CLIPPER on the small graham cracker piece. For the grass chute, cut a ½-inch triangle from each long side of the remaining piece of graham cracker.

9 Spread one of the chilled small cake squares with the black frosting and smooth. Place a chocolate-covered doughnut on its flat side in the center of the cake. Insert the pretzel end of the spice drop in the side of the cake. Return the cake to the freezer.

10 Arrange the remaining 7 chocolate sandwich cookies on a serving platter, 1 to support each recessed corner of the large cake and 3 across the center for support.

11 Place the red sugar in a large bowl. Spread the large chilled cake with some of the red frosting and smooth. Gently press handfuls of the sugar onto the sides and top of the cake to cover completely. Brush any excess sugar from the top of the cake with a pastry brush. Transfer the sugared cake on the cardboard to the top of the

cookie supports on the serving platter, adjusting the supports as necessary. Insert 4 drinking straws in a 3-inch square in the center of the sugared cake to support the 2 smaller cakes. Cut the straws flush with the top of the cake. Spread the remaining small chilled cake with the remaining red frosting and smooth. Repeat as above to coat with red sugar. For the pull-cord handle, insert the pretzel end of the sandwich cookie half in one side of the small sugared cake, pretzel side down. Return the cake to the freezer.

12 To make the wheel covers, snip a small (⅛-inch) corner from the bag with the black frosting. Pipe some of the black frosting on the cookie side of the 4 reserved creme-covered cookie halves. Press 1 cookie onto the smooth side of each of the remaining 4 chocolate-covered doughnuts, covering the hole. Refrigerate for about 10 minutes.

13 For the lawn mower handle, spray the bread sticks with the silver food decorating spray to cover on all sides.

14 Spread some black frosting on the 4 wheel insets on the cake and press on the chilled doughnut wheels, creme side facing out.

15 Use a spatula to transfer the small black-frosted cake, spice drop to the side, to the center of the large red cake, over the straw supports. Pipe a dot of black frosting on top of the doughnut. Place the small red-sugared cake, cookie pull cord to the back, on top of the doughnut. For the gas cap, place the 4-cookie stack on top of the small red-sugared cake, pressing down slightly to secure.

16 Using a toothpick, make 2 holes the width of the lawn mower handle apart near the back edge of the top of the large red cake. Gently press the ends of the handle assembly into the holes at an angle. Support each side of the handle (a can or box works well) and pipe a dot of the melted white chocolate on the cut end of one of the reserved 3½-inch pieces of bread stick. Place the bread stick under the handle for support, with the dot of chocolate against the handle (see photo). Pipe a dot of chocolate at the base of the bread stick on the platter for more stability. Repeat with the remaining 3½-inch bread stick on the other side. Allow the supports to set before removing the supporting box or can.

17 Make a small pile of green coconut on the platter to one side of the lawn mower. Press the narrow end of the graham cracker grass chute into the same side of the cake, using the mound of coconut as a support. Sprinkle the platter with the remaining green coconut, tucking some of it under the lawn mower. Attach the nameplate to the front of the lawn mower using the vanilla frosting.

SLOT MACHINE CAKE

MAKES 24 SERVINGS

A "hot" slot machine pays off with every pull—ours does it with each bite! The shape is made with cake layers covered in sparkling sugar and rolled spice drops. This one-armed bandit hits the jackpot every time.

2 recipes Perfect Cake Mix (page 289) made with yellow cake mix, baked in two 9-x-13-inch pans for 25 to 30 minutes

3 cans (16 ounces each) plus 1 cup vanilla frosting

Black food coloring (McCormick)

1 plain 9½-inch bread stick (Stella D'oro)

1 can (1.5 ounces) silver food decorating spray (Wilton)

2 whole graham crackers

½ cup white candy melting wafers (Wilton)

4 thin pretzel sticks (Bachman)

2 large red gumballs (SweetWorks)

½ cup yellow decorating sugar (Cake Mate)

1¼ cups red decorating sugar (Cake Mate)

3 bags (9 ounces each) red fruit slices, or 60 red spice drops

18 yellow, 12 white, and 6 purple spice drops

½ cup granulated sugar

¼ cup each small red and yellow pearl candies (SweetWorks)

3 light green chewy sour candy disks (Spree)

Colored-foil-covered chocolate coins (see Sources, page 296)

1 Trim the top of each cake level (see On the Level, page 14). Cut each layer in half crosswise to make four 6½-x-9-inch cakes.

2 Line a cookie sheet with wax paper. Place 1 cake piece, trimmed side up, on a work surface. Spread ½ cup of the vanilla frosting on top of the cake. Place another cake piece on top,

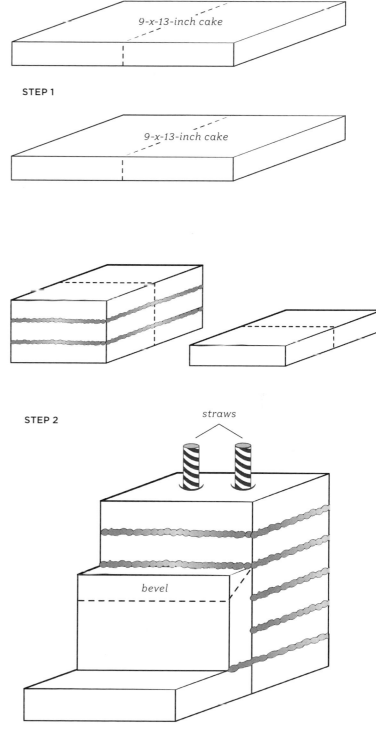

9-x-13-inch cake

STEP 1

9-x-13-inch cake

STEP 2

straws

bevel

STEP 3

trimmed side down, pressing it into the frosting. Spread the top of the stack with ½ cup of the vanilla frosting. Place another cake piece on top, trimmed side down, to make a 3-layer cake. Transfer all the cakes to the freezer to chill, about 30 minutes.

3 Cut the chilled 3-layer cake in half crosswise to make two 4½-x-6½-inch layered cakes. Spread the top of 1 stack with ⅓ cup of the vanilla frosting. Place the other stack on top to make a 6-layer cake. Cut the remaining chilled 6½-x-9-inch cake in half crosswise. Place the long side of 1 piece flush with the long side of the 6-layer cake, bottom side up (this will be the front). Stand the remaining piece on one of its long sides on top of the front piece, up against the 6-layer cake, using frosting to secure. Use a small serrated knife to bevel the top edge of the upright piece (see illustration, previous page). Place the assembled cake on a cardboard cut to fit. Push 2 drinking straws down through the stack of 6 cakes, about 2 inches

apart, for extra support, trimming the straws flush with the cake. Spread a thin crumb coating of frosting on the cake, filling any gaps, and smooth. Transfer the cake to the freezer to chill, about 30 minutes.

4 Spoon ½ cup of the remaining vanilla frosting into a freezer-weight ziplock bag. Press out the excess air and seal the bag. Tint the remaining vanilla frosting light gray with a drop or two of the black food coloring.

5 Line a cookie sheet with wax paper. As you make the parts, transfer them to the cookie sheet. For the handle, cut the bread stick into a 4½-inch length. Place the bread stick on a sheet of wax paper and spray it with the silver food decorating spray to coat on all sides; let dry.

6 Place the graham crackers on a work surface. Use a small serrated knife to cut a 5-inch-wide semicircle from each graham cracker.

7 Place the candy melts in a freezer-weight ziplock bag; do not seal the bag. Microwave the candy, massaging the bag every 10 seconds, until smooth. Snip a small (⅛-inch) corner from the bag. Pipe 4 evenly spaced lines of melted candy over 1 of the graham cracker semicircles, perpendicular to the straight edge. Place the 4 pretzel sticks on the semicircle, perpendicular to the straight edge, pressing them into the melted candy and leaving about a 2-inch overhang. Place the other semicircle on top of the pretzels, aligning it with the bottom semicircle and pressing it into the melted candy to secure. Pipe a dot of melted candy on the cut end of the silver bread stick. Press a red gumball into the melted candy to secure. Transfer the pieces to the refrigerator to set, about 5 minutes.

8 Spread melted candy, reheating it, if necessary, on both sides of the chilled graham cracker assembly and sprinkle with yellow decorating sugar to cover. Return to the refrigerator to set.

9 To make the red panels, sprinkle the work surface with some of the red sugar. Press the red fruit slices from 1 bag or 20 red spice drops together and place on the sugared surface, sprinkle with additional red sugar, and roll out the candy to roughly 6 x 7 inches, sprinkling with more sugar as necessary to prevent sticking. Repeat to make 2 more red rectangles. To make the yellow panel, use the yellow spice drops and the remaining yellow sugar and roll out a 6-inch yellow square. For the white panels, use the white spice drops and some of the granulated sugar and roll out to roughly 2½ x 5 inches. For the purple 7s, use the purple spice drops and the remaining granulated sugar and roll out to make 3 roughly 2-inch squares.

STEP 9

STEP 10

10 Line another cookie sheet with wax paper. Cut a 5½-x-6-inch rectangle from each of 2 of the red rectangles. Trim each rectangle to match the shape of the side of the slot machine, leaving a 1-inch border of cake exposed all around. Cut the remaining red rectangle into pieces measuring 3 x 5 inches, 1½ x 5 inches, and 1 x 5 inches, and 2 pieces measuring 1 x 2 inches. Cut the yellow square into a 5-inch square. Cut the white rectangle into three 1¼-x-2-inch rectangles. Cut each of the purple squares into a 1½-inch-high 7, using a small cookie cutter or a paring knife. Transfer the pieces to the cookie sheet.

11 Transfer the chilled cake to a serving platter. To keep the platter clean, place sheets of wax paper near the base of the cake. Spread the light gray frosting over the cake in an even layer, making it as smooth as possible. Spray the cake with the silver food decorating spray to give it a metallic look. Remove the wax paper and clean off any spray that may be on the platter.

12 Snip a small (⅛-inch) corner from the bag with the vanilla frosting and pipe LUCKY across the red 1½-x-5-inch panel. Use a dot of frosting to attach a purple 7 to each of the white panels, pressing to secure. Pipe some frosting on the back side of the red, yellow, and white panels and attach them to the cake, using the photo as a guide (the 3-x-5-inch red panel goes on top).

13 Use tweezers to press the small red and yellow pearl candies into the frosting, about ¼ inch apart, around the red and yellow panels. Add the green candy disks to the yellow panel, using frosting to secure.

14 For the flashing light on top, pipe a line of vanilla frosting across the straight edge on one side of the yellow graham cracker semicircle. Then pipe 5 lines radiating out from the center of the straight edge to the curved edge. Using a toothpick, poke 4 holes in the red panel on top of the cake to match the spacing of the pretzel sticks on the semicircle. Insert the pretzel ends into the cake to secure. Pipe dots of vanilla frosting along

the curved edge of the semicircle and add the remaining small red pearl candies, with the remaining large red gumball in the center.

15 For the handle, insert the pointed end of two 6-inch bamboo skewers, 2 inches apart, near the plain end of the silver bread stick. Holding the bread stick vertically, gumball up, insert the skewers into the right side of the cake.

16 Using a small knife, make a slit in the curve of the cake on the right side and add a foil-covered chocolate coin. Arrange more chocolate coins on and around the cake.

STUMP CAKE
Surprise Inside!
MAKES 12 SERVINGS

Don't be stumped by the bark or the growth rings! This cheeky twist on a bûche de Noël gets its woody look from chocolate shavings on the outside, flavor painting on top, and a wood-grain chocolate roulade inside.

¼ cup confectioners' sugar
1 recipe Perfect Cake Mix batter (page 289) made with French vanilla cake mix
1 tablespoon plus 2 teaspoons unsweetened cocoa powder
1 cup dark cocoa candy melting wafers (Wilton)
1 tablespoon vegetable shortening
1 can (16 ounces) dark chocolate frosting
1 can (16 ounces) cups vanilla frosting
1 tablespoon vodka or coffee extract (McCormick)
20 mini vanilla wafers (Mini Nilla)
20 chocolate kisses (Hershey's)

1 Preheat the oven to 350°F and prepare an 11-x-15-inch jelly-roll pan (see Please Release Me, page 12).

2 Spoon ½ cup of the batter into a small bowl. Tint the batter brown with 1 tablespoon of the cocoa powder. Spoon the cocoa batter into a freezer-weight ziplock bag. Press out the excess air and seal the bag.

3 Spoon the remaining vanilla batter into the prepared pan. Spread the batter to the edges and smooth the top.

4 Snip a small (⅛-inch) corner from the bag of cocoa batter. Pipe thin horizontal lines of the cocoa batter, crosswise, over the vanilla batter to create the wood-grain effect.

5 Bake until golden and a toothpick inserted in the center comes out clean, 15 to 17 minutes.

6 Transfer the cake to a wire rack and cool for 5 minutes. Dust a sheet of wax paper with confectioners' sugar. Invert the cake onto the prepared wax paper. Remove the pan and gently peel the wax paper from the bottom of the cake. Use a serrated knife to cut the warm cake lengthwise into quarters. While the cake is still warm, start at the short end of 1 cake strip and roll up the strip in a kitchen towel. Transfer the roll and the remaining strips to the wire rack and cool completely.

STEP 6

STEP 9

7 Microwave the candy melts and the shortening in a medium bowl, stirring every 10 seconds, until completely melted and smooth. Pour the melted candy into a 2-x-4-inch rectangular aluminum-foil container and refrigerate until firm, at least 30 minutes.

8 Spoon 2 tablespoons of the dark chocolate frosting into a ziplock bag. Press out the excess air and seal the bag.

9 Unroll the cake (it might break, but the frosting will glue it back together). Spread an even layer of dark chocolate frosting over the unrolled cake strip. Roll up the strip, chocolate side in (see photo, previous page) and transfer to the center of an 8-inch cardboard circle or a serving platter (see Getting on Base, page 14). Frost and add a second cake strip, starting where the last one ended and wrapping it around the first one. Repeat with the remaining 2 cake strips, always starting where the last strip ended. Press the sides of the cake to shape it into a circle.

10 Spread a thin crumb coating of vanilla frosting (see Got Crumbs?, page 16) over the rolled cake, filling any gaps, and smooth. Place the cake in the freezer until set, about 30 minutes.

11 Line a cookie sheet with wax paper. Unmold the candy-melt brick. Hold the brick with a paper towel to prevent it from warming. Run a vegetable peeler along the long, flat side of the chocolate, allowing the curls to fall onto the cookie sheet (see photo, opposite page). If the candy becomes too soft, return it to the refrigerator for 15 minutes and then continue making curls. Refrigerate the curls until ready to use.

12 Spread the top of the chilled cake with the remaining vanilla frosting and smooth. Return the cake to the freezer for 15 minutes to firm the frosting.

13 Tint the vodka with 1 teaspoon of the remaining cocoa powder. Use a small pastry brush to paint the vodka mixture in concentric circles on top of the cake (see Flavor Painting, page 45). Continue painting to smooth any ridges in the frosting. Tint the remaining vodka mixture darker with the remaining 1 teaspoon cocoa powder. Use a small craft brush to paint the wood grain in concentric circles (see photos, opposite page).

14 Spread the remaining dark chocolate frosting on the sides of the cake. Carefully press the chocolate curls into the frosting for the bark.

15 To make the acorns, snip a small (⅛-inch) corner from the bag with the dark chocolate frosting. Pipe a dot of frosting on the flat side of a vanilla wafer. Press the flat side of a chocolate kiss into the frosting to secure. Pipe a small dot of frosting on top of the cookie as the acorn stem. Repeat with the remaining vanilla wafers and chocolate kisses. Arrange the acorns on top of the cake and on the platter.

VACUUM CLEANER CAKE
Surprise Inside!
MAKES 16 SERVINGS

Sweet-O-Lux uses candy power to suck you in! It's made from a flavor-painted loaf cake, and it has a Golden Oreo flex hose and mini doughnut wheels. No bag needed, because the candy and cookie "dirt" are baked right in!

1 recipe Perfect Pound Cake Mix (page 289),
    Vacuum Cleaner Variation
1 can (16 ounces) vanilla frosting
Neon blue food coloring (McCormick)
2 vanilla snack-cake squares (Entenmann's Mini
    Pound Cakes)
½ cup white candy melting wafers (Wilton)
26 creme-filled vanilla sandwich cookies
    (Golden Oreos)
1 stick white gum (Extra)
1 large black spice drop
2 black licorice laces
1 tablespoon vodka or lemon extract (McCormick)
2 blue sour belts (Sour Power)
8 blue candy-coated chocolates (M&M's)
1 vanilla margherite cookie (Stella D'oro)
4 mini powdered-sugar doughnuts
Assorted small candies and cookie crumbs

1 Trim ¼ inch from all 4 top edges of the cake to round them. Place the trimmed cake, rounded side up, on a cardboard cut to fit (see Getting on Base, page 14). Spread a thin crumb coating of frosting (see Got Crumbs?, page 16) on the cake, filling any gaps, and smooth. Place the cake in the freezer until set, about 30 minutes.

2 Spoon ¾ cup of the vanilla frosting into a freezer-weight ziplock bag. Press out the excess air and seal the bag.

3 Tint the remaining vanilla frosting very pale blue with the food coloring. Cover the frosting with plastic wrap until ready to use.

4 Line a cookie sheet with wax paper. Trim 1½ inches from 1 long edge of 1 of the snack cakes and discard. Transfer the trimmed piece and the whole snack cake to the freezer for 30 minutes to chill.

5 Spread some of the blue frosting on the chilled, trimmed snack cake, leaving the cut side unfrosted, and smooth. Spread the remaining blue frosting on the chilled loaf cake and smooth. Return the cakes to the freezer for 15 minutes to chill the frosting.

6 Place the white candy melts in a freezer-weight ziplock bag; do not seal the bag. Microwave for 10 seconds to soften. Massage the candy in the bag, return to the microwave, and repeat the process until the candy is smooth. Press out the excess air and seal the bag.

7 For the cake supports, place 5 of the vanilla sandwich cookies on a cookie sheet. Snip a small (⅛-inch) corner from the bag of melted candy and pipe some of the candy on top of each cookie. Place another cookie directly on top of the candy, pressing to secure. Repeat to make 5 stacks of 3 cookies each. To make the vacuum hose, place 5 sandwich cookies on the cookie sheet. Add a pea-sized dot of melted candy near the edge of each cookie. Place a second sandwich cookie on top of the dot of candy, overhanging the edge of the bottom cookie by ½ inch, to make 5 cookie pairs (see photo, right). Refrigerate the cookie stacks until the candy is set, about 5 minutes. Reserve the remaining cookie.

8 Place one of the chilled cookie pairs on its edge. Using a dot of the melted candy, attach a second cookie pair, offsetting the cookie pairs by ½ inch. Repeat with a third cookie pair to make a row of 6 cookies, each pair offset by ½ inch. Hold the cookie assembly until set, about 3 minutes.

9 To make the plug for the vacuum, cut a ¾-inch piece, crosswise, from the stick of gum. Cut the small piece in half lengthwise; reserve the rest of the gum. Make 2 slits in the flat end of the spice drop. Insert a small cut piece of gum into each slit. To make the cord, poke a hole in the round end of the spice drop and insert the end of one of the licorice laces. Cut the remaining licorice lace into 16 pieces, each about ¾ inch long.

10 To make the on/off switch, cut the remaining piece of gum lengthwise into a ½-inch-wide strip. Press the dull side of a small knife into the strip of gum, crosswise, to mark it in half. Bend the gum slightly along the crease.

11 Arrange the 5 cookie supports on a serving platter in the approximate position of the 4 corners and the center of the vacuum cake. Snip a small (⅛-inch) corner from the bag with the vanilla frosting. Pipe a dot of vanilla frosting on top of each cookie support. Using a large spatula,

STEP 7

transfer the loaf cake to rest on top of the supports, adjusting the supports as needed.

12 Combine the vodka and a drop of the neon blue food coloring. Use a small pastry brush to paint the vodka mixture in horizontal strokes over the frosted loaf cake and snack cake (see Flavor Painting, page 45). Continue brushing to smooth any ridges in the frosting. Add a little more blue food coloring to the vodka mixture to deepen the color. Use a small craft brush to paint clusters of blue streaks onto the 2 cakes. Insert the 16 licorice pieces, in 2 rows, into the cut side of the frosted snack cake to make the brush.

13 Cut each blue sour belt into a 5-inch piece. Press a sour belt, lengthwise, on each long side of the loaf cake. Pipe SWEET-O-LUX on each sour belt with the vanilla frosting. Pipe 5 lines of vanilla frosting ¼ inch apart, crosswise, on the top at one short end of the cake, wrapping the lines about halfway around the sides. Pipe a small horizontal line on each side to join the ends of the 5 lines. Insert the licorice end of the candy plug near the bottom at the same end of the cake. Pipe some vanilla frosting on the opposite end of the cake and attach the whole unfrosted snack cake, bottom side against the cake. Push a straw through the center of the snack cake and into the loaf cake, trimming it flush with the snack cake, as added support. Pipe a decorative edge around the snack cake with vanilla frosting. To support the cookie handle, press 2 of the blue candies side by side on top of the cake and 2 more blue candies side by side 3 inches away. Pipe a dot of vanilla frosting on top of each candy and attach the flat side of the margherite cookie. Place the gum switch, crosswise, on top of the cake, midway between the handle and the snack cake, and pipe an outline of vanilla frosting around it.

14 Attach the doughnut wheels to the sides of the cake, next to the cookie supports, with some vanilla frosting. Pipe a dot of vanilla frosting in the center of each doughnut and attach one of the 4 remaining blue candies.

15 Attach the 6-cookie hose assembly to the unfrosted snack cake using vanilla frosting and balancing the hose between the snack cake and the platter. Arrange the remaining cookie and the 2 cookie pairs at the end of the hose assembly to create a flexible-looking hose, securing them with frosting. Pipe a dot of frosting on the last cookie in the assembly and attach the snack-cake brush. Pipe a decorative edge around the bristle end of the brush. Sprinkle the assorted candies and cookie crumbs in front of the brush.

PINEAPPLE CAKE

MAKES 12 SERVINGS

Check this pineapple for ripeness by tugging on a candy-coated potato-chip leaf or sniffing the yellow-and-brown marbleized frosting skin.

1 recipe Perfect Pound Cake Mix (page 289), Pineapple Variation
1 sugar cone (Joy, Keebler)
35 Pringles potato chips
1½ cups green candy melting wafers (Wilton)
1 tablespoon vegetable shortening
1 can (16 ounces) vanilla frosting
Yellow food coloring (McCormick)
1 can (16 ounces) cups chocolate frosting

One 1-inch star decorating tip (Wilton #2D, Ateco #845)

1 Use a small serrated knife to cut 1½ inches from the pointed end of the sugar cone. Discard the tip.

2 Line 2 cookie sheets with wax paper. Break the potato chips in half lengthwise by holding each long side and snapping them (they will be irregular).

3 Microwave the green candy melts and the vegetable shortening in a medium bowl, stirring every 10 seconds, until completely melted and smooth.

4 Dip a potato chip into the melted candy to cover (see photo, below). Allow the excess candy to drip back into the bowl. Transfer the chip to one of the cookie sheets. Repeat with the remaining chips, reheating the candy for several seconds if it becomes too thick. Refrigerate the coated chips until the candy is set, about 5 minutes.

5 Spoon the remaining melted candy into a freezer-weight ziplock bag; do not seal the bag. Reheat the candy in the microwave, massaging the bag every 5 seconds, until smooth. Press out the excess air and seal the bag.

6 Snip a small (⅛-inch) corner from the bag. Place the cut cone, wide opening down, on the second cookie sheet. Cut a 12-inch piece of aluminum foil and fold it in half lengthwise. Gently crumple the foil and shape it into a ring around the base of the cone (this is the support for the first row of green chips). Pipe some melted candy around the base of the cone. Attach a row of green chips, pointing upward, rounded edge against

STEP 4

STEP 6

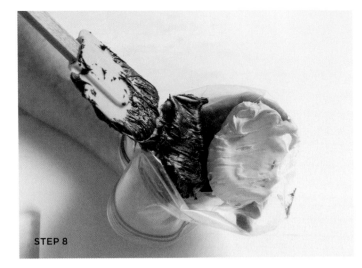

STEP 8

STEP 8

the cone, using the foil to support the chips (see photo, page 136). Transfer to the refrigerator to set, about 5 minutes. Continue adding rows of green chips up the side of the cone, reheating the candy as necessary, and chilling after each row, to cover the cone. Arrange 3 chips upright in the top opening of the cone. Refrigerate until ready to use. Reserve any extra leaves for the platter.

7 Place the loaf cake on a work surface. Trim ¼ inch from each short end with a serrated knife to make them straight. Stand the cake on one cut end and trim ½ inch from all 4 corners to round the shoulders of the cake (see photo, opposite page). Transfer the cake, in its upright position, to a serving platter and place in the freezer for 30 minutes to chill.

8 Tint the vanilla frosting yellow with the food coloring. Fit a large freezer-weight ziplock bag with the star decorating tip, if using. Hold the bag inside out in your open hand and, using a spatula,

spread half of the yellow frosting in a thick line up one side of the bag. Spread half of the chocolate frosting in a thick line up the opposite side of the bag (see photo, above left). Bring the sides of the bag up and over the frosting. Press out the excess air and seal the bag (see photo, above right).

9 Starting at the bottom, pipe a row of 1-inch stars, very close together, around the base of the cake. Repeat, piping additional rows of the frosting (see photo, opposite page). As you pipe, the colors marbleize in the star; turn the bag every few stars to vary the design. When the bag is empty, repeat with a clean freezer-weight ziplock bag and the remaining yellow and chocolate frostings, washing the star tip, and continue to cover the cake completely, including the top.

10 Transfer the pineapple crown to the top of the cake, gently pressing it into the frosting to secure. Arrange any remaining leaves on the serving platter.

bowl me over
bowl cakes

Decorating should be a ball. That's where bowl cakes come in. Put two together and cover them with frosting, and you've got the head for a plush toy rabbit, snowman, or bear staring back at you. Flip a bowl cake over and cover it with spray-painted marshmallows, and you have the shell of a seafaring turtle.

Note: *Whether you choose to bake in bowls made from metal, ceramic, or glass, make sure they are oven-safe. We based our recipes on sizes and shapes found in oven-safe glass bowls, because they are more uniform. (Baking times will not vary substantially.) But other oven-safe bowls of similar size and shape can be used, and the difference will make your design more original. (Be sure to read Baking in Glass, page 293.)*

PLUSH TOY MASTER CAKE

So cute you won't know whether to snuggle with these plush toys or eat them! Four bowl cakes combine to make the body and head. Then each toy gets its own treatment with coconut, forked frosting, flavor painting, mini marshmallows, or candy clay to create a plush, overstuffed look.

1 recipe Perfect Cake Mix batter (page 289) made with yellow cake mix or devil's food cake mix
1 cup vanilla frosting

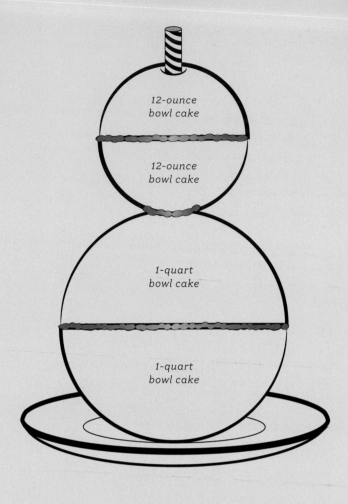

1 Preheat the oven to 350°F and prepare two 1-quart and two 12-ounce (4½-inch) oven-safe glass bowls (see Please Release Me, page 12). Spoon 1¾ cups of the batter into each of the 2 prepared 1-quart glass bowls and ¾ cup into each of the 2 prepared 12-ounce bowls. Place the bowls on a large cookie sheet and bake until the cakes are firm and a toothpick inserted in the center comes out clean, 25 to 30 minutes for the small bowls and 35 to 40 minutes for the large bowls. Transfer the cakes on the cookie sheet to a wire rack and cool for 10 minutes. Invert, remove the bowls, and cool completely.

2 Line a cookie sheet with wax paper. Trim the top of each cake with a serrated knife to level (see On the Level, page 14). Place one of the large cakes, trimmed side up, on a work surface. Spread some vanilla frosting on the trimmed side of the cake. Place the other same-size cake on top, trimmed side down, pressing to secure. Repeat the process with the smaller cakes. Spread a thin crumb coating of frosting (see Got Crumbs?, page 16) on the cakes, filling any gaps, and smooth. Transfer the cakes to the cookie sheet and place in the freezer until set, about 30 minutes.

3 Place the large chilled cake on a serving platter, flattest side down, as the body. Spread some of the frosting on top and add the smaller chilled cake, flattest side down, as the head. Insert a drinking straw down through the center of the small cake and into the large cake to help stabilize the cake, trimming the straw flush with the cake, if necessary. Return the cake assembly to the freezer to chill.

TEDDY CAKE

MAKES 12 SERVINGS

1 Plush Toy Master Cake (page 142) made with devil's food cake mix
1 cup vanilla frosting
⅓ cup creamy peanut butter
1 can (16 ounces) plus 1 cup milk chocolate frosting
6 peanut butter–filled sandwich cookies (Nutter Butter)
3 (5.25 ounces each) peanut butter cups (Reese's)
1 chocolate kiss (Hershey's)
1 roll (0.75 ounce) red fruit leather (Fruit by the Foot)
1 (5-inch) piece black licorice lace
2 black round candy-coated chocolates (Sixlets)
1 candy cane (optional)

1 Combine the vanilla frosting with the peanut butter, mixing well until smooth. Spoon the frosting into a freezer-weight ziplock bag. Spoon ¼ cup of the chocolate frosting into a freezer-weight ziplock bag. Press out the excess air and seal the bags.

2 Line a cookie sheet with wax paper. As you make the parts, transfer them to the cookie sheet. For the legs and ears, cut 5 of the peanut butter cookies in half crosswise with a serrated knife (see photo, below). For the feet, remove ¼ inch from one edge of 2 of the peanut butter cups. For the muzzle, cut ½ inch from 2 sides of the remaining peanut butter cup on an angle to create a point. For the nose, cut the chocolate kiss in half lengthwise and discard one piece.

3 Remove the chilled cake assembly from the freezer. For the ears, attach 2 of the cookie halves, cut side down, on top of the head cake, about 2 inches apart, with some milk chocolate frosting. For the muzzle, attach the pointed peanut butter cup to the head cake with some frosting,

STEP 2

rounded side down, with the point just below the center. For each leg, attach a cookie half, cut side down, against the base of the body using a dot of frosting. Attach 3 more cut cookies to each leg, and finish with a trimmed peanut butter cup, cut side down. Return the cake to the freezer.

4 For the bow, unroll the fruit leather and fold it in half crosswise to make a double thickness. Press firmly to adhere. Cut the strip into two 5-inch lengths and two 3-inch lengths. Loop each of the longer pieces in half and pinch the ends together (see photo, previous page). Overlap the pinched ends of each loop and press them together. To make the tails of the bow, cut a V-shaped notch from one short side of each of the 2 smaller pieces; reserve one of the cut-out notches. Pinch the straight end of each tail piece and press together with the pinched ends of the loops to make the bow. Attach the reserved notch in the center with a dot of water to cover the pinched area. Place the bow assembly on the cookie sheet.

5 Remove the chilled cake from the freezer. Spread some of the milk chocolate frosting on the cookie legs and smooth, leaving the flat side of the peanut butter cup unfrosted. Starting at the edge of the peanut butter cup, use a fork to pull the frosting in a downward and outward motion (see Forked Frosting, page 22), working in overlapping rows to the top of each leg. Spread some of the milk chocolate frosting on the body and smooth. Starting at the base of the body cake, continue forking the frosting in one direction, in overlapping rows, to the neck. Spread the remaining milk chocolate frosting over the head and backs of ears, leaving the peanut butter cup muzzle unfrosted, and smooth. Starting at the neck,

continue forking the frosting in one direction, in overlapping rows, up to and including the ears.

6 Starting at the platter, between the legs, press the licorice lace, vertically, in the center of the body. Snip a ¼-inch corner from the bag with the peanut butter frosting. For the chest fur, start with a narrow row in the center of the body and pipe overlapping rows of peanut butter frosting, always pulling down and out, making the rows wider as you work up to the neck to create a V-shape. Starting at the top of the cookie ears, pipe rows of the peanut butter frosting to cover the front of the ears. Pipe some peanut butter frosting over the muzzle and smooth. Let the muzzle frosting dry to the touch for about 25 minutes, then add texture to the muzzle by lightly pressing a paper towel into the frosting (see Toweled Frosting, page 23).

7 Snip a ¼-inch corner from the bag with the milk chocolate frosting. For the arms, remove and discard the filling from the remaining peanut butter cookie. Pipe milk chocolate frosting on one side of each cookie. Using a dot of frosting, attach a cookie, frosted side out, to each side of the body cake, close to the head. Starting at the bottom of the arms, use a fork to pull the frosting in a downward and outward motion, working in overlapping rows to the top of each arm. Pipe spikes of milk chocolate frosting to cover any flaws on the cake.

8 Attach the cut chocolate kiss to the muzzle, pointed end down, for the nose, using a dot of frosting to secure. Place the black candies above the muzzle for the eyes. Attach the bow to the side of the neck with a dot of frosting. Add the candy cane, if using.

RAG DOLL CAKE

MAKES 16 SERVINGS

1 Plush Toy Master Cake (page 142) made with yellow
   cake mix, prepared through step 2
1 plain doughnut (Entenmann's)
2 cans (16 ounces each) vanilla frosting
Red, black, and blue food coloring (McCormick)
½ cup dark chocolate frosting
5 creme-filled vanilla snack cakes (Twinkies)
1 roll (0.75 ounce) red fruit leather (Fruit by the Foot)
1 small red jelly bean
2 black gumdrops (Crows)
2 recipes Candy Clay (page 292) made with white
   candy melting wafers (Wilton)
1 package (14 ounces) red licorice laces (Twizzlers
   Pull 'n' Peel)
1 tablespoon small red ball decors (Wilton)
6 thin pretzel sticks (Bachman)

1 Attach the plain doughnut to the top of the
chilled large assembled body cake with some
vanilla frosting. Return the cake to the freezer.

2 Tint 1 cup of the vanilla frosting very pale pink
with the red food coloring. Spoon the pink frosting into a glass measuring cup and cover with plastic wrap until ready to use. Tint ½ cup of the vanilla
frosting red with the food coloring. Spoon the red
frosting into a freezer-weight ziplock bag. Tint the
dark chocolate frosting black with the food coloring. Spoon 3 tablespoons of the black frosting
into a freezer-weight ziplock bag and cover the
remaining frosting with plastic wrap until ready to
use. Spoon 2 tablespoons of the remaining vanilla
frosting into a freezer-weight ziplock bag. Press
out the excess air and seal the bags.

3 Line a cookie sheet with wax paper and
place a wire rack on top. For the shoes, cut 1
snack cake in half crosswise. Place the snack cake
halves, cut side down, on the rack. Microwave
the remaining black frosting, stirring every few
seconds, until it has the texture of lightly whipped
cream, about 7 seconds. Pour the melted black
frosting over the 2 snack cake halves to cover
completely, allowing the excess to drip onto the
pan (see Pouring and Flooding, page 41). For the
legs, trim ¼ inch from one short side of 2 of the
remaining snack cakes. Arrange the snack cakes
on the wire rack, flat side down. Microwave ½ cup
of the remaining vanilla frosting, stirring every few
seconds, until it has the texture of lightly whipped
cream, about 7 seconds. Pour the melted vanilla
frosting over the trimmed snack cakes to cover
completely, allowing the excess to drip onto the
pan. For the head and arms, place the chilled
small assembled head cake on a work surface.
Trim ½ inch from the flattest side and place the
cake, trimmed side down, on the wire rack with
the remaining 2 snack cakes, flat side down (see
photo, below). Microwave the light pink frosting,

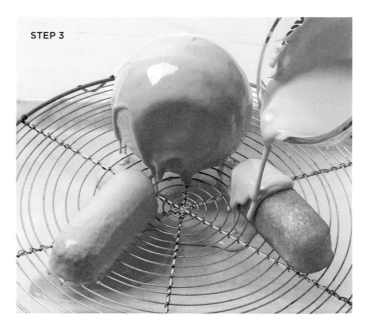

STEP 3

stirring every few seconds, until it has the texture of lightly whipped cream, about 10 seconds. Pour the melted pink frosting over the cakes to cover completely, allowing the excess to drip onto the pan. Place the cakes in the refrigerator to set, about 30 minutes.

4 Line a cookie sheet with wax paper. As you make the parts, transfer them to the cookie sheet. Unroll the fruit leather and fold the strip in half crosswise, making a double thickness. Press firmly to adhere. Cut the fruit leather into two 4½-inch lengths and trim the long sides to straighten the edges. Trim each piece to a ⅓-inch-wide strip and cut into 3 equal lengths for the socks. Cut a 1-x-1-x-½-inch triangle from the remaining fruit leather for the nose. Cut the red jelly bean in half lengthwise for the mouth and discard one piece. Cut ⅛ inch from the flat end of each black gumdrop for the eyes.

5 Tint half (1 recipe) of the candy clay blue with the food coloring. Leave the other half (1 recipe) white.

6 For the dress, roll out two thirds of the blue candy clay to a 13-inch circle, trimming to even the edges. Roll out the remaining blue candy clay to a 5¾-x-9¼-inch rectangle. Trim to even the edges. Cut two ½-x-9-inch strips from the rectangle. For the blue sleeve ruffles, start at one end of each 9-inch strip and gather the candy clay into pleats to make a 5-inch length. Cut the remaining piece of the rectangle in half crosswise for the sleeves. Roll out half of the white candy clay to a 5¼-x-9¼-inch rectangle. Trim to even the edges. Cut the rectangle lengthwise to get a 3-inch-wide piece. Cut the 3-inch-wide piece in half crosswise for the bloomers. Cut the remaining piece of the rectangle lengthwise into four ½-x-9-inch-wide strips. For the white ruffles for the neck and bloomers, start at one end of each 9-inch strip and gather the candy clay into pleats to make a 5-inch length. For the apron, roll out the remaining white candy clay to roughly a 5-inch square. Trim to straighten the sides and to taper the square slightly at 2 adjacent corners. Attach a red licorice lace to the apron, crosswise, ¼ inch from the wide end, using a drop of water to moisten, if necessary, and trimming to fit. Press the red ball decors in rows above the licorice lace, using a drop of water, if necessary, to secure.

7 For the legs, starting at the trimmed end, place a strip of the fruit leather across the white-frosted snack cake, trimming any excess, as a stripe on the sock (see photo, below). Repeat, spacing the strips ½ inch apart, to make 3 stripes on each leg. Wrap a bloomer piece of clay loosely around the rounded end of the leg, pressing it into the frosting. Brush the straight edge of the bloomer at the top of the sock with some water and attach the gathered edge of a white ruffle, pressing to secure. Repeat to attach a bloomer and a ruffle to the other leg.

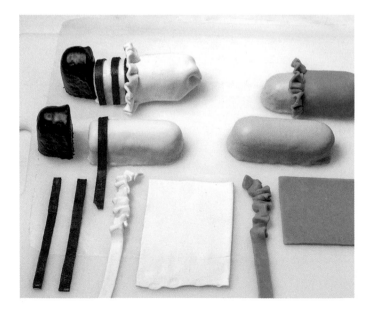

8 For the arms, wrap a blue rectangle around one of the pink-frosted snack cakes, 1½ inches up from one end and positioned so that the edges of the sleeve come together under the arm, on the flat side of the snack cake (see photo, opposite page). Press the edges flat into the frosting. Gather and pinch together any excess candy clay at the top of the arm as the cap of the sleeve. Brush the straight edge at the bottom of the sleeve with a drop of water and attach the gathered edge of a blue ruffle, pressing to secure. Starting from the top, insert 3 pretzel sticks into the flat side under the arm, about 1 inch apart and perpendicular to the arm, leaving 1½ inches of the pretzels exposed. Repeat with the other arm.

9 To assemble the rag doll, snip a very small (¹⁄₁₆-inch) corner from the bags with the black, red, and vanilla frostings. Transfer the chilled body cake to a serving platter. Spread the remaining vanilla frosting over the cake and doughnut and smooth. Place the leg snack cakes in front of the body, about 2 inches apart, with the untrimmed ends against the cake. For the shoes, attach the flat sides of a black frosted snack cake half, cut side down, to the trimmed end of each leg with some of the black frosting.

10 Soften the large blue candy clay circle by hand and drape it over the top of the frosted cake, making soft pleats for the dress; trim any areas that are too long, if necessary. Place the apron over the front of the dress, positioning the narrow end near the top of the cake and gathering it slightly at the neck. Using the red frosting, pipe 5 red dots in a circular cluster with a dot in the center to make small flowers evenly spaced over the blue dress. Attach the remaining 2 white ruffles in a circle at the top of the dress to form the neck opening.

11 Use a large spatula to transfer the chilled head cake to the top of the doughnut, trimmed side down. Insert 3 drinking straws down through the head, close together, into the body cake as support. Trim the straws flush with the top of the cake.

12 Using a dot of vanilla frosting, attach the cut jelly bean to the front of the head cake, crosswise, for the mouth, cut side against the cake, and add the fruit-leather triangle, short side down, for the nose. Pipe two ½-inch circles of vanilla frosting for the eyes. Press the 2 gumdrop slices into the frosting, cut side down, for the pupils. Pipe a white dot on each eye as a highlight. Squeeze several drops of red food coloring in a small bowl. Touch the tip of a small dry craft brush into the coloring for just a hint of color. Dab the brush on a paper towel before lightly painting circles on the face, about 2 inches apart, for rosy cheeks (see photo, previous page). Using the black frosting, pipe a curved line on each side of the mouth for the smile with a smaller curve at the end for the dimples. Add the eyelashes below the eyes and the eyebrows with the black frosting.

13 For the hair, trim the red licorice laces into 2- to 5-inch lengths. Pinch the ends of one longer strand together to make a loop. Make several more loops and set aside. Pipe some of the red frosting on the top and back of the head. Starting at the bottom of the head and working from one side to the other, press the longer licorice pieces into the frosting to secure. Continue work-

ing in overlapping rows to the top of the head. Arrange the shorter strands as the bangs, piping more red frosting, as necessary. Add the licorice loops to the top of the head.

14 To attach the arms, hold an arm in position at the shoulder and lightly press the pretzels into the dress to mark the candy clay. Using a toothpick, poke 3 holes in the clay at the marks. Insert the pretzel ends into the holes and through the cake, securing with frosting, as necessary. Pipe red frosting flowers over the blue sleeves.

SNOWMAN CAKE

MAKES 12 SERVINGS

1 Plush Toy Master Cake (page 142) made with
   devil's food cake mix
¼ cup dark chocolate frosting
1 can (16 ounces) plus 1 cup vanilla frosting
¼ cup light blue decorating sugar (Cake Mate)
20 white, 2 red, and 4 orange spice drops
1 tablespoon granulated sugar
1 thin pretzel stick (Bachman)
1 bag (10 ounces) mini marshmallows
3 light blue pearlized gumballs (SweetWorks)
2 pretzel rods (Bachman)
2 brown candy-coated chocolates (M&M's)
1 (4-inch) piece black licorice lace
2 chocolate-covered marshmallow cookies
   (Mallomars)
1 unfrosted chocolate cupcake
1 Dutch cocoa cookie (Archway)

1 Spoon the chocolate frosting and 3 tablespoons of the vanilla frosting into separate freezer-weight ziplock bags. Press out the excess air and seal the bags.

2 Line a cookie sheet with wax paper. As you make the parts, transfer them to the cookie sheet. Sprinkle a work surface with some of the light blue sugar. Press the 20 white spice drops together, sprinkle with additional blue sugar, and roll out to roughly a 4-x-10-inch rectangle, about ⅛ inch thick, sprinkling with more blue sugar, if necessary, to prevent sticking. Sprinkle a work surface with the granulated sugar. Press the 2 red spice drops together and roll out to a ⅛-inch thickness. Press the 4 orange spice drops together and shape into a 2-inch-long cone for the nose. Insert the thin pretzel stick into the flat end of the orange cone (see photo, above).

3 For the necktie, cut a ¾-x-10-inch strip from the blue candy for the neck of the snowman. For the tie, cut a 1½-x-9-x-9-inch triangle. Trim ½ inch from the narrow end. Remove a ¾-inch corner from each side of the wide end to make the pointed end of the tie (see photo, above). Cut a 1-inch circle from the blue candy, rerolling the scraps, as necessary, to have enough candy. Follow the template below to cut 2 skate blades from the blue candy. Cut two 1¼-inch circles from the red candy for the cheeks.

4 Remove the chilled cake assembly from the freezer. Spread some vanilla frosting on the large body cake and smooth. Starting at the base of the cake, press the mini marshmallows all over the cake, very close together, to completely cover. Frost the head cake with the remaining vanilla frosting and smooth. Repeat the process with the remaining mini marshmallows to completely cover.

5 For the buttons, remove 3 marshmallows from the front of the body in a vertical row, equally spaced. Press the light blue gumballs in their place. For the arms, remove a marshmallow from opposite sides of the body, close to the neck. Insert the end of a pretzel rod into each space, leaving 3 to 4 inches of the pretzel showing.

6 Snip a small (⅛-inch) corner from the bags with the chocolate and vanilla frostings. For the necktie, pipe a thin line of vanilla frosting around the base of the neck and attach the long strip of blue candy, trimming it if necessary. Attach the narrow end of the tie to the strip at a jaunty angle with some vanilla frosting. Use a dot of frosting to attach the 1-inch circle of blue candy to cover where the tie and strip join.

7 Insert the pretzel end of the orange candy into the center of the head cake as the nose. Pipe some of the vanilla frosting to attach the 2 brown candies for the eyes, the black licorice lace for the mouth, and the 2 red candy circles for the cheeks.

8 Pipe 2 dots of chocolate frosting on the flat side of each marshmallow cookie and attach the blue candy skate blades. Arrange the marshmallow cookies at the base of the cake, securing them with a dot of vanilla frosting.

9 For the hat, pipe some chocolate frosting on top of the cupcake and smooth. Pipe a dot of chocolate frosting on top of the cocoa cookie and attach the bottom of the cupcake to the cookie.

10 Just before serving, pipe a dot of vanilla frosting on the top of the cake and add the hat.

24-CARROT BUNNY CAKE

MAKES 12 SERVINGS

1 Plush Toy Master Cake (page 142) made with
   devil's food cake mix
2 cans (16 ounces each) vanilla frosting
4 anisette toasts (Stella D'oro)
1 tablespoon pink decorating sugar (Cake Mate)
1 bag (14 ounces) sweetened flaked coconut
8 thin pretzel sticks (Bachman)
26 orange circus peanuts
3 chocolate-covered creme-filled devil's food
   cakes (Ring Dings)
¼ cup mini marshmallows
¼ teaspoon vodka or lemon extract (McCormick)
¼ teaspoon gold luster dust (see Sources, page 294)
2 white mint gum rectangles (Orbit White,
   Dentyne Ice)
1 stick pink gum (Extra)
6 green sour belts (Sour Power)
2 flat pink mint cremes (Jelly Belly)
1 black jelly bean
2 brown candy-coated chocolates (M&M's)
6 (3-inch) pieces black licorice lace

1 Spoon ½ cup of the vanilla frosting into a freezer-weight ziplock bag. Press out the excess air and seal the bag.

2 Line a cookie sheet with wax paper. As you make the parts, transfer them to the cookie sheet. For the ear supports, insert the pointed end of a 4-inch bamboo skewer about 1 inch into the end of 2 toasts. Spread some vanilla frosting over the toasts and smooth. Place the toasts on the cookie sheet, curved sides facing out. Sprinkle the front of each toast with the pink decorating sugar. Press coconut into the frosting on the sides and back of each toast.

3 For the front feet, insert a pretzel stick into the flat side at one end of 2 of the circus peanuts (see photo, below). Spread the 2 circus peanuts with vanilla frosting. Press coconut into the frosting. For the hind legs and thighs, cover the 2 remaining anisette toasts and 2 of the chocolate-covered cakes with vanilla frosting. Press coconut into the frosting. For the tail, spread vanilla frosting on the remaining chocolate-covered cake and press the mini marshmallows into the frosting, very close together, to cover.

4 For the gold tooth, combine the vodka and the gold luster dust in a small bowl. Use a small craft brush to paint one of the white gum rectangles gold (or use a yellow rectangle of gum). For the bow tie, cut a 1¾-inch length from the stick

of pink gum. Pinch the center of this piece. Cut the remaining small piece of gum in half lengthwise, and discard one half. Wrap the small piece around the center of the large piece to cover the pinched area (see photo, below right).

5 For the carrot tops, cut the sour belts crosswise into twenty-four 2½- to 3-inch pieces. Use scissors to cut small notches in the long sides and top of each sour-belt piece (see photo, opposite page). Pinch the bottom end into a point. To shape the carrots, place a circus peanut on its side and trim and discard ¼ inch from the long dimpled side to flatten. Pinch one end of the candy into a point. Use the back of a small knife to press crosswise lines into the untrimmed bottom side of the circus peanut. Using the knife, cut a slit in the

rounded end of the circus peanut and insert the pointed end of a green sour belt piece. Repeat to make 24 carrots.

6 Remove the chilled cake assembly from the freezer. Spread some of the vanilla frosting on the cake and smooth. Starting at the base of the cake and working to the top of the head, press coconut into the frosting to cover completely. Brush excess coconut from the serving platter. Snip a ¼-inch corner from the bag with the vanilla frosting. For the thighs, attach the 2 frosted chocolate-covered cakes on opposite sides of the lower portion of the body. To secure the thigh cakes, insert 2 pretzel sticks, 1 inch apart, through each cake and into the body cake, covering the holes with coconut. For the hind legs, arrange the

whole frosted anisette toasts in front of the thigh cakes. Insert the pretzel end of the front feet near the neck of the cake, about 2 inches apart, using frosting to secure. Pipe a dot of frosting to the back of the tail cake. Secure the tail by inserting 2 thin pretzel sticks, 1 inch apart, through the tail cake and into the body cake, covering the hole with a marshmallow.

7 For the face, using frosting to secure, attach the flat pink cremes for the upper lip, the black jelly bean nose, and the brown candy eyes. Pipe a white dot for the highlight in each eye.

Attach the 2 gum rectangles below the upper lip for the teeth. For the whiskers, insert 3 pieces of black licorice lace on each side of the upper lip. Attach the pink bow tie just below the neck with some vanilla frosting. Attach 1 circus-peanut carrot, scored side out, near 1 front foot.

8 Add the anisette-toast ears on top of the cake, pink sugar side facing the front, pushing the skewers down into the cake and adding vanilla frosting to secure. Arrange the remaining 23 circus peanut carrots, scored side up, around the base of the cake.

ARMADILLO CAKE

MAKES 12 SERVINGS

Funny-looking but sweet! Our armadillo wears mini-marshmallow armor coated in cocoa powder and has a band of chocolate Necco wafers around his middle. The tip of his sugar-cone snout has a cereal-O mouth.

1 recipe Perfect Cake Mix (page 289) made with devil's food cake mix, baked in a 2½-quart oven-safe glass bowl for 45 to 50 minutes

1 can (16 ounces) plus 1 cup chocolate frosting

1 sugar cone (Joy, Keebler)

1 tablespoon light pink decorating sugar (Wilton)

1 jumbo marshmallow

2 thin pretzel sticks (Bachman)

2 tablespoons unsweetened cocoa powder

2 cups mini marshmallows

2 brown candy-coated chocolates (M&M's)

3 rolls (2.02 ounces each) chocolate flat candy wafers (Necco)

1 red cereal O (Froot Loops)

12 yellow banana-shaped hard candies (Runts)

1 Line a cookie sheet with wax paper. Trim the top of the cake level (see On the Level, page 14); reserve the cake trimmings for the dirt. Place the cake, trimmed side down, on a work surface. For the body, cut a 2-inch-wide piece from opposite sides of the cake. For the head, place one 2-inch-wide piece upright on the work surface. Measure 3 inches in from each side, along the straight edge, and make 2 angled cuts to the curved outer edge, leaving a wedge in the center that tapers from 1¼ inches to 3 inches (see illustration, page 160). Split the 2 end pieces in half lengthwise to make the 4 feet. Trim ½ inch from the long side of the remaining 2-inch-wide piece and reserve with the other trimmings. The

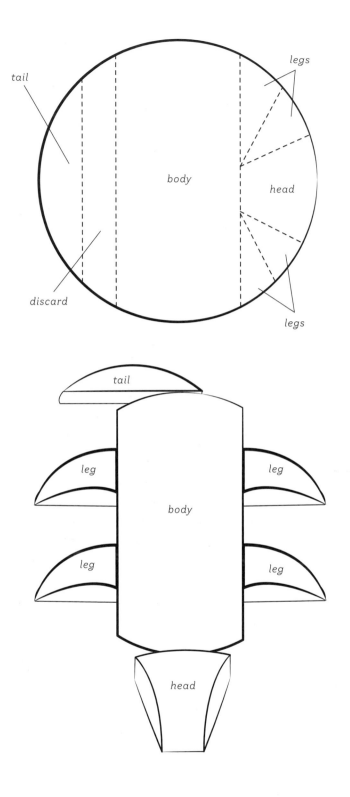

larger piece is for the tail. Arrange the body cake, rounded side up, and the 6 cake pieces (see illustration, below left) on a serving platter. Spread a thin crumb coating of chocolate frosting (see Got Crumbs?, page 16) on the cake, filling any gaps, and smooth. Place the cake in the freezer until set, about 30 minutes.

2 Line a cookie sheet with wax paper. As you make the parts, transfer them to the cookie sheet. For the snout, cut and discard a ½-inch piece from the wide end of the sugar cone with a serrated knife and ½ inch from the pointed end (see photo, below). For the ears, place the pink sugar in a small bowl. Cut ¼ inch from each flat end of the jumbo marshmallow with scissors, discarding the center. Press the cut side of each marshmallow piece into the sugar. Press a pretzel stick into the narrow edge of each marshmallow piece for the ear supports. Brush some of the cocoa powder on the outside edge of the marshmallow ears with a small craft brush. For

STEP 2

(between the legs) and smooth. Starting on the frosting closer to the tail end and working forward, shingle 6 or 7 rows of the chocolate candy wafers on this frosted section for the large scales, overlapping slightly and pressing the ends into the frosting to secure. Spread more of the chocolate frosting on the rear third of the body cake, the rear legs, and the tail and smooth. Starting from the tip of the tail and working up to the middle section, shingle rows of the cut mini marshmallows, cut side down, overlapping the rows to cover the frosting.

4 Using long strokes, spread some chocolate frosting over the trimmed sugar cone and smooth. Attach the wide end of the cone to the front of the head cake, securing with frosting. Spread the remaining chocolate frosting over the front third of the body cake, the head, and the front legs and smooth. Starting where the chocolate candy scales end, shingle rows of the cut mini marshmallows, cut side down, overlapping the rows to cover all but the snout area of the frosting. Remove several marshmallows from the top of the head and add 3 shingled chocolate candy scales in their place. Insert the pretzel end of a marshmallow ear on each side of the head scales, with the sugared sides facing forward. Snip a small (⅛-inch) corner from the bag with the chocolate frosting and attach the candy eyes at the top of the snout with a dot of frosting. Pipe a dot of frosting at the end of the snout and attach the cereal O for the nose. Pipe 3 dots of frosting at the end of each foot and attach 3 banana-shaped candies, rounded side up, for the claws. Crumble the reserved cake trimmings and sprinkle the crumbs around the cake on the platter for the dirt.

the eyes, cut a mini marshmallow in half crosswise. Press a brown candy onto the sticky side of each half. Place the remaining mini marshmallows in a freezer-weight ziplock bag with the remaining cocoa powder. Seal the bag and shake well until the marshmallows are light brown and evenly coated. Remove the marshmallows and cut them in half crosswise for the small scales.

3 Spoon 2 tablespoons of the remaining chocolate frosting into a freezer-weight ziplock bag. Press out the excess air and seal the bag. Spread some of the remaining chocolate frosting over the middle third of the body cake

BUNNY HILL CAKE
Surprise Inside!
MAKES 12 SERVINGS

The marshmallows on Bunny Hill seem to multiply like rabbits. The parents are regular size, and their juniors are miniature. Stashed away inside their hill is a sweet mound of candy carrots.

1 recipe Perfect Cake Mix batter (page 289) made with devil's food cake mix, baked in a 2½-quart oven-safe glass bowl for 45 to 50 minutes
¼ cup dark chocolate frosting
1 can (16 ounces) vanilla frosting
Green and yellow food coloring (McCormick)
½ cup light pink decorating sugar (Wilton)
6 marshmallows
1 bag (10 ounces) mini marshmallows
¾ cup white candy melting wafers (Wilton)
Small pink heart-shaped decors (see Sources, page 294)
1 cup small carrot-shaped candies (Jelly Belly Peas & Carrots)
¼ cup green candy melting wafers (Wilton)
3 tablespoons green sprinkles (Wilton)

1 Spoon the dark chocolate frosting into a freezer-weight ziplock bag. Spoon 2 tablespoons of the vanilla frosting into a freezer-weight ziplock bag. Press out the excess air and seal the bags. Tint the remaining vanilla frosting light green with the green and yellow food coloring. Cover with plastic wrap to prevent drying.

2 Line a cookie sheet with wax paper. As you make the parts, transfer them to the cookie sheet. Place the pink sugar in a small bowl. For the large bunny ears, use sharp craft scissors to cut 1 of the large marshmallows crosswise into 4 thin slices, allowing the 4 pieces to fall into the pink

sugar. Shake the bowl and press the cut sides of the marshmallow pieces into the sugar to coat. Remove the pieces from the sugar bowl and brush any excess sugar off the sides. Repeat with 25 of the mini marshmallows to make 100 small bunny ears. For the large bunny legs, cut a ½-inch piece from each flat end of 1 large marshmallow, discarding the center. Cut each piece in half crosswise, to make 4 semicircles. For the small bunny legs, cut 50 mini marshmallows in half crosswise.

3 Place the white candy melts in a freezer-weight ziplock bag; do not seal the bag. Microwave for 10 seconds to soften, massage the candy in the bag, return to the microwave, and repeat the process until smooth, about 30 seconds. Press out the excess air and seal the bag. Snip a small (⅛-inch) corner from the bag.

STEP 4

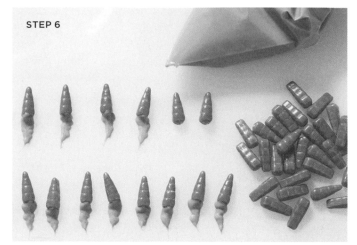

STEP 6

4 To assemble the bunnies, pipe a dot of melted candy on the flat side of a whole marshmallow for the body. For the head, press another whole same-size marshmallow into the candy on its side. Lay the partially assembled bunny on its back, pipe a dot of melted candy on each side of the body near the bottom, and attach the leg pieces cut from the same-size marshmallow. Pipe a dot of melted candy on the top of the head and arrange 2 sugared marshmallow ears made from same-size marshmallows, sugar side facing forward (see photo, above). Repeat to make 2 large and 50 baby bunnies. Refrigerate until the melted candy is set, about 5 minutes.

5 Snip a very small (⅟₁₆-inch) corner from the bags with the dark chocolate and vanilla frostings. For the nose, attach a heart decor to the front flat side of each marshmallow head with a dot of vanilla frosting. Pipe the eyes with the dark chocolate frosting.

6 Line a cookie sheet with wax paper. Arrange the carrot-shaped candy in rows on the cookie sheet. Place the green candy melts in a freezer-weight ziplock bag; do not seal the bag. Microwave for 10 seconds to soften, massage the

candy in the bag, return to the microwave, and repeat the process until smooth. Press out the excess air and seal the bag. Snip a small (⅛-inch) corner from the bag. Pipe a ½-inch-long wavy line onto one end of each candy as the leafy top (see photo, above). Refrigerate until the melted candy is set, about 5 minutes.

7 Place the chilled cake, flat side up, on a work surface. Trim the top of the cake level (see On the Level, page 14); reserve the cake trimmings for the dirt. Using a small knife, cut a 3-inch circle, about 2½ inches deep, from the center of the cake. Reserve the removed cake for the dirt.

STEP 8

8 Gently remove the carrots from the wax paper. Fill the opening in the cake with the carrots (see photo, opposite page). Cut a cardboard circle to fit on top of the cake, place it on the cake, and invert the cake, rounded side up. Place the cake on a serving platter. Spread the light green frosting on the cake and make soft swirls with an offset spatula or the back of a spoon (see Classic Swirled Frosting, page 23). Stand the marshmallow bunnies all over the cake, pressing them into the frosting to secure. Add patches of green sprinkles for grass. Crumble the reserved cake pieces and sprinkle the crumbs around the cake as dirt.

LADYBUG CAKE
Surprise Inside!
MAKES 14 SERVINGS

Ladybugs are real crowd-pleasers, and this one is so cute, she may attract a swarm to your next garden party! Her spots are made from chocolate doughnut holes, and surprise, she even has spots on the inside!

1 recipe Perfect Cake Mix batter (page 289) made
   with French vanilla cake mix
Red and black food coloring (McCormick)
17 chocolate doughnut holes (Munchkins)
1 can (16 ounces) vanilla frosting
Red paste food coloring (Wilton)
1 cup dark chocolate frosting
2 black licorice twists (Twizzlers)
1 black licorice lace
10 creme-filled chocolate sandwich cookies (Oreos)
6 thin pretzel sticks (Bachman)
2 mini chocolate-covered mints (Junior Mints)

1 Preheat the oven to 350°F and prepare a 16-ounce and a 1½-quart oven-safe glass bowl (see Please Release Me, page 12). Tint the batter bright pink using the liquid red food coloring. Spoon ⅔ cup of the batter into the 16-ounce bowl. Press 3 doughnut holes into the batter and top with another ⅔ cup of the batter, covering the doughnut holes, and smooth (see photos, below). Reserve 3 doughnut holes for the ladybug's wings. Spoon some of the remaining batter into the 1½-quart bowl. Add 4 or 5 doughnut holes. Repeat the layering to use the remaining batter and the remaining doughnut holes, making sure that the doughnut holes are completely covered with batter (see photo, below right). Smooth.

2 Place the bowls on a cookie sheet and bake until the cakes are firm and a toothpick inserted in the center comes out clean, 30 to 35 minutes for the small bowl and 45 to 50 minutes for the large bowl. Transfer the cakes on the cookie sheet to a wire rack to cool for 10 minutes. Invert, remove the bowls, and cool completely.

3 Line a cookie sheet with wax paper. Trim the top of each cake level (see On the Level, page 14). Place the cakes, trimmed side down, on a work surface. Trim ¾ inch from 1 edge of each cake and discard the trimmings. Place each cake on a cardboard cut to fit (see Getting on Base, page 14), rounded side up, and transfer to the cookie sheet. Place the cakes in the freezer to chill, about 30 minutes.

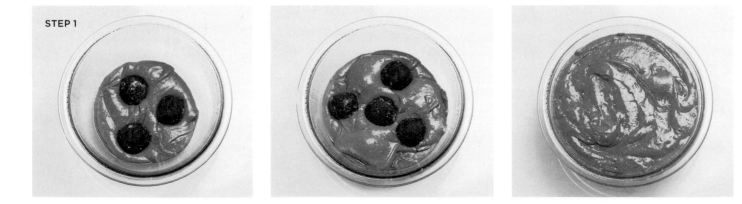

STEP 1

4 Tint the vanilla frosting red with the paste food coloring and spoon into a glass measuring cup. Cover with plastic wrap to prevent drying. Tint 3 tablespoons of the dark chocolate frosting black with the food coloring and spoon into a freezer-weight ziplock bag. Press out the excess air and seal the bag.

5 Line a cookie sheet with wax paper. As you make the parts, transfer them to the cookie sheet. For the legs, cut the black licorice twists into six 3-inch pieces. For the antennae, cut the licorice lace in half, twisting each piece into a curve at one end. Remove a cookie side from 2 of the chocolate sandwich cookies; reserve the creme-covered sides for the eyes. Place the 2 plain cookie sides and the remaining 8 chocolate sandwich cookies in a food processor and pulse until finely ground, or place the cookies in a freezer-weight ziplock bag (do not seal the bag) and crush with a rolling pin until finely ground. For the spots on the wings, place the cookie crumbs in a medium bowl. Cut the reserved 3 doughnut holes in half. Place them, cut side down, on a sheet of wax paper. Spread the tops with a thin layer of dark chocolate frosting and smooth. Press the frosted side of the doughnuts in the cookie crumbs to cover. Spread the remaining dark chocolate frosting over the small chilled cake and smooth. Press the cookie crumbs into the frosting to cover. Place the doughnuts and the cake in the freezer until set, about 30 minutes.

6 Line a cookie sheet with wax paper and place a wire rack on top. Place the large chilled cake on the wire rack. Microwave the red frosting,

stirring every 5 seconds, until it has the texture of lightly whipped cream, about 20 seconds. Pour the melted frosting over the cake to cover completely, allowing the excess to drip onto the pan. Place the cake in the refrigerator to set the frosting, about 30 minutes.

7 Use a large spatula to transfer the large cake to a serving platter. For the head, arrange the small cake against the large cake, trimmed edges together.

8 Use a long wooden skewer to score an indentation down the center of the large cake, starting at the head. Snip a small (⅛-inch) corner from the bag with the black frosting and pipe a line along the score mark.

9 To position the spots on the wings, use a toothpick to make 6 marks in the red frosting, mirroring one another on each side of the large cake and leaving enough space so that the doughnuts do not touch. Insert a pretzel stick into the cut side of each halved doughnut. Push the end of the pretzels into the marks on the cake, pressing the doughnuts flush with the cake. Use your finger to smooth any dents in the cookie crumbs on the doughnuts.

10 Using a dot of black frosting, attach the 2 creme-covered cookies on the small cake for the eyes. Use another dot of black frosting to attach the chocolate mints for the pupils. For the legs, add the 6 cut black licorice twists, 3 on each side of the body. For the antennae, insert 1 licorice lace into the head behind each eye.

SEA TURTLE CAKE

MAKES 12 SERVINGS

Our sea turtle is such a beautiful specimen, it may end up on the endangered cake list! One of our favorite candies, the marshmallow, is spray-painted with food color to mimic the leatherback's shell.

1 recipe Perfect Cake Mix (page 289) made with yellow cake mix, 1 cup batter baked in an 8-ounce oven-safe glass bowl for 30 to 35 minutes and 4 cups batter baked in a 2½-quart oven-safe glass bowl for 45 to 50 minutes

1 can (16 ounces) plus 1 cup vanilla frosting

Neon blue and yellow food coloring (McCormick)

10 jumbo marshmallows

1 can (1.5 ounces) each blue and green food decorating spray (Wilton, Cake Mate)

¼ cup each blue, green, and yellow candy-coated chocolates (M&M's)

2 white flat candy wafers (Neccos)

2 mini chocolate-covered mints (Junior Mints)

25 brown candy-coated chocolates (M&M's)

2 brown candy-coated chocolate-covered sunflower seeds (Sunny Seed Drops)

2 anisette toasts (Stella D'oro)

3 tablespoons light blue decorating sugar (Wilton)

1 Spoon 1 tablespoon of the vanilla frosting into a freezer-weight ziplock bag. Press out the excess air and seal the bag. Tint 1¼ cups of the remaining vanilla frosting light blue with the food coloring. Tint the remaining vanilla frosting yellow with the food coloring. Cover the frosting with plastic wrap until ready to use.

2 Line a cookie sheet with wax paper. Trim ½ inch off the top of each bowl cake to make a flat surface to support the cake. Place the cakes, trimmed side down, on a work surface. For the head, cut 1 inch from the edge of the small cake and discard. Starting 1 inch from the end of the first cut, make a second 1-inch cut from the edge, to give the head a V shape, and discard. For the body, cut 1½ inches from the edge of the large cake. Starting 2 inches from the end of the first cut, make a second 1½-inch cut from the edge, to taper the tail end of the body. For the front flippers, place each 1½-inch trimmed piece, cut side down, on a cardboard cut to fit. Place the head

and body cakes on cardboards cut to fit, trimmed side down. Spread a thin crumb coating of the yellow frosting (see Got Crumbs?, page 16) over the head and body cakes making sure to cover any exposed underside, and the front flippers, filling any gaps, and smooth. Transfer the cakes to the cookie sheet and place in the freezer until set, about 30 minutes.

3 Line a cookie sheet with wax paper. Cut the marshmallows in half lengthwise. Transfer 13 halves, cut side down and spaced about 1 inch apart, to the cookie sheet. Cut the remaining 7 halves on the diagonal to make 14 triangles, and transfer 10 triangles to the cookie sheet. Cut ¼ inch from the cut edge of the 4 remaining triangles and transfer the smaller triangles to the cookie sheet (see photo, opposite page).

4 Using the food decorating spray, add spots of blue and green color to the marshmallow pieces to create the mottled coloring of the turtle shell (see photo, opposite page). Let the marshmallows dry.

5 Place the cake on a serving platter. For the shell, spread the top of the cake with the light blue frosting and smooth. Press a single row of the yellow candy-coated chocolates where the blue and yellow frostings meet.

6 To assemble the shell, position the cake in front of you, tapered tail end to the back. Starting at the front of the cake, attach a row of colored marshmallow halves, crosswise, ¼ inch apart, down the center. Continue with 2 more rows to the right of the center row and 2 more to the

left, offsetting the marshmallows by ½ inch and filling in at the end of the rows with triangles to match the curve of the shell. Attach a marshmallow triangle at the back end for the tail.

7 For the head, snip a small (⅛-inch) corner from the bag with the vanilla frosting. Spread the small chilled cake with some of the yellow frosting and smooth. For the eyes, place the white candy wafers on top of the cake, one near each cut edge. Use some vanilla frosting to attach the chocolate-covered mints for the pupils. Pipe a small white highlight on each eye. Press some of the blue, green, and brown candy-coated chocolates in clusters on the head cake as scales. Press the 2 candy-coated sunflower seeds on the front of the cake as the nostrils. Using a small spatula, transfer the head cake to the front of the body cake on the platter.

8 For the front flippers, spread the 2 chilled cake pieces with some yellow frosting and smooth. Transfer the frosted pieces to the platter, positioning one on each side of the body about 2 inches from the head, curved edge facing forward, and tuck them under the shell. Press some of the blue, green, and brown candy-coated chocolates in clusters on each flipper. For the back flippers, use a small serrated knife to remove a 2-inch piece from one end of each anisette toast and discard. Place the toasts side by side on a work surface, rounded sides facing outward. Spread the top and sides of the toasts with the remaining yellow frosting and smooth. Place 1 toast on each side at the back of the cake, cut end against the cake, with the straight edge facing the tail. Press the remaining candy-coated chocolates in clusters on top of the back flippers as scales. Sprinkle the platter with the light blue sugar.

ORNAMENT CAKE

MAKES 14 SERVINGS

Favorite ornaments deserve special placement—like on a dessert plate. Smashed sugar turns a bowl cake, a cupcake, doughnuts, and a sugar cone into the prettiest festive bauble.

1 recipe Perfect Cake Mix (page 289) made with devil's food cake mix, ⅓ cup batter baked in a foil cupcake liner for 12 to 15 minutes and 4⅔ cups batter baked in a prepared 1½-quart oven-safe glass bowl for 45 to 50 minutes

3 plain doughnuts (Entenmann's)

2 cans (16 ounces each) vanilla frosting

Red, yellow, and green food coloring (McCormick)

1½ cups coarse white decorating sugar (Wilton)

1 sugar cone (Joy, Keebler)

1 teaspoon peppermint extract (McCormick)

1 strand jelly-filled red licorice (Welch's)

1 marshmallow

18 small white pearlized jelly beans (Jelly Belly)

1 Line a cookie sheet with wax paper. As you make the parts, transfer them to the cookie sheet. Cut ¼ inch from one edge of each doughnut and discard (see photo, right). Trim the top of the cake and the cupcake level (see On the Level, page 14). Place the cake, trimmed side down, on a cardboard cut to fit (see Getting on Base, page 14). Trim ¾ inch from opposite edges of the cake (this is where the cake and the doughnuts will come together). Spread a thin crumb coating of the vanilla frosting (see Got Crumbs?, page 16) on the cake, filling any gaps, and smooth. Place the cake, the cupcake, and the doughnuts in the freezer to chill for 30 minutes.

2 Tint ¾ cup of the vanilla frosting red with the food coloring. Tint ¾ cup of the vanilla frosting bright green with the yellow and green food coloring. Spoon the red, green, and 1 cup of the remaining vanilla frosting into separate freezer-weight ziplock bags. Press out the excess air and seal the bags.

3 Place the decorating sugar in a large bowl. Snip a ¼-inch corner from the bags with the frosting. Pipe some of the green frosting on 2 of the chilled doughnuts. Spread the frosting over the doughnuts, except the cut side, and smooth. Lightly press the sugar into the frosting to cover completely (see Smashed Sugar, page 37). Repeat with the remaining doughnut and some of the red frosting. Return the sugared doughnuts to the cookie sheet, cut side down. Pipe some vanilla frosting on top of the cupcake. Gently dip the top of the cupcake in the sugar to coat. Pipe alternating lines of colored frosting and white frosting, lengthwise, on the sugar cone. Gently press the sugar into the frosting to cover (see photo, below). Transfer to the cookie sheet.

4 Transfer the chilled cake to a serving platter, with the trimmed ends top and bottom. Use a toothpick to score stripes of straight and wavy lines, crosswise, on the cake. Alternating the vanilla, red, and green frostings, fill in the scored stripes in an even layer. Lightly press the sugar into the frosting to cover completely. Use a pastry brush to remove any excess sugar. Lightly press the sugared cake to smooth and flatten any ridges in the frosting.

5 To make the golden reflector in the center, use a 3-inch round cookie cutter or a small knife to cut a 2-inch-deep cone (tapered) shape in the top of the cake. Use a small knife or fork to remove the cake inside the cut. Spread some of the remaining vanilla frosting over the exposed cake and smooth. Score the tapered sides with the tip of a toothpick. Place the cake in the freezer for 15 minutes to chill.

6 Tint the peppermint extract yellow with the food coloring. Use a small craft brush to lightly paint the frosted center of the reflector with the yellow extract (see Flavor Painting, page 45).

7 For the hanger, poke 2 holes, about 1½ inches apart, in the foil base of the cupcake with a chopstick. Insert the ends of the licorice strand to make a 1½-inch loop.

8 To assemble, place a green doughnut, cut side down, against the cut side at the top of the cake. Insert a 6-inch wooden skewer through the doughnut and into the cake leaving 1½ inches exposed. For the hanger, push the frosted side of the cupcake onto the exposed skewer and up against the doughnut. Repeat the process on the bottom half of the cake, starting with a red, then a green doughnut. Insert a 6-inch wooden skewer through the doughnuts into the cake, leaving 2 inches exposed. Place the sugar cone with the open end against the green doughnut, to cover the skewer. Arrange the marshmallow under the cone for extra support.

9 Pipe a thin line of vanilla frosting around the edge of the yellow reflector and attach the jelly beans, end to end.

UP, UP, AND AWAY CAKE

MAKES 12 SERVINGS

Little balloon cakes take flight on strings of licorice lace. They are baked in three sizes of small bowls and get a lift from a coating of vibrantly colored frosting. The balloon knot is shaped from fruit chews in colors to match.

1 recipe Perfect Cake Mix (page 289) made with yellow cake mix, a scant ¾ cup batter each baked in two 10-ounce oven-safe glass bowls for 30 to 35 minutes, ½ cup batter each baked in six 6-ounce oven-safe glass bowls for 25 to 30 minutes, and ⅓ cup batter baked in a 5-ounce oven-safe glass bowl for 20 to 23 minutes
1 can (16 ounces) plus 1 cup vanilla frosting
Red, green, blue, and yellow food coloring (McCormick)
2 each red, green, blue, and yellow fruit chews (Jolly Rancher, Tootsie)
9 thin pretzel sticks (Bachman)
9 yellow licorice laces (Rips Whips)

1 Line a cookie sheet with wax paper. Trim the top of each cake level (see On the Level, page 14). Place the cakes, trimmed side down, on cardboards cut to fit (see Getting on Base, page 14). Transfer the cakes to the cookie sheet and chill in the freezer for about 30 minutes.

2 Spoon 1 tablespoon of the vanilla frosting into a freezer-weight ziplock bag. Press out the excess air and seal the bag. Divide the remaining vanilla frosting among 4 bowls. Tint each bowl a different primary color with the food coloring: red, green, blue, and yellow. Spoon each color of frosting into a separate freezer-weight ziplock bag. Press out the excess air and seal the bags.

3 Line a cookie sheet with wax paper. As you make the parts, transfer them to the cookie sheet. Microwave the fruit chews for 3 seconds to soften. Press the 2 like-color fruit chews together and roll out to a ⅛-inch thickness. Cut out two 1½-inch circles from the blue, the green, and the yellow and 3 circles from the red, rerolling the scraps as needed.

4 Poke the end of a pretzel stick into the center of a candy circle and thread the candy through to within ½ inch of the other end of the pretzel, pinching the top around the end to look like the balloon knot. Insert a strand of yellow licorice lace at the open end as the rope, pressing to secure. Repeat with the remaining candy circles and pretzels.

5 Line a cookie sheet with wax paper and place a wire rack on top. Arrange 2 cakes on the wire rack (use 3 small cakes for the red frosting). Microwave 1 color of frosting, stopping to massage the bag, until it has the texture of lightly whipped cream, about 7 seconds. Snip a ¼-inch corner from the bag. Pipe the melted frosting over the cakes to cover completely. Allow the excess frosting to drip onto the pan. Use a spatula and return the frosted cakes to the original cookie sheet. Repeat the process with the remaining cakes and colored frosting, coating 3 small cakes red and 2 cakes each yellow, blue, and green. Refrigerate until the frosting is just set, about 30 minutes.

6 When ready to serve, arrange the cakes close together on a serving platter, raising some cakes up on a juice glass or small inverted bowl, to make a tight cluster. Insert the pretzel end of a same-color balloon knot into the bottom of each cake, orienting them all in the same direction. Gather the yellow laces together on the platter below the cakes.

7 Snip a small (⅛-inch) corner from the bag with the vanilla frosting. Pipe a small white highlight on the same side of each cake for a reflection.

measure for measure

measuring-cup cakes

For good measure, add more shapes using oven-safe measuring cups from your everyday kitchen arsenal. They are perfect for designs that need a cylindrical shape. Picture a 1-cupper as the head of a zebra, reindeer, or piñata. Or stack a 1-cupper, a 4-cupper, and a 1-quart bowl cake to build an egg shape that works as well for a Fabergé egg as for a baby in diapers.

Note: *Just like bowls, measuring cups come in a variety of materials, including glass, metal, and ceramic. Whatever you use, make sure it is oven-safe. (Be sure to read Baking in Glass, page 293.) We based our recipes on sizes and shapes found in oven-safe glass measuring cups because they are more uniform. But other oven-safe vessels of similar size and shape can be used, and the difference will make your design original.*

STABLEMATES MASTER CAKE

These thoroughbreds are similar enough to share a stable, but beyond their measuring-cup heads and loaf-pan bodies lies a world of candy difference!

1 recipe Perfect Cake Mix batter (page 289) made with French vanilla cake mix
¼ cup white candy melting wafers (Wilton)
20 creme-filled sandwich cookies (Oreos)

1 Preheat the oven to 350°F and prepare a 1-cup oven-safe measuring cup and a 9-x-5-inch loaf pan (see Please Release Me, page 12). Spoon 1 cup of the batter into the prepared measuring cup and pour the remaining batter into the prepared loaf pan. Spread to the edges and smooth. Bake until the cakes are firm and a toothpick inserted in the center comes out clean, 25 to 30 minutes for the measuring cup and 45 to 50 minutes for the loaf pan. Transfer the cakes to a wire rack and cool for 10 minutes. Invert, remove the measuring cup and the loaf pan, and cool completely.

2 Line a cookie sheet with wax paper. Place the loaf cake, bottom side down, on a cardboard cut to fit. Place the cakes on the cookie sheet and transfer to the freezer to chill, about 30 minutes.

3 Line a cookie sheet with wax paper. Place the candy melts in a freezer-weight ziplock bag; do not seal the bag. Microwave for 10 seconds to soften. Massage the candy in the bag, return to the microwave, and repeat the process until the candy is smooth. Press out the excess air and seal the bag. Place 4 sandwich cookies on a cookie sheet. Snip a small (⅛-inch) corner from the bag and pipe some melted candy on top of each of the 4 cookies. Place another cookie directly on top, pressing to secure. Repeat to make 4 stacks of 5 cookies each for the legs. Transfer to the cookie sheet and place in the freezer to chill, about 15 minutes.

VARIATIONS

ZEBRA: Divide the batter in half and tint one half with ¼ cup unsweetened cocoa powder. Spoon 3 tablespoons of the vanilla batter into the prepared measuring cup. Spread to the edges and smooth. Top with 3 tablespoons of the cocoa batter and smooth. Repeat the process, alternating the flavors, to make 5 layers of batter (about 1 cup). Alternate the remaining batters to make 7 layers in the prepared loaf pan (see photos, below). Bake and chill as directed.

PIÑATA: Divide the batter into 5 bowls and, using food coloring, tint each batter a different color: orange with yellow and red food coloring;

lime green with yellow and green food coloring; yellow; pink with neon pink food coloring; and blue with neon blue food coloring. Spoon 3 tablespoons of one color into the prepared measuring cup as in the zebra variation. Spread to the edges and smooth. Repeat the process with the 4 remaining colors to make 5 layers of batter (about 1 cup). Alternate the remaining batter to make 5 layers in the prepared loaf pan. Bake and chill as directed.

REINDEER: Substitute 1 recipe Perfect Cake Mix batter (page 289) made with devil's food cake mix, ¼ cup dark cocoa candy melting wafers (Wilton), and 20 creme-filled chocolate sandwich cookies (Oreos).

PIÑATA CAKE
Surprise Inside!
MAKES 12 SERVINGS

1 Stablemates Master Cake (page 182) made with
   Piñata Variation
1 can (16 ounces) plus 1 cup vanilla frosting
1 jumbo marshmallow
5 thin pretzel sticks (Bachman)
1 jumbo ice-cream wafer cup (Joy)
50 each orange, green, and yellow spice drops
100 white spice drops
1 cup each orange, light green, yellow, pink, and blue
   decorating sugar (Cake Mate)
1 anisette toast (Stella D'oro)
¼ cup white candy melting wafers (Wilton)
2 white flat candy wafers (Necco)
2 mini chocolate-covered mints (Junior Mints)
1 plain 9½-inch bread stick (Stella D'oro)

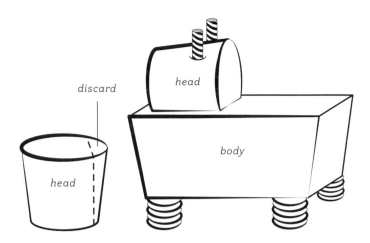

1 Spoon 1 cup of the vanilla frosting into a freezer-weight ziplock bag. Press out the excess air and seal the bag.

2 For the head, place the measuring-cup cake upright and starting ½ inch in from the edge at the top, cut straight down to the bottom (see illustration, above). Spread some vanilla frosting on top of the chilled loaf cake at one end. Place the chilled measuring-cup cake, cut side down, into the frosting lengthwise, 1 inch from the edge of the cake, wide end toward the center.

3 Push 2 drinking straws through the measuring-cup cake, one on each side, and into the loaf cake for stability (see illustration, above). Trim the top of the straws flush with the cake. Snip the marshmallow in half on the diagonal to make the ears. Insert a pretzel stick into the flat uncut side of each marshmallow piece. Insert the remaining 3 pretzel sticks into the front end of the measuring-

STEP 3

cup cake. Trim and discard 1 inch from the open end of the ice-cream cup. Attach the cut side of the cone to the front end of the measuring-cup cake, using the pretzels for support and securing with frosting (see photo, above). Attach the ears by pushing the pretzels into the top back edge of the measuring-cup cake, cut side to the back, and securing with frosting. Return the cake to the freezer to chill.

4 Line a cookie sheet with wax paper. As you make the parts, transfer them to the cookie sheet. To make the fringe, work with 10 like-color spice drops at a time. Sprinkle the work surface

with the matching colored sugar. (With the white spice drops, use half of them with the pink decorating sugar and half with the blue sugar.) Press 10 spice drops together and place on the sugared surface, sprinkle with additional sugar, and roll out the candy to roughly a 2½-x-6-inch rectangle, sprinkling with more sugar, as necessary, to prevent sticking. Repeat with the remaining sugar and spice drops (you will have 5 rectangles of each sugar color). Trim the long sides of each rectangle to straighten. Cut the rectangles in half lengthwise. To create the fringe on each strip, use small scissors to make cuts ⅛ inch apart along one long side, keeping ¼ inch of the strip uncut on the opposite side. Cut the strips into 1½- and 2½-inch-wide pieces.

5 For the tail, cut the anisette toast in half crosswise and discard 1 piece. Insert the pointed end of a 4-inch wooden skewer into the straight edge of the toast piece, near the tapered end. Place the candy melts in a freezer-weight ziplock bag; do not seal the bag. Microwave for 10 seconds to soften. Massage the candy in the bag, return to the microwave, and repeat the process until the candy is smooth. Snip a small (⅛-inch) corner from the bag. Pipe some of the melted candy on the toast piece. Starting at the cut end, wrap a row of pink fringe around the cookie, trimming any excess and allowing it to overhang the end by ½ inch. Repeat with another row of pink fringe, overlapping the first row by ½ inch. Continue, adding 2 rows of green and 2 rows of yellow. Pipe a line of melted candy around the

bottom of a chilled cookie stack. Attach a row of the pink fringe, trimming any excess. Pipe more melted candy and add 3 rows of yellow fringe to cover the sides of the cookie stack. Repeat with the remaining 3 cookie stacks. Refrigerate for 5 minutes to set.

6 Snip a small (⅛-inch) corner from the bag of vanilla frosting. Arrange the fringed cookie legs on a serving platter, one stack for each corner of the body. Pipe a dot of vanilla frosting on top of each stack. Using a large spatula, transfer the chilled cake on its cardboard to rest on top of the cookie legs. Adjust the cookie legs, as needed, to support the cake.

7 Spread some vanilla frosting over the body cake and smooth. Press a row of green fringe around the bottom edge of the body, allowing it to overhang the cake slightly. Repeat with a second row of green. Repeat, adding rows of orange fringe to the front and back third of the cake, with rows of pink fringe for the center third and a row of blue fringe at the base of the head and the tail area (see photo, page 185).

8 Spread the remaining vanilla frosting over the head, muzzle, and ears and smooth. Starting at the bottom, attach 3 rows of blue fringe to the front of the muzzle, trimming to round the top row of fringe. On the sides of the head, starting at the neck, attach 3 rows of yellow fringe. Continue to cover the sides with rows of green fringe. Add more green fringe to the top of the muzzle, up to the eye area. Add several rows of blue fringe up the back of the head and the back of the ears, trimming to fit the small areas. Add rows of pink

fringe to cover the forehead between the eyes. Add orange fringe to cover the front of the ears.

9 Reheat the candy melts in the microwave, massaging the bag if necessary. Pipe a dot of melted candy on each side of the head and attach a white candy wafer for the eyes, holding the candy until set, about 2 minutes. Use a dot of melted candy to attach the chocolate mints as the pupils. Attach the tail to the back of the cake, inserting the skewer all the way into the cake.

10 Serve with the plain bread stick as the bat for the piñata.

REINDEER CAKE

MAKES 12 SERVINGS

1 Stablemates Master Cake (page 182), Reindeer
   Variation
1 can (16 ounces) plus 1 cup chocolate frosting
1 cup vanilla frosting
3 marshmallows
3 thin pretzel sticks (Bachman)
1 box (12 ounces) gingersnap cookies
4 thin pretzel twists (Bachman)
¼ cup white candy melting wafers (Wilton)
1 large red gumball (SweetWorks)
12 candy spearmint leaves
2 white flat candy wafers (Necco)
1 roll (0.75 ounce) red fruit leather (Fruit by the Foot)
15 each small red and brown candy-coated
   chocolates (M&M's Minis)
2 brown candy-coated chocolates (M&M's)
Finely chopped sweetened flaked coconut
   (optional)

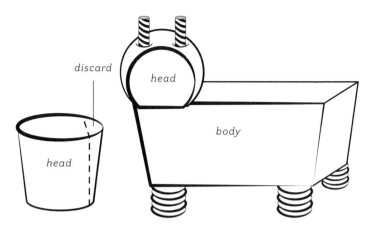

1 Spoon ¼ cup of the chocolate frosting into a freezer-weight ziplock bag. Spoon the vanilla frosting into a freezer-weight ziplock bag. Press out the excess air and seal the bags.

2 Place the measuring-cup cake upright and, starting ½ inch in from the edge at the top, cut straight down to the bottom (see illustration, above). For the ears, cut 1 marshmallow in half on the diagonal. Insert a pretzel stick into the flat end of each piece. Transfer the chilled measuring-cup cake, cut side down, to a work surface. Press the pretzel end of a marshmallow ear into the wide end of the cake, one on each side at the top, securing with some chocolate frosting. Return the cake to the freezer for 30 minutes to chill.

STEP 3

3 Line a cookie sheet with wax paper. As you make the parts, transfer them to the cookie sheet. For the antlers, position the 4 pretzel twists with the rounded side and the inverted V at the bottom. Using a serrated knife, cut the pretzels crosswise to remove the top and leave the inverted V intact (see photo, above). Discard the tops. For the muzzle, trim ¼ inch from one side of a gingersnap cookie with a small serrated knife. For the tail, using the serrated knife, remove ½ inch from one side of a gingersnap. Starting at one end of the cut, remove ½ inch, on the diagonal, from the opposite side to make a V shape.

4 Place the remaining gingersnap cookies in a food processor and pulse until finely ground. Place the cookie crumbs in a large bowl.

5 Place the white candy melts in a freezer-weight ziplock bag; do not seal the bag. Microwave for 10 seconds to soften. Massage the candy in the bag, return to the microwave, and repeat the process until the candy is smooth. Press out the excess air and seal the bag.

6 For the muzzle, pipe a dot of the melted candy in the center of the cut edge of the gingersnap. Press the gumball into the candy. For the tail, pipe a dot of the melted candy on the wide end of the V-shaped tail cookie and press the end of a pretzel stick into the candy, rotating it to coat and allowing it to overhang about 2 inches. For the antlers, pipe a dime-size dot of melted candy on one cut end of 1 pretzel twist on the cookie sheet. Place a marshmallow on the pretzel. Place another pretzel twist, oriented exactly like the first one, on top, supported by the marshmallow, with a cut end in the melted candy (see photo, previous page). Repeat to make another antler. Transfer to the refrigerator to set, about 5 minutes.

7 Cut the spearmint leaves in half horizontally to make 24 leaf shapes. Cut and discard one third from each white candy wafer for the eyes.

8 Spread some chocolate frosting over the sides of the chilled cookie legs. Roll the cookies in the cookie crumbs to coat.

9 Line a cookie sheet with wax paper. Spread the chilled loaf cake with some chocolate frosting and smooth. Place the cake on the cookie sheet. Gently press handfuls of the cookie crumbs into the sides and top of the cake to cover completely. Brush any excess crumbs from the top of the cake.

10 Arrange the cookie legs on a serving platter, 1 stack for each corner of the body. Snip a small (⅛-inch) corner from the bag with the chocolate frosting. Pipe a dot of chocolate frosting

on top of each cookie leg. Using a large spatula, transfer the body cake on the cardboard to rest on top of the cookie legs, adjusting the legs, as needed, to support the cake.

11 Place the chilled measuring-cup cake, cut side down, on the cookie sheet. Insert a drinking straw halfway into the top of the cake to help secure the cake later. Spread the measuring-cup cake and the marshmallow ears with some chocolate frosting and smooth. Attach the cookie and gumball to the front tapered end of the cake as the muzzle. Supporting the cake with the straw, gently press handfuls of the cookie crumbs into the sides and top of the cake, including the ears, to cover completely and smooth. Brush any excess crumbs from the cake. With a large spatula, transfer the cake, cut side down, to one end of the body cake, turning the head cake to one side, perpendicular to the body cake (see illustration, page 189). Carefully press the straw into the body cake. Insert another straw about 2 inches away for extra support. Trim the straws flush with the top of the cake and cover the holes with cookie crumbs.

12 Spread the remaining chocolate frosting over the tail cookie. Coat with the cookie crumbs. Insert the pretzel end of the tail, pretzel side down, into the back end of the body cake.

13 Gently peel the pretzel antlers from the wax paper and remove the supporting marshmallows. Insert the candy end of the antlers into the top of the head, between the ears, securing with more frosting. Snip a small (⅛-inch) corner from the bag with the vanilla frosting and pipe tufts of fur between the antlers. Pipe short vertical lines of chest fur on the front end of the cake under the head, always pulling the frosting down. Pipe fur along the bottom edge on both sides of the cake at the belly and on the underside of the tail cookie.

14 Fold the fruit leather in half lengthwise, pressing firmly. Wrap the fruit-leather strip around the muzzle, trimming to fit. Add the spearmint leaves, sugared side up, and the small red candies around the base of the head, securing with some vanilla frosting. Press the small brown candies along the back as spots. For the eyes, use the chocolate frosting to attach the white flat candies, cut side down, on either side of the head. Outline the white candy with chocolate frosting and attach the large brown candies as the pupils. Pipe eyelashes above each eye. Pipe a small vertical line under the nose and a curve for the mouth.

15 Sprinkle the platter with chopped coconut as snow, if using.

ZEBRA CAKE
Surprise Inside!
MAKES 12 SERVINGS

1 Stablemates Master Cake (page 182), Zebra
  Variation
1 can (16 ounces) dark chocolate frosting
Black food coloring (McCormick)
1 can (16 ounces) plus 1 cup vanilla frosting
1 jumbo marshmallow
6 thin pretzel sticks (Bachman)
2 anisette toasts (Stella D'oro)
3 creme-filled chocolate sandwich cookies (Oreos)
½ cup dark cocoa candy melting wafers (Wilton)
2 cups coarse white decorating sugar (Wilton)
6 mini marshmallows
2 brown candy-coated chocolates (M&M's)
2 large squares shredded wheat (Post Original Big
  Biscuit)

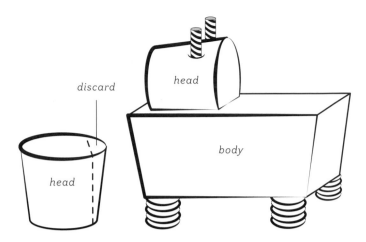

1 Tint the dark chocolate frosting black with the food coloring. Spoon ¾ cup of the black frosting into each of 2 freezer-weight ziplock bags. Spoon ¾ cup of the vanilla frosting into a freezer-weight ziplock bag. Press out the excess air and seal the bags.

2 Line a cookie sheet with wax paper. As you make the parts, transfer them to the cookie sheet. For the ears, cut the jumbo marshmallow in half crosswise. Insert a pretzel stick into the edge of one narrow end of each half. For the tail, use a small serrated knife to cut a 2-inch piece, crosswise, from 1 anisette toast. Reserve the remaining piece for the mane. Insert the pointed end of a 4-inch wooden skewer into the bottom straight edge of the 2-inch tail piece, near the cut end. For the mane, cut a 1½-inch piece, measured from the cut edge, from the reserved anisette toast piece; discard the tip. Make a hole large enough for the end of a pretzel stick in the center

of the bottom straight edge of the 1½-inch piece and of the remaining whole anisette toast (see photo, page 194).

3 Place the chocolate sandwich cookies on a work surface. Use the serrated knife to remove ¼ inch from the edge of 2 cookies and ½ inch from the edge of the remaining cookie. Transfer the cookie pieces to the cookie sheet. Place the candy melts in a freezer-weight ziplock bag; do not seal the bag. Microwave for 10 seconds to soften. Massage the candy in the bag, return to the microwave, and repeat the process until the candy is smooth. Press out the excess air and seal the bag. Snip a small (⅛-inch) corner from the bag. Press the cut edges of the 2 larger sandwich cookie pieces together to make a figure-eight shape and pipe some melted candy on top of the cookies and along the edges where they meet. For the bottom of the muzzle, pipe some melted candy on top of the remaining cookie piece and place 2 pretzel sticks into the melted candy, rotating to coat and allowing them to overhang the cut side of the cookie. For the mane, pipe some melted candy on one end of each of the remaining 2 pretzel sticks and insert them into the holes in the 1½-inch toast and the whole toast (see photo, page 194).

4 Line a cookie sheet with wax paper. Place the white decorating sugar in a large bowl. Snip a small (⅛-inch) corner from the bags with the black frosting. Spread the sides of a chilled cookie leg with some vanilla frosting and smooth. Pipe horizontal uneven lines of black frosting around the leg. Hold the leg over the bowl of sugar and gently press the sugar into the frosting, flattening the black lines and smoothing the frosting (see Smashed Sugar, page 37). Repeat with the remaining 3 cookie legs. Transfer the legs to the cookie sheet.

5 Place the chilled loaf cake on the cookie sheet. Spread the cake with vanilla frosting and smooth. Pipe uneven lines of black frosting, about 1 inch apart, on the cake to create the zebra stripes (to make wider stripes, pipe several adjacent rows of the black frosting). Gently press handfuls of the sugar into the sides and top of the cake to cover completely. Brush any excess sugar from the top of the cake.

6 Arrange the cookie legs on a serving platter, 1 stack for each corner of the body. Snip a small (⅛-inch) corner from the bag with the vanilla frosting. Pipe a dot of vanilla frosting on top of each cookie leg. Using a large spatula, transfer the body cake from the cardboard to rest on top of the cookie legs, adjusting the legs, as needed, to support the cake.

7 Place the measuring-cup cake upright and, starting ½ inch in from the edge at the top, cut straight down to the bottom (see illustration, page

STEP 7

192). Place the chilled measuring-cup cake, cut side down, on the cookie sheet. Insert a drinking straw halfway into the top of the cake to help secure the cake later. Spread the measuring-cup cake with the remaining vanilla frosting and smooth. Pipe zigzag lines of black frosting, about ¾ inch apart, to create the zebra stripes (see photo, opposite page). Supporting the cake with the straw, gently press handfuls of the sugar into the sides and top of the cake to cover completely and smooth. Brush any excess sugar from the cake. With a large spatula, transfer the head cake, cut side down, to the body cake, positioning it lengthwise, 1 inch from the edge of one end of the cake, wide end toward the center. Carefully press the straw through the head and into the body cake. Insert another straw about 2 inches away for extra support. Trim the straws flush with the top of the cake.

8 For the mane, push the pretzel end of the 1½-inch anisette toast piece into the top of the head, aligning the end of the toast with the edge of the cake (see photo, opposite page). Position the whole anisette toast directly behind the first piece, overlapping it to line up the top of the tapered end with the top of the first piece, and push the pretzel into the cake (see photo, opposite page). Starting at the front with vanilla frosting, pipe alternating vertical stripes of the black and vanilla frosting, about ½ inch wide, along one side to the end of the mane and up the other side. Pipe dots of frosting on the top of the mane to match the alternating stripes and cover the toasts. Use a small knife to remove a section of sugared frosting the size of one sandwich cookie from the top of the head cake at the tapered end. Pipe some vanilla frosting on the cleaned area and attach the figure-eight cookies, lengthwise, candy-melt side down, leaving about half a cookie overhanging the front edge of the cake. Insert the pretzel ends of the

bottom muzzle cookie into the head cake, pretzel side down, about ½ inch below the overhanging cookie. Using a dot of black frosting, attach the mini marshmallows, between the muzzle cookies, flat side against the cookies, for the teeth.

9 Pipe vertical lines of black and vanilla frosting, about ½ inch apart, over the marshmallow ears to create stripes (see photo, opposite page). Gently press the marshmallows into the sugar to cover. Insert the pretzel end of the ears into the head cake on either side of the front of the mane.

10 For the tail, pipe horizontal lines of black and vanilla frosting over the tail piece, then coat with sugar, pressing to smooth. Insert the skewer on the tail into the end of the body cake, near the top. Pipe several rows of black frosting at the tip of the tail for tufts of hair.

11 Use a dot of black frosting to attach the brown candies as the eyes and pipe a line of black frosting around each eye to outline. Gently break up the shredded wheat and arrange it around the base of the cake to create the dry grass.

PAT THE POODLE CAKE

MAKES 14 SERVINGS

Nothing says pampered like a sassy pink poodle. The marshmallow poodle cut, wafer-cone ears and snout, and sparkling Twinkie toes are all pretty in pink.

1 recipe Stablemates Master Cake (page 182) made with French vanilla cake mix, prepared through step 2
2 cans (16 ounces each) cups vanilla frosting
2 tablespoons dark chocolate frosting
Neon pink food coloring (McCormick)
3 creme-filled vanilla snack cakes (Twinkies)
4 creme-filled vanilla sandwich cookies (Golden Oreos)
2 ice-cream wafer cones (Joy, Keebler)
1 cup light pink decorating sugar (Wilton)
3 plain 9½-inch bread sticks (Stella D'oro)
1 bag (10 ounces) pink marshmallows
1 black jelly bean
1 yellow flat candy wafer (Necco)
1 teaspoon pink small round sprinkles (Wilton)
2 brown candy-coated chocolates (M&M's)

1 Spoon 2 tablespoons of the vanilla frosting into a freezer-weight ziplock bag. Spoon the dark chocolate frosting into a freezer-weight ziplock bag. Tint the remaining vanilla frosting light pink with the neon pink food coloring. Spoon ½ cup of the pink frosting into a freezer-weight ziplock bag. Press out the excess air and seal the bags. Cover the remaining pink frosting with plastic wrap until ready to use.

2 Line a cookie sheet with wax paper. Remove the cardboard from the chilled loaf cake and place the cake, bottom side down, on a work surface. Starting 1½ inches in from one end of the cake, cut straight down. This 1½-inch piece will be used as support behind the cake. To straighten the other end, start ¼ inch in from the uncut end and cut straight down. Discard this trimming. Working on the same short end of the cake and using a serrated knife, remove a ¾-inch triangle from each corner (see illustration, below top).

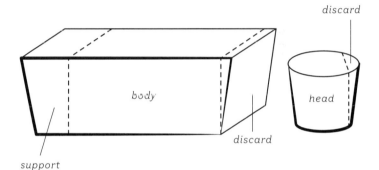

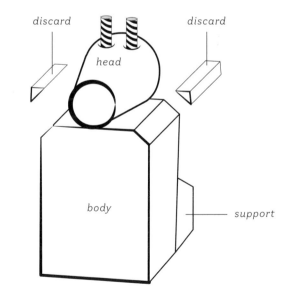

3 Place the large cake, beveled side up, and the support cake, cut side against the flat back side of the large cake, on a cardboard cut to fit. Secure the cakes with some pink frosting. Place the measuring-cup cake upright and, starting ½ inch in from the edge at the top, cut straight down to the bottom (see illustration, previous page, bottom). Attach the chilled head cake, cut side down, on top of the body, tapered end to the front, using frosting to secure. Insert 2 drinking straws side by side, about 2 inches apart, into the center of the head cake and down into the body cake for support; trim the straws flush with the top of the cake. Spread a thin crumb coating of pink frosting (see Got Crumbs?, page 16) on the cake, filling any gaps, and smooth. Place the cake in the freezer until set, about 30 minutes.

4 Line a cookie sheet with wax paper. As you make the parts, transfer them to the cookie sheet. For the front paws, cut 1 of the snack cakes in half crosswise. Leave the remaining 2 snack cakes whole for the back legs (see photo, left). For the haunches, spread some pink frosting on top of 2 of the vanilla sandwich cookies. Place another cookie on top of each to make 2 stacks of 2 cookies. Place the snack cakes and cookie stacks in the freezer for 30 minutes to chill.

5 To make the muzzle, use a serrated knife to cut 1 inch from the open end of 1 ice-cream cone (see photo, left). For the ears, cut the remaining ice-cream cone in half lengthwise. Place the pink decorating sugar in a large bowl. Spread the outside of the muzzle and the ears with a thin layer of pink frosting and sprinkle with the pink sugar to coat. Cut 2 of the bread sticks into 7-inch lengths. Spread the 2 cut bread sticks and the remaining whole bread stick with a thin layer of pink frosting and smooth. Sprinkle the bread sticks with the pink sugar to coat.

6 Spread a thin layer of pink frosting on the chilled snack cakes and cookie stacks. Sprinkle with the pink sugar to coat.

7 Set aside 10 of the pink marshmallows. Cut the remaining marshmallows into ½-inch pieces for the poodle cut. Cut the black jelly bean in half lengthwise and discard 1 piece.

8 Transfer the chilled cake to a serving platter. Spread the remaining pink frosting over the cake in an even layer and smooth.

2 inches from the body, rounded side forward. Position the cut side of the trimmed bread sticks on top of the paws, near the cut edge, and lean them against the front of the cake, near the shoulders, using frosting to secure at each end.

11 Snip a very small (¹⁄₁₆-inch) corner from the bag with the chocolate frosting and pipe PAT on the yellow flat candy for the dog tag. Pipe a line around the edge on top of the tag with the pink frosting and press the pink sprinkles into the frosting. Use a dot of frosting to attach the tag to the front of the cake body.

12 Use the pink frosting to attach the marshmallow pieces for the poodle cut around the neck and ankles, the tip of the ears, and one end of the remaining bread stick for the tail. Using some pink frosting, attach the 10 reserved pink marshmallows on the head, between the ears, for the topknot.

13 Snip a small (¹⁄₈-inch) corner from the bag with the vanilla frosting. Pipe 2 dots of vanilla frosting above the muzzle and attach the brown candies for the eyes. Pipe a dot of vanilla frosting at the top of the front of the muzzle and press the cut side of the black jelly bean, horizontally, into the frosting for the nose.

14 When ready to serve, insert the bread-stick tail, marshmallow end up, into the support cake at the back.

9 Snip a small (¹⁄₈-inch) corner from the bag with the pink frosting. Press the open end of the muzzle cone into the front end of the head cake and secure with pink frosting. Add the cone ears, narrow end toward the top of the head cake, near the back, securing with pink frosting.

10 Arrange the whole snack cakes on either side of the cake as the back legs. For the haunches, add a cookie stack on top of each snack cake, flat side against the body cake, securing with pink frosting. Arrange the paws at the front,

SIAMESE CAT CAKE

MAKES 12 SERVINGS

Purrr-fect by any measure, but baked in a measuring cup and a loaf pan, our kitty really stacks up! The shorthair look is created using a fork to "comb" the frosting, and her distinctive chocolate points are Oreo cookie crumbs.

1 recipe Stablemates Master Cake (page 182) made with yellow cake mix, prepared through step 2
1 can (16 ounces) plus 1½ cups vanilla frosting
3 tablespoons dark chocolate frosting
Neon blue food coloring (McCormick; optional)
1 jumbo marshmallow
2 thin pretzel sticks (Bachman)
¼ cup pink decorating sugar (Cake Mate)
12 white spice drops
2 4-inch round oatmeal cookies (Archway)
¼ cup white candy melting wafers (Wilton)
5 orange circus peanuts
3 plain 9½-inch bread sticks (Stella D'oro)
2 tablespoons blue decorating sugar (Cake Mate)
20 bite-size creme-filled chocolate sandwich cookies (Mini Oreos)
18 small white pearl candies (SweetWorks)
1 black gumdrop (Crows)
2 brown candy-coated chocolates (M&M's)
1 unfrosted cupcake (optional)

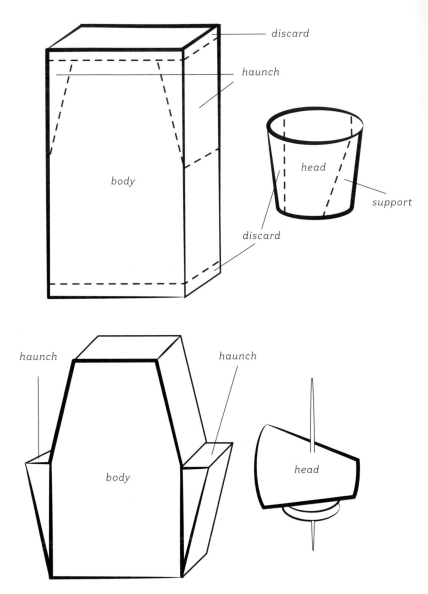

1 Spoon 2 tablespoons of the vanilla frosting into a freezer-weight ziplock bag. Spoon 2 tablespoons of the dark chocolate frosting into a freezer-weight ziplock bag. If using the optional cupcake, tint ¼ cup of the vanilla frosting light blue with the blue food coloring. Spoon the blue frosting into a freezer-weight ziplock bag. Press out the excess air and seal the bags. Tint the remaining vanilla frosting beige with the remaining tablespoon of dark chocolate frosting. Cover the frosting with plastic wrap until ready to use.

2 Line a cookie sheet with wax paper. For the head, place the chilled measuring-cup cake upright on a work surface. Place the measuring-cup cake upright and, starting ½ inch in from the edge at the top, cut straight down to the bottom (see illustration, above top). On the side opposite the trimmed side, cut a wedge that starts at the outside edge at the top and angles to 1½ inches in from the bottom edge on the same side. Reserve this wedge to support the body cake. Place the head cake on the cookie sheet, straight trimmed

STEP 4

STEP 7

side down, angled trimmed side up. For the ears, cut the marshmallow in half on the diagonal. Insert a pretzel stick into the flat end of each marshmallow piece. Insert the pretzel end of a marshmallow ear into each side on the wide end of the head cake, securing with some beige frosting. Place the cake in the freezer for 30 minutes to chill.

3 For the body, remove the cardboard from the chilled loaf cake and place the cake, bottom side down, on a work surface. Trim ¼ inch from each short side to straighten the ends. Starting at one short end, 1 inch in from one long side, cut a triangle that ends at the midpoint of the same side (see illustration, page 200). Repeat, starting at the top, 1 inch in from the opposite long side, to cut another triangle. Trim 1 inch from the tapered end of each triangle. Stand the loaf cake on end, wide side down, on a cardboard cut to fit. Spread some

beige frosting on the back of the cake. As added support, press the reserved wedge of cake from the head into the frosting on the back of the body cake, cut side against the cake, tapered end up. For the haunches, spread the lower sides of the loaf cake with some frosting and attach the triangle-shaped cake pieces, cut sides against the cake, trimmed tapered ends down (see illustration, page 200). Place the cake in the freezer for 30 minutes to chill.

4 Line a cookie sheet with wax paper. As you make the parts, transfer them to the cookie sheet. To make the collar, sprinkle the work surface with some of the pink sugar. Press 10 white spice drops together and roll them out, adding more sugar to prevent sticking, to a ½-x-11-inch strip. Trim the long sides to make even (see photo, above left). Stack the 2 oatmeal cookies on top of each other. Use a chopstick to poke a hole in the middle of the stack, making it large enough for a wooden skewer to pass through the hole.

5 Place the white candy melts in a freezer-weight ziplock bag; do not seal the bag. Microwave for 10 seconds to soften. Massage the candy in the bag, return to the microwave, and repeat the process until the candy is smooth. Press out the excess air and seal the bag.

6 Snip a small (⅛-inch) corner from the bag with the melted candy. Pipe some of the melted candy on top of one of the oatmeal cookies, avoiding the hole. Place the other oatmeal cookie on top, bottom side down, lining up the holes. Pipe a line of the melted candy around the outside edge of the cookies. Press the pink candy collar into the melted candy to cover the edge of the cookies, pressing to secure and trimming the ends. Transfer to the cookie sheet and refrigerate until set, about 5 minutes.

7 To make the paws, place 4 of the circus peanuts on a work surface, flat side down. Trim ½ inch from one end of each peanut. For the tail, trim ¼ inch from one end of the remaining circus peanut (see photo, opposite page). Roll the circus peanut between your hands to form a log about the same thickness as the bread stick and shape it into a curve. Pipe a dot of melted candy on the cut end of the rolled circus peanut and attach it to the end of a bread stick. For the whiskers, pipe 2½-inch-long curved lines of the melted candy on the wax paper, pulling the end into a point; make about 10 in case of breakage. Refrigerate until the candy is set, about 5 minutes.

8 For the eyes, sprinkle a work surface with some of the blue sugar. Press the remaining 2 white spice drops together and place on the sugared surface. Sprinkle with additional blue sugar, and roll out to a 2-inch circle, sprinkling with more sugar, as necessary, to prevent sticking. Cut the rolled candy into two ¾-x-1¼-inch ovals with tapered ends.

9 Reserve 2 whole bite-size sandwich cookies for the upper lips. Remove a cookie side from one of the bite-size sandwich cookies and reserve for the lower lip. Transfer the creme-covered cookie side and the remaining cookies to a food processor and pulse until finely ground. (Or place the cookies in a large freezer-weight ziplock bag; do not seal the bag. Use a rolling pin to finely crush the cookies.) Place the cookie crumbs in a large bowl.

10 Spread an even layer of beige frosting over the front, back, and sides of the chilled body cake and smooth. Sprinkle cookie crumbs over the haunches (it is okay to see some of the frosting through the crumbs), being careful not to get the crumbs all over the cake. Transfer the cake to a serving platter.

11 Starting at the base of the cake, use a fork to gently pull the crumb-free frosting in a downward motion away from cake to create a fur texture (see Forked Frosting, page 22). Repeat this process, working in horizontal, slightly overlapping rows, to completely cover the body cake.

12 Spread some frosting on the top of the body cake. Press the cookie collar onto the top of the cake. Transfer the cake to the refrigerator to chill.

13 Spread an even layer of beige frosting over the chilled head cake, including the ears, and smooth. Press cookie crumbs on both sides of the ears and on the front of the face around the muzzle. Starting at the top edge of the cake and working toward the muzzle, use a fork to gently pull the crumb-free frosting in an upward motion away from the cake. Continue working in slightly overlapping rows just up to the cookie-crumb muzzle. Sprinkle a line of cookie crumbs up the center from the muzzle.

14 Insert a 6-inch wooden skewer into the center of the top of the head cake until you see the skewer poking through the bottom of the cake (see illustration, page 200). Use a spatula to transfer the head cake to the top of the cookie collar on the body cake. Continue pressing the skewer through the head, through the holes in the cookies, and into the body cake for extra stability. Cover the hole in the head cake with some beige frosting. Return the cake to the refrigerator to chill.

15 For the legs, snip a small (⅛-inch) corner from the bag with the dark chocolate frosting. Spread some beige frosting over the 4 circus-peanut paws and smooth. Roll the paws in the cookie crumbs to coat. Spread the 2 remaining bread sticks with an even layer of beige frosting. Sprinkle a little more than half of each bread stick with cookie crumbs, making the crumbs heavier at the end of the bread stick. Starting where the crumbs end, use a fork to gently pull the frosting in a downward motion away from the bread stick. Continue working in overlapping rows to the top of the bread stick. Press the frosting end of the bread-stick legs against the front of the cake, about 1 inch apart. Pipe a dot of dark chocolate frosting at the end of each bread stick on the platter and at the front of the haunches and attach the circus-peanut paws, rounded side to the front.

16 Spread an even layer of beige frosting over the tail assembly. Starting at the curved end of the tail, sprinkle a little more than half of

the bread stick with cookie crumbs, making the crumbs heavier at the curved end. Starting where the crumbs end, use a fork to gently pull the frosting in a downward motion away from the bread stick. Continue working in overlapping rows to the end of the bread stick. Press the frosted end of the bread stick against the back of the cake.

17 Snip a small (⅛-inch) corner from the bag with the vanilla frosting. Pipe dots of vanilla frosting around the center of the collar. Attach a pearl candy to each dot of frosting. For the bottom lip, pipe a dot of dark chocolate frosting on the lower front edge of the muzzle. Press the reserved cookie side into the frosting. Pipe some dark chocolate frosting above the bottom lip and attach the 2 reserved bite-size sandwich cookies, side by side, as the upper lip. For the nose, attach the black gumdrop, tapered end down, above and centered between the upper lip.

18 Attach the blue candy eyes at an angle in the frosting above the cookie-crumb muzzle. Pipe a line of dark chocolate frosting around the eyes, and add a few eyelashes. Pipe a dot in the center of each eye, and attach the brown candies for the pupils.

19 Carefully peel the candy whiskers from the wax paper. Press 3 whiskers, pointed ends out, into the frosting on each side of the upper lips.

20 For the optional ball of yarn, snip a small (⅛-inch) corner from the bag with the light blue frosting. Pipe some frosting on top of the cupcake and smooth. Pipe random lines of frosting back and forth over the cupcake to look like strands of yarn. Pipe a line of frosting leading from the ball of yarn to the cake platter.

RUX THE WONDER DOG CAKE

MAKES 12 SERVINGS

It doesn't take much training to master this little champ. She responds to treats—like marshmallows, cookies, Junior Mints, Jordan almonds, and spice drops. For a Scooby-Doo bone, she might even speak!

1 recipe Stablemates Master Cake (page 182) made with devil's food cake, prepared through step 2
1 can (16 ounces) plus 1 cup chocolate frosting
1 can (16 ounces) vanilla frosting
1 tablespoon light pink decorating sugar (Wilton)
5 jumbo marshmallows
2 thin pretzel sticks (Bachman)
5 large red spice drops
1 each large yellow and large black spice drop
¼ cup red decorating sugar (Cake Mate)
8 mini marshmallows
½ cup white candy melting wafers (Wilton)
2 3-inch round oatmeal cookies (Archway)
8 mini chocolate chips
3 cups chocolate jimmies (Cake Mate, Wilton)
1½ cups white jimmies (Wilton)
5 S-shaped breakfast treats (Stella D'oro)
2 mini chocolate-covered mints (Junior Mints)
12 white Jordan almonds
Bone-shaped cookies (Scooby-Doo)

1 Line a cookie sheet with wax paper. Remove the cardboard from the chilled loaf cake and place the cake, bottom side down, on a work surface. Starting 3 inches in from one short end of the cake, cut straight down (see illustration, right top). This 3-inch piece will be used as support behind the body cake. To straighten the other end, start ¼ inch in and cut straight down. Discard this trimming. Position the large cake with the wider cut

side down. Using a serrated knife held at an angle, bevel the 2 edges at the top of the cake, from front to back, by ¾ inch (see illustration, bottom left). Place the support cake, cut side down, flush against the back side of the body cake (see illustations), on cardboard cut to fit (see Getting on Base, page 14). Secure the cakes with some chocolate frosting. Transfer the cake assembly to the freezer to chill, about 30 minutes.

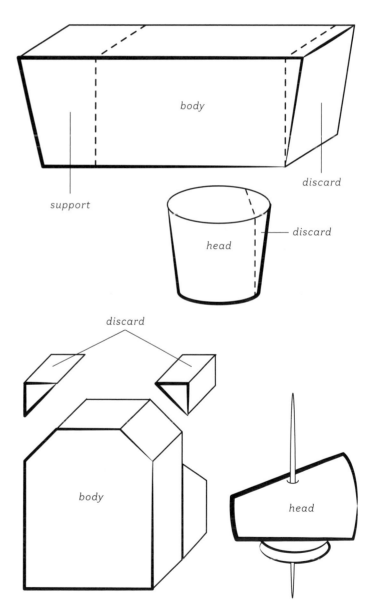

2 Spoon ½ cup of the chocolate frosting into a freezer-weight ziplock bag. Spoon the vanilla frosting into 2 separate freezer-weight ziplock bags. Press out the excess air and seal the bags.

3 Line a cookie sheet with wax paper. As you make the parts, transfer them to the cookie sheet. Place the pink sugar in a small bowl. For the ears, cut 1 jumbo marshmallow in half on the diagonal. Press the sticky side of the marshmallow halves into the sugar to coat. Insert a pretzel stick into the flat end of each marshmallow piece (see photo, right). Cut a ¼-inch slice from 3 flat ends of 2 jumbo marshmallows and set aside for the muzzle and the mouth. For the tail, cut the remaining larger marshmallow pieces in half crosswise. For the teeth, cut 2 long, ¼-inch-thick slices from the remaining pieces of marshmallow. For the tongue, cut a ⅛-inch slice from the flat end of a red spice drop. Make a line down the center of the sticky side with a small knife and pinch one end to make a teardrop shape. For the nose, cut the black spice drop in half lengthwise and discard one half.

4 For the collar, sprinkle the work surface with some of the red sugar. Press the remaining 4 red spice drops together and roll them out, adding more sugar to prevent sticking, to a ¾-x-11-inch strip (see photo, opposite page). Trim the long sides to make even. Snip the mini marshmallows in half on the diagonal for the studs on the collar. For the dog tag, cut a ¼-inch slice from the flat end of the yellow spice drop. Snip a very small (1/16-inch) corner from the bag with the chocolate frosting. Pipe RUX on the sugared side of the yellow slice.

5 Place the white candy melts in a freezer-weight ziplock bag; do not seal the bag. Microwave for 10 seconds to soften. Massage the

candy in the bag, return to the microwave, and repeat the process until the candy is smooth. Press out the excess air and seal the bag. Snip a small (⅛-inch) corner from the bag.

6 Pipe some melted candy on top of 1 oatmeal cookie. Place the other oatmeal cookie on top, bottom side down, and use a chopstick to poke a hole through the center of the cookie stack. Pipe a line of the melted candy around the outside edge of the cookies. Press the red candy collar into the melted candy to cover the edge of the cookies, pressing to secure and trimming any excess. Pipe dots of melted candy around the collar and attach the marshmallow studs, wide end down. Refrigerate until set, about 5 minutes.

7 For the mouth, place 1 marshmallow slice, cut side down, on a sheet of wax paper. Pipe some melted candy on the top of the marshmallow. Add the red candy tongue to the center, pinched end up. Place the 2 remaining marshmallow slices, cut side down, above and on either side of the tongue as the muzzle. Pipe a dot of melted candy on each side of the tongue and attach the marshmallow teeth, pointed end up. Pipe a dot of melted candy above the tongue, centered between the 2 muzzle pieces, and attach the black spice drop nose, cut side down. Attach the mini chocolate chips to the muzzle as the freckles. Refrigerate until set, about 5 minutes.

8 Line a cookie sheet with wax paper. As you make the parts, transfer them to the cookie sheet. Place the chocolate and white jimmies in separate large bowls. For the back legs, cut 1 breakfast treat in half crosswise. For the haunches, remove ½ inch from one end of 2 breakfast treats. Spread some chocolate frosting on the rounded tops of the back legs, the haunches, and 1 whole breakfast treat and on the flat bottom of the remaining breakfast treat. Press the frosted side of the breakfast treats into the chocolate jimmies to cover. Spread the marshmallow tail with chocolate frosting and cover with chocolate jimmies.

9 Snip a small (⅛-inch) corner from the bag with the vanilla frosting. For the paws, cut 1 jumbo marshmallow in half to make 2 circles and then again to get 4 semicircles. Pipe some vanilla frosting on the marshmallow paws and smooth. Press the marshmallows into the white jimmies to cover.

STEP 4

10 Pipe some vanilla frosting on the front of the chilled cake, from the belly area to the beveled shoulders, and smooth. Press the white jimmies into the frosting to cover. Spread the rest of the body and the support cake with chocolate frosting and smooth. Press the chocolate jimmies into the frosting to cover.

11 Transfer the body cake to a serving platter. Attach the haunches on either side of the body cake, flat side against cake, trimmed end down, using some chocolate frosting to secure. Arrange the back legs in front of the haunches. For the front legs, use some vanilla frosting to attach the 2 whole breakfast treats, jimmie-coated sides out (they will be mirror images; see photo, page 208) on the front of the chest and resting on the platter. Attach the collar cookie assembly to the top front of the cake with some chocolate frosting. Transfer the cake to the freezer to chill while decorating the head.

12 Line a cookie sheet with wax paper. Place the chilled head cake, cut side down, on the cookie sheet. Insert a wooden skewer in the center of the top of the head and push it into the top of the cake as far as it will go, leaving some of the skewer exposed. Insert the pretzel end of the marshmallow ears on either side of the wide end of the head, sugared side facing out. Starting from between the ears, pipe a 1-inch-wide line of vanilla frosting down the middle of the head to the narrow end. Press the white jimmies into the vanilla frosting to cover. Spread the remaining chocolate frosting in an even layer over the marshmallow ears, avoiding the sugared area, and the head, except the front of the muzzle area. Press the chocolate jimmies into the frosting to cover.

13 Enlarge the snip in the bag with the chocolate frosting to ⅛ inch. Pipe some chocolate frosting on top of the cookie in the assembled collar. Transfer the head cake to the top of the cookie collar, using the exposed skewer to stabilize the cake. Press the wooden skewer down through the hole in the cookies and into the body cake for support. Fill in the hole in the head cake with some jimmies. Pipe a line of chocolate frosting along the bottom of the marshmallow mouth and add some chocolate jimmies to cover. For the eyes, cut ¼ inch from each flat end of the remaining jumbo marshmallow, discarding the center piece. Cut the slices into 1½-inch circles. Pipe a line of chocolate frosting around the outside edge of the marshmallow eyes and press the cut side and the edge into the chocolate jimmies. Cut a wooden skewer to a 3-inch length. Insert one end of the skewer into the back side of the spice drop nose. Pipe some chocolate frosting over the front of the head cake and press the muzzle assembly into the frosting, pushing the skewer into the cake to secure. Pipe some chocolate frosting above the muzzle on either side of the white strip and attach the marshmallow eyes. Add a dot of frosting to each eye and attach a chocolate mint for the pupil. Add a dot of frosting below the collar at the front and attach the dog tag.

14 Arrange 3 Jordan almonds in front of each leg, about ½ inch away. Place a white marshmallow paw on top of the almonds, flat side down, securing with some vanilla frosting. Place the marshmallow tail on the platter against the back side of the cake. Arrange the cookie bones on the platter.

HIPPO CAKE

MAKES 12 SERVINGS

Baked in a loaf pan and a measuring cup, this fat fellow is taking a cool dip and creating ripples of flooded frosting. He also has poured frosting for his hide. Spice drops make easy work of his ears and teeth, as well as the birds.

1 recipe Stablemates Master Cake (page 182) made with devil's food cake mix, prepared through step 2
2 cans (16 ounces each) vanilla frosting
Blue, pink, and purple neon food coloring (McCormick)
6 thin honey wheat sticks (Pringles Stix)
1 chocolate chew (Tootsie Rolls)
2 green licorice twists (Kenny's Juicy Twists)
6 yellow, 1 orange, 4 white, and 7 purple spice drops
6 small blue nonpareils
2 tablespoons purple decorating sugar (Wilton)
3 pink marshmallows
2 small brown candy-coated chocolates (M&M's Minis)
3 small brownie snacks (Entenmann's Little Bites)

1 Line a cookie sheet with wax paper. Remove the cardboard from the chilled loaf cake and place the cake, bottom side down, on a work surface. For the body, trim the cake into an hourglass shape by removing a 5-inch-long, ¾-inch-deep curve from each long side of the cake (see illustration, below left). Trim the corners and remove ½ inch around the top edge of the cake to round it. Discard the

trimmings. Place the cake on a cardboard cut to fit (see Getting on Base, page 14) and transfer to the cookie sheet. For the head, place the chilled measuring-cup cake upright and cut the cake in half from top to bottom (see illustration, below right). Place one piece on a cardboard cut to fit, cut side down, and transfer it and the other piece, cut side down, to the cookie sheet. Spread a thin crumb coating of vanilla frosting over the 3 cakes, filling any gaps, and smooth. Place the cakes in the freezer until set, about 30 minutes.

2 Spoon ¼ cup of the vanilla frosting into a freezer-weight ziplock bag. Tint ⅓ cup of the vanilla frosting light blue with the food coloring. Spoon the frosting into a freezer-weight ziplock bag. Tint ½ cup of the vanilla frosting a darker blue. Spoon the frosting into a freezer-weight ziplock bag. Tint 3 tablespoons of the vanilla frosting light pink with the food coloring. Spoon the frosting into a freezer-weight ziplock bag. Press out the excess air and seal the bags. Tint the remaining vanilla frosting light purple with the food coloring. Spoon the purple frosting into a 2-cup microwavable measuring cup and cover with plastic wrap until ready to use.

3 Line a cookie sheet with wax paper. As you make the parts, transfer them to the cookie sheet. For the cattails, cut 1 wheat stick in half crosswise. Microwave the chocolate chew for 3 seconds to soften. Cut the chocolate chew into quarters; slightly flatten 2 pieces into rectangles. Discard the other 2 pieces. Wrap a chocolate-chew rectangle around the top of each wheat-stick half, leaving ¼ inch of the stick showing, pressing gently to secure (the wheat sticks are fragile). To make the reeds, cut the green licorice twists into 1- to 1½-inch pieces, then cut each piece on the diagonal.

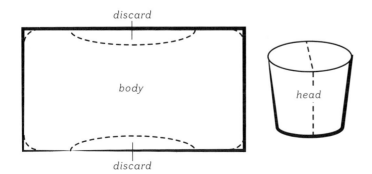

discard

body

discard

head

4 For the birds, slice a thin piece from the flat end of each yellow spice drop, reserving the slices for the wings. Press the cut ends of the spice drops together to make 3 birds. For the wings, press 1 thin spice-drop slice, sticky side down, on each side of the bird bodies. For the legs, cut 2 of the remaining wheat sticks into 6 equal pieces. Press 2 wheat-stick pieces into the bottom end of each bird body. For the beak, snip 3 small triangle pieces from the orange spice drop and press one against the front of each bird body, just above where the spice drops are joined. For the eyes, press 2 blue nonpareils into the spice drop above the beak.

5 For the hippo teeth, cut a wheat stick into quarters. Insert a cut wheat stick into the rounded end of each white spice drop. For the nostrils, cut ¼ inch from the flat side of 2 purple spice drops and discard the rounded ends. Place the pieces, sticky side down, on a piece of wax paper and remove a small hole from the center of each piece using a pastry tip or a thin drinking straw. For the eyelids, press 2 purple spice drops together and shape into a 1-inch circle. Cut the circle in half crosswise to make 2 semicircles. Cut a wheat stick in half and insert one piece into the cut side of each semicircle. Sprinkle the work surface with some of the purple sugar (reserve 1 teaspoon of the sugar for sprinkling the body). Press 2 purple spice drops together. Roll out the candy to a 1½-x-3-inch rectangle, sprinkling with more sugar, as necessary, to prevent sticking. Cut out two 1-inch-long ovals, pinching one short end of each for the ears. For the tail, roll the remaining purple spice drop to a 1-x-1½-inch rectangle. Using small scissors, make 1-inch-deep cuts every ⅛ inch on a short side of the rectangle, leaving ½ inch uncut. Wrap the candy, overlapping slightly, around the end of the remaining wheat stick, pressing lightly to secure.

6 Line a cookie sheet with wax paper and place a wire rack on top. Place the 3 chilled cakes on the wire rack, 2 on their cardboard pieces and 1 large cut side down. Microwave the purple frosting, stirring every 5 seconds, until it has the texture of lightly whipped cream, about 20 seconds. Dip the purple spice-drop eyelids into the melted frosting to cover. Allow the excess frosting to drip back into the cup. Transfer the pieces to the wire rack. Pour the remaining melted frosting over the cakes to cover completely, allowing the excess to drip onto the pan (see Pouring and Flooding, page 41). Lightly sprinkle the body cake with the reserved 1 teaspoon of the purple sugar. Place the cakes in the refrigerator to set, about 30 minutes.

7 Using a large spatula, place the chilled body cake, lengthwise, at one end of a rimmed serving platter. For the lower jaw, place the head-cake half without the cardboard at the other end of the platter, frosted side down, flat edge 1 inch away from the body. Place a pink marshmallow in the space between the jaw and the body cake to support the head. Snip a small (⅛-inch) corner from the bags with the vanilla and pink frostings. Pipe pink frosting on top of the exposed cake on the lower jaw. Carefully spread the frosting to the edge and smooth. Place the remaining 2 pink marshmallows lengthwise in the center of the pink frosting as the tongue. Pipe several lines of vanilla frosting along the edge of the jaw. Insert the wheat-stick end of 2 of the white spice-drop teeth along the piped edge near the front of the lower jaw, about 3 inches apart.

8 Press the purple spice-drop nostrils, cut side down, into the wide, rounded end of the remaining head-cake half. To add the ears, use a toothpick to poke a hole on each side at the back of the head cake. Insert the pinched end of a purple spice-drop ear into each hole. Attach the eyelids by inserting the wheat sticks at an angle just in front of the ears. Pipe dots of vanilla frosting on the tongue, the support marshmallow, and the front end of the body. Use a spatula to transfer the head, with the cardboard, to the back of the lower jaw, resting on the 3 marshmallows and flush against the end of the body. Insert the wheat-stick end of the remaining 2 teeth into the bottom edge of the front of the top jaw, about 2½ inches apart. Pipe a dot of vanilla frosting on the front side of the eyelids and add the small brown candies for pupils. Insert the wheat-stick end of the tufted tail into the back edge of the body cake.

9 Microwave the bags of light and dark blue frosting for 3 seconds, massaging the bags, until just softened. Snip a small (⅛-inch) corner from the bags. Starting with the light blue frosting, pipe a 1-inch ring of frosting close to the hippo cake. Pipe an irregular 1-inch ring of the dark blue frosting next to the light blue. Continue piping 1-inch rings of alternating blue frostings to cover the bottom of the platter.

10 Press the large flat sides of the brownie snacks into the blue frosting around the cake. Insert the wheat-stick ends of the 2 cattails and a few green licorice reeds into one brownie. Insert 1 bird and some reeds into each of the remaining 2 brownies. Insert the remaining reeds into the frosting surrounding the brownies. Insert the remaining bird on top of the hippo cake.

EGG MASTER CAKE

Our basic egg shape hatches a cartonful of ideas. Whether you need an egghead for a baby shower or a ghost for a haunting or are planning a party of your own invention, let this shape egg you on to delicious fun. Get cracking!

1 recipe Perfect Cake Mix batter (page 289) made with the cake mix specified in the recipe
1 cup vanilla frosting

1 Preheat the oven to 350°F and prepare a 1-cup and a 4-cup oven-safe measuring cup and a 1-quart oven-safe glass bowl (see Please Release Me, page 12). Pour 1 cup batter into the 1-cup oven-safe measuring cup, 2 cups batter into the 4-cup oven-safe measuring cup, and the remaining batter into the 1-quart oven-safe glass bowl.

2 Bake the cakes on a cookie sheet until golden and a toothpick inserted in the center comes out clean, 25 to 30 minutes for the measuring cups and 30 to 35 minutes for the bowl. Transfer the cakes on the cookie sheet to a wire rack and cool for 10 minutes. Invert, remove the cups and bowl, and cool completely.

3 Trim the top of each cake level (see On the Level, page 14). To assemble the egg shape, place the bowl cake, trimmed side up, on a small saucer for support (the assembled and decorated cake will remain in the saucer through serving). Spread some vanilla frosting on top. Add the large measuring-cup cake on top, trimmed side

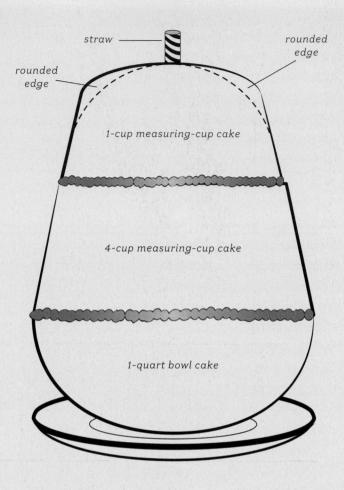

straw

rounded edge

rounded edge

1-cup measuring-cup cake

4-cup measuring-cup cake

1-quart bowl cake

down. Spread some frosting on top. Add the small measuring-cup cake on top, trimmed side down. Trim the edge of the top cake to round it slightly (see illustration, above).

4 Insert a drinking straw down the center of the cakes for support; trim the straw flush with the top of the cake. Spread a thin crumb coating of frosting (see Got Crumbs?, page 16) on the cake, filling any gaps, and smooth. Place the cake in the freezer until set, about 30 minutes.

EGGHEAD BABY CAKE

MAKES 12 SERVINGS

1 Egg Master Cake (page 216) made with yellow
  cake mix
2 cans (16 ounces each) vanilla frosting
Red food coloring (McCormick)
3 egg jumbo cookies (Stella D'oro)
2 pink marshmallows
4 mini pink marshmallows
2 black licorice laces
1 large and 1 small yellow spice drop
3 white marshmallows
4 thin pretzel sticks (Bachman)
2 large brown candy-coated chocolates (Peanut
  Butter M&M's)
1 pink jelly bean
1 mini yellow marshmallow

1 Use some of the vanilla frosting to spread an
even layer over the cake and smooth. Return
the cake to the freezer to chill. Spoon 1 cup of the
vanilla frosting into a freezer-weight ziplock bag.
Tint the remaining vanilla frosting light pink with
the red food coloring and spoon 2 tablespoons
into a freezer-weight ziplock bag. Press out the
excess air and seal the bags. Spoon the remaining
pink frosting into a microwavable measuring cup
and cover with plastic wrap to prevent drying.

2 Line a cookie sheet with wax paper and place
a wire rack on top. For the arms, cut one of
the egg jumbo cookies in half crosswise. Arrange
the cookie halves and the remaining 2 cookies, flat
side down, on the wire rack. Transfer the chilled
cake on the saucer to the wire rack.

3 Microwave the measuring cup of pink frosting,
stirring every 5 seconds, until it has the texture
of lightly whipped cream, about 20 seconds.
Working on the cookies first, pour the melted
frosting over the cookies to cover them completely,
allowing the excess to drip onto the pan. Spoon
the excess frosting back into the measuring cup.
Reheat the frosting as necessary. Pour the melted
frosting over the cake to cover the top two thirds
of the cake, allowing the excess to drip onto the
pan (see photo, below). Place the cake and the
cookies in the refrigerator to set, about 30 minutes.

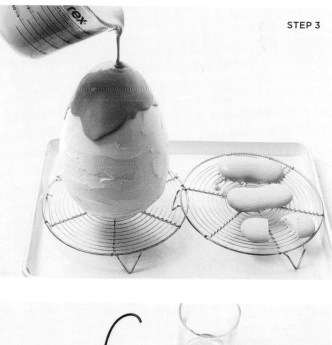

STEP 3

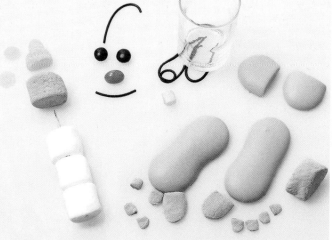

4 Line a cookie sheet with wax paper. As you make the parts, transfer them to the cookie sheet. To make the big toes, cut a ¼-inch slice from each flat end of 1 pink marshmallow and discard the center. Cut and discard a ¼-inch piece from the side of each slice. For the small toes, cut the mini pink marshmallows in half crosswise. Transfer the 2 chilled coated whole cookies to the cookie sheet. Snip a small (⅛-inch) corner from the bag with the pink frosting. Pipe 5 dots of frosting at the same end of each cookie foot and attach the big toe, trimmed side against the cookie, cut side down, on the side with the slight dip. Attach the mini marshmallow halves, cut side down (see photo, page 217).

5 Cut the licorice laces into one 7-inch piece, two 3-inch pieces, and one 1½-inch piece. Microwave the pieces of licorice for 3 to 4 seconds to soften. For the diaper pin, make a loop in the middle of the 7-inch piece by wrapping it around your finger, place it on the cookie sheet, and put a small glass on top to hold the licorice until it cools (see photo, page 217). Bend 1 of the 3-inch pieces in half for the front of the pin and place a glass on top to hold. Curl the remaining 3-inch piece to make the hair. Shape the 1½-inch piece into a semicircle for the mouth.

6 To make the bottle, cut a ⅛-inch piece from the rounded end of the large spice drop and a ⅛-inch piece from the flat side of the small spice drop. Press the cut sides together to make the nipple for the bottle. Insert a 4-inch wooden skewer into the flat end of the large spice drop. Thread the remaining pink marshmallow and the 3 white marshmallows onto the skewer (see photo, page 217).

7 To mark the top of the diaper, use a toothpick and a ruler to score a line around the chilled cake, about 3½ inches from the base. Find the best side of the cake to use as the front. Snip a ¼-inch corner from the bag with the vanilla frosting. Pipe a line of frosting along the score mark. Fill in the area below the mark with vanilla frosting. Use an offset spatula to spread the frosting, horizontally, around the cake. Refrigerate the cake for 15 minutes to firm.

8 Pipe vertical lines of vanilla frosting to make the front flap of the diaper, about 2½ inches wide. Use the offset spatula to smooth into vertical lines.

9 Pipe a dot of pink frosting on the cut edges of the arm cookies. Press 1 cookie, crosswise, on each side of the cake, resting it on the diaper. Insert 2 pretzel sticks under each arm and into the cake for support.

10 Pipe dots of vanilla frosting for the eyes and place the large brown candies for the pupils. Add the pink jelly bean, crosswise, for the nose, using a dot of frosting to secure. Lightly brush the back of the licorice lace mouth with a drop of water and press it onto the cake. Use a toothpick to poke a hole at the top of the cake and insert the licorice hair. Insert the ends of the remaining 2 licorice pieces into the front of the diaper, about 2 inches apart, for the diaper pin. Pipe a dot of frosting on the front piece of the diaper pin and add the mini yellow marshmallow as the safety closure.

11 Using a large spatula, transfer the cake to a serving platter. Arrange the cookie feet, big toes to the center, 1 flat on the serving platter and 1 raised and pressed into the cake, adding more frosting to secure, if necessary. Place the bottle next to the baby cake, resting against 1 arm.

FABERGÉ EGG CAKE

MAKES 12 SERVINGS

1 Egg Master Cake (page 216) made with devil's
   food cake mix
12 sticks pink gum (Extra)
2 tablespoons white chocolate chips
1 can (16 ounces) vanilla frosting
3 cups small orange, dark pink, light pink, and white
   pearlized jelly beans (Jelly Belly)
1 can (1.5 ounces) pearl food decorating spray
   (Wilton)

1 Line a cookie sheet with wax paper. As you make the parts, transfer them to the cookie sheet. For the tail of the bow, cut a V-shaped notch from one end of 2 sticks of gum (see photo, above right). Pinch the uncut ends. For the loops of the bow, cut and discard a ¾-inch piece from one end of 4 sticks of gum. Fold the 4 trimmed and the remaining 6 whole sticks of gum in half crosswise to make loops. Pinch the ends of each loop.

2 Place the white chocolate chips in a freezer-weight ziplock bag; do not seal the bag. Microwave for 10 seconds to soften, massage the chips in the bag, return to the microwave, and repeat the process until smooth, about 30 seconds. Press out the excess air and seal the bag. Snip a small (⅛-inch) corner from the bag.

3 To make the bow, arrange the pinched ends of the 6 large loops of gum on the cookie sheet in a circle. Pipe a large dot of the melted chocolate in the center to cover the ends. Add 3 of the small loops to the center, on top of the first set of loops,

pressing the pinched ends into the melted chocolate (see photo, above). Finish the bow with the remaining small loop, pinched end down into the center of the cluster, securing with melted chocolate, as necessary. Transfer to the refrigerator to set, about 5 minutes.

4 Starting at the base of the cake and working on one small section at a time, spread an even layer of vanilla frosting over the chilled cake and smooth. Arrange the jelly beans, end to end, in a swirling pattern to create a decorative design, completely covering the cake (use a toothpick or a wooden skewer to make small adjustments to the jelly-bean design). Using a large spatula, transfer the cake to a serving platter.

5 Lightly spray the assembled bow and V-notched pieces with the pearl decorating spray. Gently peel the bow from the wax paper and attach it to the top of the cake, using frosting to secure. Attach the 2 V-notched pieces below the bow for the tail.

GHOST EGG CAKE

MAKES 12 SERVINGS

1 Egg Master Cake (page 216) made with devil's food
  cake mix
1 can (16 ounces) plus 1 cup vanilla frosting
2 marshmallows
1 9½-inch bread stick (Stella D'oro)
½ recipe Candy Clay (page 292) made with white
  candy melting wafers (Wilton)
2 cups white pearlized jimmies (Wilton)
¼ cup dark chocolate frosting

1 Using some vanilla frosting, attach a marshmallow, on its rounded side, near one edge of the top of the chilled cake. Cut 1 marshmallow in half on the diagonal. Discard one half and attach the other half, pointed end up, on top of the marshmallow on the cake, using frosting to secure, to make a peak (see photo, below). Using a serrated knife, cut the bread stick in half crosswise. For the arms, insert the cut ends of the bread-stick halves at the top of the middle cake, one on each side, leaving 3 inches exposed. Transfer the cake assembly to the freezer for 30 minutes to chill.

2 Roll out the white candy clay on a sheet of wax paper to ⅛ inch thick. Cut two 2-x-3-x-3-inch triangles and one 4-x-5-x-5-inch triangle, rerolling the scraps, if necessary.

3 Line a cookie sheet with wax paper. Place the chilled cake on the cookie sheet. Spread some vanilla frosting along the underside of the breadstick arms and on each side of the cake under the bread sticks. To make the draped arms, press a small candy-clay triangle into the frosting on each bread stick and on the side of the cake (see photo, below left). For the tail, spread some frosting at the base of the cake on the side to which the marshmallow on the head points. Attach the large candy-clay triangle to the frosting, bending and shaping the tail to look as if it is moving.

4 Place the jimmies in a large bowl. Spread the remaining vanilla frosting over the cake, including the marshmallows, arms, and tail. Lightly press the jimmies into the frosting to coat completely. Brush off any excess jimmies. Lightly press the surface of the cake to smooth and flatten any ridges. Using a large spatula, transfer the cake to a serving platter.

5 To make the eyes, use a small melon scoop or a 1¼-inch round cookie cutter to cut two 1-inch-deep circles from the front of the cake near the top. Remove the inside of the circles with a small knife or a spoon. Spoon the dark chocolate frosting into a ziplock bag. Press out the excess air and seal the bag. Snip a small (⅛-inch) corner from the bag. Pipe the frosting into the eye openings and smooth.

MONKEY CAKE

MAKES 12 SERVINGS

Go bananas with our Egg Master Cake by adding a tangle of arms, legs, and tail made from breakfast-treat cookies. Forked-frosting fur isn't monkey business—it's evolutionary!

1 Egg Master Cake (page 216) made with devil's food cake mix, prepared through step 2

1 can (16 ounces) chocolate frosting

1 can (16 ounces) vanilla frosting

5 gingersnaps, about 2 inches wide (Nabisco)

1 marshmallow

½ cup dark cocoa candy melting wafers (Wilton)

10 thin pretzel sticks (Bachman)

5 S-shaped breakfast treats (Stella D'oro)

½ cup red decorating sugar (Cake Mate)

20 red and 2 yellow spice drops

3 tablespoons small yellow pearl candies (SweetWorks)

2 brown candy-coated chocolates (M&Ms) or 1 black jelly bean, halved lengthwise

1 tube (4.25 ounces) black decorating icing (Cake Mate)

1 Combine the chocolate frosting and 1 cup of the vanilla frosting in a bowl and stir until well blended. Spoon ¼ cup of the light brown frosting into a freezer-weight ziplock bag. Spoon the remaining vanilla frosting into a freezer-weight ziplock bag. Press out the excess air and seal the bags. Cover the remaining light brown frosting with plastic wrap to prevent drying.

2 Trim the top of the bowl cake and the 4-cup measuring-cup cake level (see On the Level, page 14).

3 To assemble the monkey shape, place the bowl cake, trimmed side up, on a small saucer for support. Spread some brown frosting on top. Add the 4-cup measuring-cup cake on top, trimmed side down. Spread some brown frosting on top. Add the 1-cup measuring-cup cake on top, trimmed side down, wide end facing forward and slightly overhanging the edge. Insert a drinking straw down through the center of the 3 cakes for support; trim the straw flush with the top of the cake. Spread a thin crumb coating of brown frosting on the cake (see Got Crumbs?, page 16), filling any gaps, and smooth. Place the cake in the freezer for 30 minutes to chill.

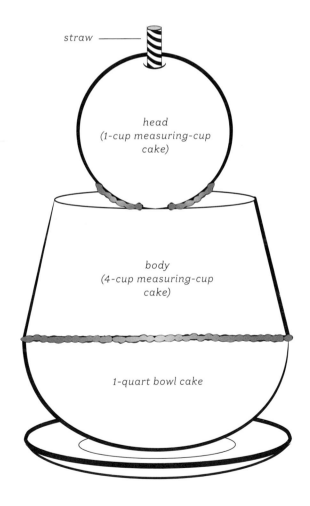

straw

head
(1-cup measuring-cup cake)

body
(4-cup measuring-cup cake)

1-quart bowl cake

6 For the eyes, pipe a 1½-inch circle of the melted candy on the cookie sheet. Place the eye cookies, flat side down, on top of the melted candy and press the long cut edge of the cookies together making sure the bottom cut edges line up (see photo, left). For the lower part of the mouth, place the remaining cookie half, bottom side down, on the cookie sheet. Pipe a line of melted candy on the top of the cookie, along the cut edge. Place the remaining large trimmed cookie, bottom side down, into the melted candy, allowing the cut edge to slightly overlap the bottom cookie.

7 To make the arms, legs, and tail, place the 5 breakfast treats, bottom side up, on the cookie sheet and pipe a dot of the melted candy on one end of each breakfast treat. Press the end of 2 pretzel sticks into the candy, turning them to coat and allowing them to overhang about 2 inches (see photo, above left). Refrigerate until set, about 5 minutes.

8 To make the red vest and hat, sprinkle the work surface with some of the red sugar. Press 15 of the red spice drops together and roll out to a 3-x-15½-inch rectangle about ⅛ inch thick, sprinkling with more sugar, as necessary, to prevent sticking. Repeat with the remaining 5 red spice drops to make a 1½-x-4½-inch rectangle. Trim the long sides of each rectangle to even the edges.

9 Round the corners of the large red candy rectangle to shape the vest. From the scraps cut a ¼-x-1-inch semicircle for the mouth. To make the hat, place the small red rectangle on a work surface, with one long side at the top. Starting at the top, ¼ inch in from the right edge, make an angled cut to the bottom corner on the right. Starting at the top, ¼ inch in from the left edge, make an angled cut to the bottom corner on the left. Discard the

4 Line a cookie sheet with wax paper. As you make the parts, transfer them to the cookie sheet. To make the ears and the lower part of the mouth, cut 2 gingersnaps in half using a small serrated knife; discard 1 of the pieces. Cut ¾ inch from the edge of the remaining 3 cookies; discard the small pieces. Reserve 1 of the 3 trimmed cookies for the upper part of the mouth (see photo, above). For the eyes, place the remaining 2 trimmed cookies side by side, flat side down, cut edge to cut edge. Cut ½ inch horizontally from the bottom of each of the 2 adjacent cookies. For the whites of the eyes, cut a ⅛-inch slice from each flat end of the marshmallow; discard the center. Trim and discard ¼ inch from the short end of each marshmallow slice.

5 Place the candy melts in a freezer-weight ziplock bag; do not seal the bag. Microwave for 10 seconds to soften, massage the candy in the bag, return to the microwave, and repeat the process until smooth, about 30 seconds. Press out the excess air and seal the bag. Snip a small (⅛-inch) corner from the bag.

trimmings. Press the 2 angled ends together to secure. Trim the wide end opening to make it straight. Press the remaining scrap pieces together, flatten, and cut into a 1-inch circle. Attach the red candy circle to the smaller opening to make the top of the hat. For the hat tassel, flatten 1 yellow spice drop to a 1-inch square. Cut the piece into a ½-x-1-inch rectangle. Using small scissors, make ¾-inch cuts lengthwise, every ⅛ inch along one side, leaving ¼ inch uncut. Pinch the uncut end together. Trim ¼ inch from the flat side of the remaining yellow spice drop and discard. Place the pinched end of the tassel on top of the hat and add the trimmed spice drop, cut side down, to secure.

STEP 10

10 Place the chilled cake on a serving platter. Spread an even layer of light brown frosting on the body and smooth. Starting at the bottom of the cake, use a fork to gently pull the frosting in a downward motion, away from the cake, to create a fur texture (see photo, right). Continue forking the frosting in horizontal, slightly overlapping rows, working from the bottom edge to the neck. Spread the remaining light brown frosting over the head. Starting at the outer edge of the face and working to the center, use a fork to pull the frosting in a downward motion, away from the cake, in slightly overlapping concentric rows. Repeat for the back of the head. For the ears, press a gingersnap half to each side of the head, cut side against the cake.

11 Snip a small (⅛-inch) corner from the bags with the vanilla and light brown frostings. Wrap the red candy vest around the top third of the body, pressing it into the frosting to secure. Pipe dots of the vanilla frosting around the edge of the vest, about ¾ inch apart, and add the yellow pearl candies. Arrange the candy hat at a jaunty angle on top of the head. Using the light brown frosting, as necessary, attach the cookie eyes, flat

side down, straight edge at the bottom, to the top half of the face. Attach the mouth cookies, flat side down, cut edge horizontal, with the larger cookie at the top, to the bottom half of the face, overlapping the cookie eyes. Use a dot of vanilla frosting to attach the marshmallow slices to the eye cookies, cut side down, trimmed edge at the bottom. Pipe a dot of vanilla frosting on the lower part of the marshmallow slices and attach the M&M's or jelly-bean halves, touching the mouth cookie. Using the light brown frosting, pipe tufts of fur on top of the head. Using the black decorating icing, pipe the nostrils on the upper portion of the mouth cookie. Attach the red candy semicircle mouth on the lower portion of the mouth cookie.

12 Just before serving, use a toothpick to make a hole in each side of the vest at the arm position. Attach the cookie arms, pushing the pretzels into the cake.

QUEEN BEE CAKE

MAKES 12 SERVINGS

Friends and family will swarm all over this honey of a cake. The queen bee rules her hive with a Yodel and a doughnut hole, while the worker bees buzz around the basket-weave hive on strands of uncooked spaghetti.

1 recipe Perfect Cake Mix (page 289) made with yellow cake mix, 1½ cups batter baked in a 2-cup oven-safe measuring cup for 35 to 40 minutes and 3½ cups batter baked in a 4-cup oven-safe measuring cup for 40 to 45 minutes
2 cans (16 ounces each) vanilla frosting
Red and yellow food coloring (McCormick)
¼ cup chocolate frosting
1 plain doughnut hole (Munchkins)
1 chocolate-coated creme-filled rolled snack cake (Yodel)
10 marshmallows
½ cup yellow decorating sugar (Cake Mate)
1 tablespoon small white nonpareils

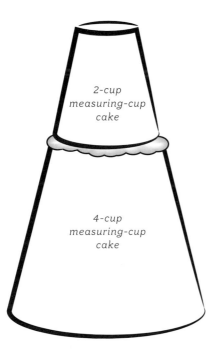

2-cup measuring-cup cake

4-cup measuring-cup cake

4 each small orange and yellow spice drops
½ cup white candy melting wafers (Wilton)
4 thin pretzel sticks (Bachman)
4 chocolate chews (Tootsie Rolls)
38 yellow candy-coated chocolates (M&M's)
38 sliced almonds
19 strands uncooked spaghetti
1 large yellow spice drop
1 tube (4.25 ounces) black decorating icing (Cake Mate)
1 small red heart-shaped decor (see Sources, page 294)

1 Trim the top of each cake level. Place the large cake, trimmed side down, on a cardboard cut to fit. Spread some vanilla frosting on top of the cake. Add the small cake, trimmed side down. Spread a crumb coating of frosting on the cake, filling any gaps, and smooth. Every 1¼ inches around the base of the cake, mark a line from the bottom to the top by pressing a long wooden skewer into the cake (see photo, opposite page). Place the cake in the freezer until set, about 30 minutes.

2 Spoon 3 tablespoons of the vanilla frosting into a small glass bowl and tint pale pink with the red food coloring. Cover with plastic wrap to prevent drying. Spoon ½ cup of the vanilla frosting into a freezer-weight ziplock bag. Tint the remaining vanilla frosting golden yellow with some yellow food coloring and 1 tablespoon of the chocolate frosting. Divide the yellow frosting evenly between 2 freezer-weight ziplock bags. Spoon the remaining chocolate frosting into a freezer-weight ziplock bag. Press out the excess air and seal the bags.

3 Line a cookie sheet with wax paper. As you make the parts, transfer them to the cookie sheet. For the queen's head, insert the tines of a

small fork into the doughnut hole. Microwave the pink frosting, stirring often, until it has the texture of lightly whipped cream, about 3 seconds. Dip the doughnut hole in the melted frosting to cover, allowing the excess frosting to drip back into the bowl. Refrigerate the doughnut hole until the frosting is set, about 30 minutes.

4 For the queen's torso, remove a 2-inch piece from one end of the chocolate snack cake and discard. Using large scissors, cut a ¼-inch slice from one flat end of 1 marshmallow and discard the rest of the marshmallow. For the collar, press the cut side of the marshmallow slice on one end of the trimmed snack cake. To make the sleeves, cut 1 marshmallow in half on the diagonal. Press the cut side of the marshmallow halves on either side of the snack cake, tapered end near the collar.

5 For the flowers, place the yellow sugar in a medium bowl. To make the petals, cut each of the remaining 8 marshmallows crosswise into 5 thin slices, allowing the pieces to fall into the sugar (see photo, below). Shake the bowl and press the cut sides of the marshmallows into the sugar to coat. Place the white nonpareils in a small bowl. Remove and discard a ⅛-inch slice from the flat end of each small spice drop. Press the cut ends of the spice drops into the nonpareils to coat. Place the candy melts in a freezer-weight ziplock bag; do not seal the bag. Microwave for 10 seconds to soften, massage the candy in the bag, return to the microwave, and repeat the process until smooth, about 30 seconds. Press out the excess air and seal the bag. Snip a small (⅛-inch) corner from the bag. Pipe a dot about the size of a dime onto a lined cookie sheet. Arrange 5 marshmallow slices in the melted candy

in the shape of a flower, sugared side up and over-lapping slightly. Repeat to make 8 flowers. Refrigerate the flowers until set, about 5 minutes. Pipe a dot of melted candy in the center of each flower and add a spice drop, sprinkle side out. Return to the refrigerator until set, about 5 minutes.

6 Make a copy of the wing template below, enlarging it 200 percent. Place the wing template on a cookie sheet and cover with wax paper. Using the melted candy, pipe an outline of the 2 wings on the wax paper. Press the end of a pretzel stick into the melted candy at the pointed end of each wing, perpendicular to the wing, and pipe more melted candy on top to cover (see photo, opposite page). Repeat the process to make another set of wings. Transfer to the refrigerator until the candy is set, about 5 minutes.

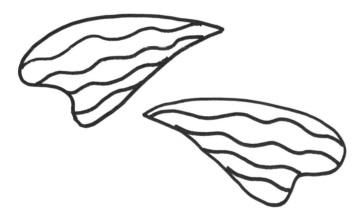

7 To make the worker bees, microwave the chocolate chews for 3 seconds to soften. Cut each chew crosswise into 6 small slices. Shape 19 of the slices into ¼-inch balls. Place a yellow candy on each side of a ball and press together until the chocolate chew is flush with the sides of the candies. Insert the pointed ends of 2 almond slices into the edge of the chew for the wings. Insert the end of a spaghetti strand into the chew, on the side opposite the wings (see photo, opposite page). Repeat the process to make 19 bees.

8 For the door to the hive, press the remaining 5 chocolate-chew slices together. Roll out on a sheet of wax paper to a ⅛-inch thickness and cut into a 1-x-1½-inch rectangle. Trim the corners of one short end to create an arch for the door.

9 For the queen's crown, make 5 rounded cuts around the edge of the flat side of the large yellow spice drop to scallop the edge.

10 To pipe the basket weave for the hive, transfer the chilled cake to a serving platter. Snip a small (⅛-inch) corner from the bag with the vanilla frosting. Snip a ¼-inch corner from the bags with the yellow frosting. Starting at the top of the cake, pipe a vertical line of vanilla frosting over one of the scored lines on the cake. Using the yellow frosting, start at the bottom edge of the cake and pipe a horizontal dash that starts at the scored line to the left of the white piped line of frosting, crosses the white line, and ends at the scored line to the right of the white line. Move up, leaving a space equal to the width of the previous dash, and repeat the process (see photo, page 233). Continue piping dashes, with spaces between them, to the top of the cake. Starting at the top, pipe a second vertical line of vanilla frosting over the scored line to the right of the first white line, crossing over the ends of the dashes. Starting at the bottom, in the space left between the first and second yellow dashes, pipe a horizontal yellow dash that starts at the first white line of frosting, crosses the second white line, and ends at the scored line to the right of the second white line. Repeat this process, filling in the spaces left between the first set of yellow dashes, to the top of the cake. Continue working in this pattern from left to right around the cake to cover completely.

11 For the queen's torso, press the chocolate snack cake, collar side up, on top of the cake, using vanilla frosting to secure. Pipe a dot of vanilla frosting on the marshmallow collar. Remove the dipped doughnut hole from the fork, taking care not to smudge one side, and place on top of the collar, with the smoothest side as her face. Insert a wooden skewer straight down through the doughnut hole and the torso and into the cake for support.

12 Snip a small (⅛-inch) corner from the bag with the chocolate frosting and pipe hair on the top, back, and sides of the doughnut hole, including a small point of hair at the front. Add the spice-drop crown on top of the head, pressing into the frosting. Pipe little white points on the tips of the crown. Pipe white dots for the eyes.

Use the black decorating icing to pipe the pupils and eyelashes. Attach the red heart decor for the mouth with a dot of vanilla frosting. Pipe a decorative edge of yellow frosting around the collar and at the end of the sleeves.

13 Using a toothpick, poke 4 holes in the top of the skirt cake behind the snack-cake torso for the wings. Carefully peel the candy wings from the wax paper. Insert the pretzel ends into the holes, overlapping the wings on each side. Place the chocolate-chew door near the bottom on the front of the cake. Arrange the 8 marshmallow flowers around the base of the cake.

14 Just before serving, insert the spaghetti ends of the candy bees all over the cake, cutting the spaghetti to different lengths.

BEDAZZLED CHRISTMAS TREE CAKE

MAKES 12 SERVINGS

Deck the tree with garlands of Swedish fish, gumballs, Sixlets, spice drops, and marshmallows, in red, green, and white, all the way up to the tippy-top of its waffle-cone peak.

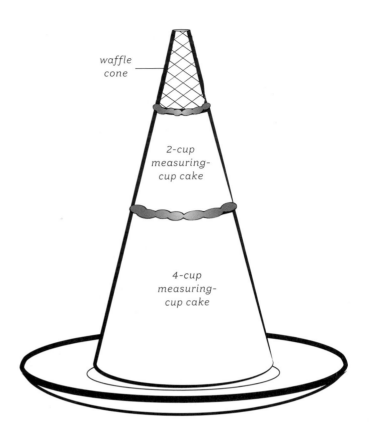

waffle cone

2-cup measuring-cup cake

4-cup measuring-cup cake

1 recipe Perfect Cake Mix (page 289) made with yellow cake mix, 1½ cups batter baked in a 2-cup oven-safe measuring cup for 35 to 40 minutes and 3½ cups batter baked in a 4-cup oven-safe measuring cup for 40 to 45 minutes
1 can (16 ounces) plus 1 cup vanilla frosting
Green and yellow food coloring (McCormick)
1 waffle cone (Joy, Keebler)
½ cup granulated sugar
10 marshmallows
70 mini red Swedish fish
1 cup light green pearlized gumballs (SweetWorks)
1 cup each white and red round candy-coated chocolates (Sixlets)
1 cup red spice drops
1 large green pearlized gumball (SweetWorks)

1 Tint the vanilla frosting light green with the green and yellow food coloring. Spoon ¼ cup of the frosting into a freezer-weight ziplock bag. Press out the excess air and seal the bag. Cover the remaining frosting with plastic wrap to prevent drying.

2 Trim the wide end of the waffle cone level with a serrated knife. Trim ¾ inch from the tip of the cone.

3 Trim the top of each cake level (see On the Level, page 14). Place the large cake, trimmed side down, on a cardboard cut to fit. Spread some green frosting on the top of the cake. Add the small cake, trimmed side down. Insert a drinking straw down through the center of both cakes. Spread a thin crumb coating of frosting on the cake (see Got Crumbs?, page 16), filling any gaps, and smooth. Place the cake in the freezer until set, about 30 minutes.

4 Line a cookie sheet with wax paper. Place the granulated sugar in a medium bowl. Use large scissors to cut each marshmallow crosswise into 5 thin slices (clean off the scissors periodically to prevent sticking), allowing the slices to fall into the sugar. Shake the bowl and press the cut sides of the marshmallows into the sugar to coat. Transfer the slices to the cookie sheet.

5 Transfer the chilled cake to a serving platter. Spread some green frosting on the top of the cake and add the cone, wide end down.

6 Starting at the base of the cake, spread an even layer of green frosting over the bottom 4 inches of the cake. Working quickly before the frosting dries, press 1 row of marshmallow slices, sugared side out, lengthwise and side by side into the frosting. Add 1 row of Swedish fish, slightly overlapping the marshmallows. Continue adding rows in the following order: 1 row of light green gumballs, 2 rows of white candies, 1 row of red candies, 1 row of spice drops, flat side against the cake, and 1 row of red candies (see photo, page 235). Add frosting to the next 4 inches of the cake and, starting with the marshmallow slices, repeat the pattern of rows 2 more times to cover the cake completely.

7 Snip a small (⅛-inch) corner from the bag with the green frosting. Pipe a dot of frosting on the top of the tree and attach the large gumball. Use the remaining green frosting in the bag to secure any loose candies.

Variation made with sugared marshmallow slices and Sixlets.

pound of fun

store-bought pound cakes

Call it geniosity or laziness, but we think using store-bought pound cake is a brilliant way to get decorating fast. We love the taste of freezer-case pound cake, like Sara Lee, and the firm texture is perfect for holding decorations. This cake is versatile too, whether you add a simple coating of frosting and sugar to make the Nerds' Dance Cake or use it as the stepping-off point for the shape of the Work Boot Cake.

BOOT MASTER CAKE

Give boring party cakes the boot, and cobble together footgear that suits your guest of honor. With store-bought pound cake and ready-made doughnuts, you can start decorating right away.

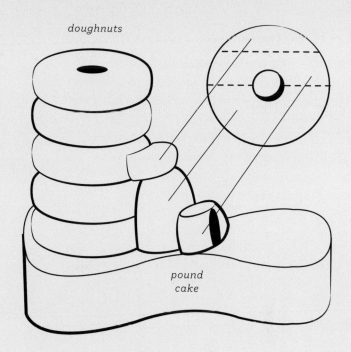

doughnuts

pound cake

1 family-size (16-ounce) frozen all-butter pound cake, thawed (Sara Lee)
6 cake doughnuts (flavor specified in the recipe)
1 can (16 ounces) vanilla frosting

1 Place the pound cake on a work surface. Make a copy of the sole template at left, enlarging it 200 percent. Use the template to cut the cake into the foot shape. Trim the top edge of the cake to slightly round it. Place the cake on a cardboard cut to fit (see Getting on Base, page 14).

2 Line a cookie sheet with wax paper. Reserve 1 doughnut to form the instep of the boot. Spread the top of a doughnut with some frosting. Arrange another doughnut on top. Repeat the process 3 more times to make a stack of 5 doughnuts. (For the Work Boot, make a stack of 4 doughnuts and reserve 1 doughnut for use in the recipe.) Spread the top of the heel area of the cake with some frosting and place the stack of doughnuts on top.

3 Cut the reserved doughnut in half, crosswise, to make 2 semicircles. (For the Work Boot, there will be 1 additional doughnut remaining for use in the recipe.) Cut 1 inch from the rounded top

of 1 doughnut half, reserving both pieces. Using frosting to secure the pieces, attach the semicircle doughnut piece, crosswise, to the top of the cake, cut ends down and one flat side against the stacked doughnuts. Attach the trimmed semicircle piece, crosswise, cut ends down, in front of the semicircle piece. Attach the remaining piece, crosswise, to the top of the intact semicircle, cut side against the stacked doughnuts (see illustration, above).

4 Insert a drinking straw down the center of the doughnut stack and into the cake. Trim the straw with scissors and push it down to cover completely. Spread the remaining vanilla frosting over the cake and doughnuts, mounding it over the top of the toe area, and smooth. Transfer the cake to the freezer for 30 minutes to chill.

Got sole?

The sole of your boot may be hidden on the bottom, but finding the right candy for it will go a long way to making your design look real. You need a candy or snack that is firm enough to hold the weight of the pound cake and doughnuts stacked above. Once you choose your candy, creating the sole is fairly simple.

1 Cut a sole shape from the cardboard lid of the frozen pound cake or from any light cardboard.

2 Pipe a few dots of frosting on the cardboard sole, then arrange the candy along the edge of the sole, placing it with the most soleful side facing out. For the licorice bites in the Rain Boot Cake (page 246), that would be the open end, with the holes.

3 Fill in the center of the sole with additional candies or cookies to make a solid support for the cake.

4 Transfer the chilled cake to the sole, adjusting the candies as necessary to support the cake.

5 If you're using chocolate-covered wafer bars, like Kit Kats, line them up on a work surface and pipe some dots of frosting on top. Place the cardboard sole or the trimmed cake on top and use a serrated knife to trim the wafers to fit.

WORK BOOT CAKE

MAKES 12 SERVINGS

1 Boot Master Cake (page 241) made with 6 chocolate-covered cake doughnuts (Entenmann's)
1 can (16 ounces) vanilla frosting
Yellow food coloring (McCormick)
1 teaspoon unsweetened cocoa powder
¼ cup dark chocolate frosting
61 soft caramels (Kraft)
16 extra-large chocolate-covered wafer bars (two 4.5-ounce Kit Kats)
14 small yellow candies with a hole in the center (from a candy necklace)
2–3 yellow licorice laces (Rips Whips)
½ cup chocolate cookie crumbs (Oreos)

1 Tint ½ cup of the vanilla frosting light brown with the yellow food coloring and ½ teaspoon of the cocoa powder and spoon into a freezer-weight ziplock bag. Spoon the dark chocolate frosting into a freezer-weight ziplock bag. Press out the excess air and seal the bags.

2 Line 2 cookie sheets with wax paper. As you make the parts, transfer them to the cookie sheets. For the toe of the boot, soften 24 of the caramels in the microwave for 2 to 3 seconds. Press the caramels together and roll out on a sheet of wax paper to an 11-inch oval, about ⅛ inch thick. Make a copy of the toe template on page 240, enlarge it to 200 percent, and use it to cut the caramel with scissors or a small knife. Repeat the process to cut out the remaining boot pieces, using 5 caramels for the boot tongue, 10 caramels for each side, and 10 caramels for the heel. Roll out 1 caramel for each of the 2 logos and cut them into 1-inch circles.

3 Place the chilled cake on a work surface. Spread the remaining vanilla frosting over the cake assembly, rounding the top of the toe, and smooth. Starting with the toe piece, drape the caramel over the front of the boot, centering the caramel on the toe and allowing it to extend to the bottom of the cake at the front. Gently press into the frosting to secure (see photo, below). Press the sides of the toe piece into place, making sure that the caramel extends to the bottom edge of the cake. Rub gently with your fingertips to remove any creases or bubbles, stretching the caramel to fit, if necessary. Place the tongue piece, lengthwise, on the front center of the cake, with the wide end slightly overlapping the toe piece and the tapered end extending about 1 inch beyond the doughnut stack. Add the 2 side pieces, slightly overlapping the tongue on the front of the boot, with the top edges extending about 1 inch beyond the doughnut stack. Press the caramel into the frosting to secure. At the top of the boot, make a 1-inch vertical cut in the extended caramel about 1 inch in from the curved front edge of each side piece to create the eyelet flaps. Gently fold the excess caramel over the doughnut stack,

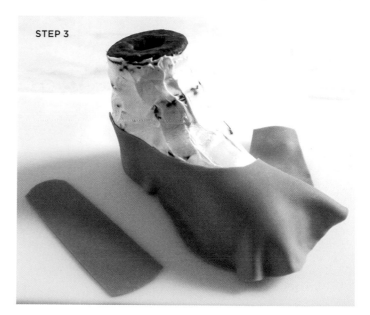

STEP 3

leaving the eyelet flaps loose (see photo, opposite page). Add the heel piece at the back of the cake, overlapping the 2 side pieces and extending to the bottom of the cake. Use a small knife to cut a clean edge of caramel along the base of the cake, removing and discarding any excess. Use a drop of water between the caramel pieces to secure to each other, as necessary.

4 Snip a small (⅛-inch) corner from the bag with the dark chocolate frosting. Arrange the chocolate-covered wafer bars, side by side, bottom side up, on a serving platter. Pipe some dark chocolate frosting over the wafers.

5 Transfer the cake from the cardboard with a large spatula and place it on top of the wafers. Use a small serrated knife to trim the wafers flush with the cake for the waffled sole of the boot. Brush away the crumbs.

6 Use a drop of water to attach 7 of the yellow candies, evenly spaced, along the outside edge of each eyelet flap. Use a toothpick to poke a hole in the caramel through the hole in each candy. Gently thread the yellow licorice through the holes as the laces. Tie a knot at the end of each lace.

7 For the logo, use a toothpick to score the outline of a tree on each caramel circle (or to customize your cake, adding initials or numbers). Lightly rub the scored circles with the remaining ½ teaspoon cocoa powder to enhance the tree shape. Use a drop of water to attach 1 circle to each side of the boot.

8 Pipe some dark chocolate frosting on top of the doughnut stack (and any folded-over caramel). Add the remaining chocolate-covered doughnut and pipe a decorative edge around the base of the doughnut to secure.

9 Snip a very small (¹⁄₁₆-inch) corner from the bag with the light brown frosting. Pipe a line of frosting around the base of the cake, where the caramel meets the wafer sole. For the stitching, pipe a ¼-inch dashed line just above the piped line at the base of the cake and along the straight edge of the 2 side pieces and the 2 vertical edges of the heel piece.

10 Sprinkle some of the chocolate cookie crumbs on the serving platter around the base of the boot to resemble dirt.

RAIN BOOT CAKE

MAKES 12 SERVINGS

1 Boot Master Cake (page 241) made with 6 glazed
  cake doughnuts
1 can (16 ounces) vanilla frosting
¼ cup dark chocolate frosting
Yellow and green food coloring (McCormick)
1 recipe Candy Clay (page 292)
Confectioners' sugar
60 bite-size black licorice pieces (Twizzlers Bites)
2 black licorice twists (Twizzlers)
4 thin pretzel sticks (Bachman)
1 marshmallow
2 mini chocolate-covered mints (Junior Mints)
1 6½-inch piece black licorice lace
6 small green candy-coated chocolates (M&M's Minis)
½ cup coarse white decorating sugar (Wilton;
  optional)
Blue teardrop-shaped hard candies (Cry Baby Tears;
  optional)

1 Spoon ½ cup of the vanilla frosting into a
freezer-weight ziplock bag. Spoon the dark
chocolate frosting into a freezer-weight ziplock
bag. Press out the excess air and seal the bags.
Tint the remaining vanilla frosting yellow with the
food coloring. Tint three quarters of the candy
clay bright yellow with the food coloring. Tint the
remaining candy clay lime green with the green
and yellow food coloring. Cover the candy clay
with plastic wrap until ready to use.

2 Line 3 cookie sheets with wax paper. As
you make the parts, transfer them to the
cookie sheets. Divide the yellow candy clay into
4 equal pieces. Lightly dust a work surface with
confectioners' sugar and roll out each piece to a
⅛-inch thickness. Using the templates on page 240
and enlarging them to 200 percent, cut out the
toe, sides, tongue, and heel pieces with a paring

knife, rerolling the scraps, as necessary. Cover with
plastic wrap. For the decorative edges and straps,
divide the green candy clay in half. Lightly dust a
work surface with confectioners' sugar and roll out
1 piece to a 1½-x-10-inch strip, about ⅛ inch thick.
Cut a ½-inch-wide strip, lengthwise, for the top of
the boot. Cut the remaining strip in half crosswise
into two 1-x-5-inch strips for the cinches. Roll the
remaining piece of green candy clay into a rope,
then flatten it out to a 1-x-24-inch strip for the
base of the boot. Trim the edges of the 4 strips to
straighten.

3 Snip a small (⅛-inch) corner from the bag with
the vanilla frosting. For the cinches, round the
ends of the two 1-x-5-inch green strips. Loosely
fold each strip, crosswise, so that the folded-over
end is about 1 inch from the other end and there
is a small loop at the fold (see photo, page 248).
Attach a bite-size piece of black licorice, crosswise,
to each looped strip with a dot of vanilla frosting.
For the boot straps, cut each black licorice twist
into a 6-inch-long piece. Insert a pretzel stick
about ½ inch into each end of the 2 pieces.

4 Use the enlarged sole template from the Boot
Master Cake to cut out a piece of cardboard
and place it on a serving platter. Snip a small
(⅛-inch) corner from the bag with the dark
chocolate frosting. Pipe a few dots of dark
chocolate frosting on the template, then arrange
the remaining bite-size licorice pieces, side by
side, along the edge of the sole shape, pressing
them together and making sure the ends with the
holes are facing out. Trim the pieces with a small
knife, as necessary, to match the curved shape.
Arrange any extra licorice pieces inside the edged
area, evenly spaced, for additional support. Pipe
dark chocolate frosting over the licorice pieces to
help secure.

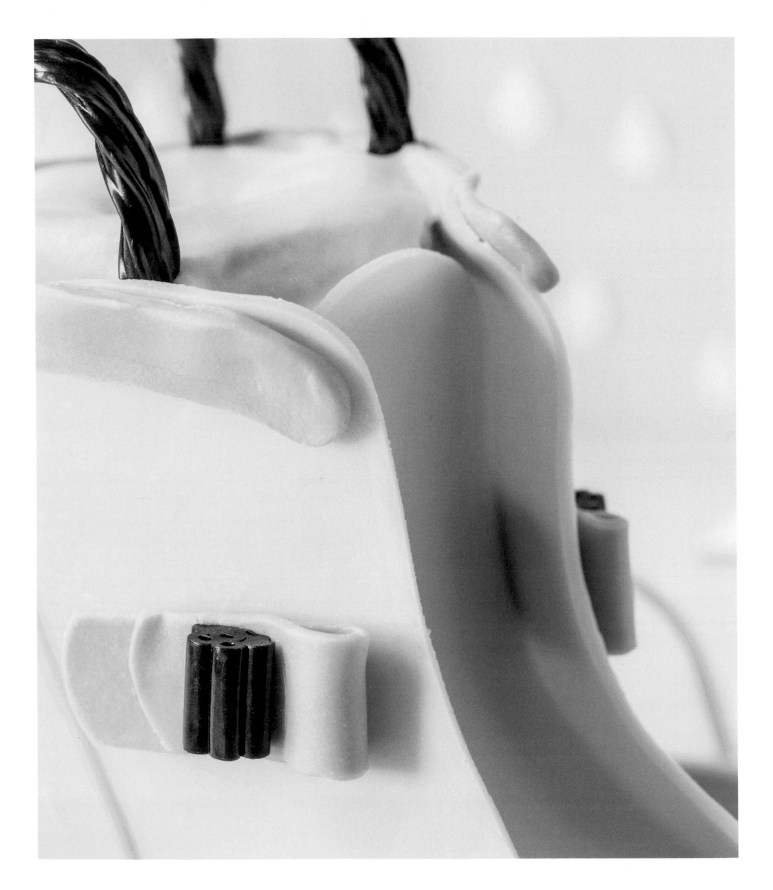

5 Place the chilled cake on a work surface. Spread the yellow frosting over the cake assembly, rounding the top of the toe, and smooth. Starting with the toe piece, drape the yellow candy over the front of the boot, centering the candy on the toe and allowing it to extend to the bottom of the cake at the front. Gently press into the frosting to secure. Press the sides of the toe piece into place, making sure that the candy extends to the bottom edge of the cake. Rub gently with your fingertips to remove any creases or bubbles, stretching the candy to fit, if necessary. Place the tongue piece, lengthwise, on the center of the cake, with the wide end slightly overlapping the toe piece and the tapered end ending about halfway up the last doughnut in the stack. Add the 2 side pieces, slightly overlapping the tongue on the toe of the boot, with the top edges level with the last doughnut in the stack. Press the candy into the frosting to secure. Add the heel piece at the back of the cake, overlapping the 2 side pieces and extending to the bottom of the cake. Use a small knife to cut a clean edge of candy along the base of the cake, removing and discarding any excess. Use a drop of water between the candy pieces to secure to each other, if necessary.

6 Use a drop of water to moisten one side of the 1-x-24-inch strip of green candy. Pressing the moistened side against the yellow candy, wrap the strip around the bottom edge of the cake and trim any excess. Repeat with the ½-x-10-inch strip, attaching it along the top edge of the boot.

7 Use a large spatula to remove the cake from the cardboard and place it on top of the licorice sole on the serving platter. Pipe a line of vanilla frosting around the base of the cake, just above the green band.

8 For the straps, bend each licorice twist in half to form a loop and insert the pretzel ends into the doughnut at the top of the stack, 1 strap on each side.

9 For the eyes, cut the marshmallow in half crosswise to make 2 circles. Using a dot of vanilla frosting, attach the marshmallows, cut side down, to the rounded toe at the front of the boot. For the pupils, attach the mini chocolate-covered mints to the marshmallows, using a dot of frosting. For the eyelashes, cut the licorice lace into four 1-inch pieces and attach 2 pieces above each eye. Shape the remaining 2½-inch piece of licorice lace into a semicircle for the mouth and attach it at the front of the cake, using a drop of water. For the freckles, attach 3 of the small green candies on each side of the smile with a dot of vanilla frosting.

10 Just before serving, use a dot of vanilla frosting to attach a green cinch, crosswise, to each side of the cake, about 3 inches below the green trim at the top. Sprinkle the serving platter with the decorating sugar, if desired, and add the blue teardrop-shaped candies.

HIGH-TOP SNEAKER CAKE

MAKES 10 SERVINGS

1 Boot Master Cake (page 241) made with 6 powdered-
sugar doughnuts
1 recipe Candy Clay (page 292)
Neon blue and pink food coloring (McCormick)
Confectioners' sugar
1 can (16-ounce) vanilla frosting
2 tablespoons light corn syrup
3 tablespoons coarse white decorating sugar (Wilton)
20 small candies with a hole in the center (from a
candy necklace)
1 roll (2 ounces) pink bubble-gum tape (Hubba Bubba)

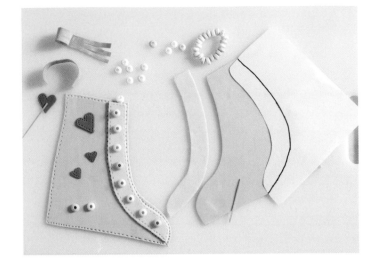

1 Line 3 cookie sheets with wax paper. As you make the parts, transfer them to the cookie sheets. Tint two thirds of the candy clay light blue with the food coloring. Tint one third of the remaining candy clay pink with the food coloring. Leave the remaining candy clay white. Cover the candy clay with plastic wrap until ready to use.

2 Lightly dust a sheet of wax paper with confectioners' sugar. Roll out the pink candy clay to a scant ⅛-inch thickness. Use a paring knife to cut a 1-x-2½-inch rectangle from the clay. Cut two 2½-inch, six 1-inch, and three ½-inch heart shapes with small cookie cutters or a paring knife, rerolling the scraps, as necessary. Use the wide end of a flat toothpick to press the stitching around the edge of the hearts and to write LOVE on the rectangle (see photo, page 252). Transfer the pieces to a cookie sheet and cover with plastic wrap.

3 Lightly dust a work surface with confectioners' sugar and roll out the white candy clay to a scant ⅛-inch thickness. Using the templates on page 240 and enlarging them to 200 percent,

cut out the tongue, and the eyelets. Rerolling the scraps as necessary, cut out a 5-inch-diameter circle and cut the circle in half to make 2 semicircles. One semicircle is for the toe cap; cut the second in half crosswise for the heel. Transfer the pieces to a cookie sheet and cover with plastic wrap.

4 Lightly dust a work surface with confectioners' sugar and roll out the blue candy clay to a scant ⅛-inch thickness. Using the templates on page 240, cut out the toe, sides, and heel pieces with a paring knife, rerolling the scraps as necessary. Transfer to a cookie sheet and cover with plastic wrap.

5 Transfer the chilled cake on the cardboard to a serving platter. Spread the vanilla frosting over the cake assembly, leaving the top of the doughnut stack unfrosted, and smooth. Starting with the blue toe piece, drape the candy over the front of the sneaker, centering the candy on the toe and allowing it to extend to the bottom of the cake at the front. Gently press into the frosting to secure. Press the sides of the toe piece into place, making sure that the candy extends to the bottom edge of the cake. Rub gently with your fingertips

to remove any creases or bubbles, stretching the candy to fit, if necessary. Place the white tongue piece, lengthwise, on the center of the cake, with the wide end slightly overlapping the blue toe piece and the tapered end extending about 1 inch beyond the last doughnut in the stack. Add the 2 blue side pieces, slightly overlapping the tongue on the toe of the sneaker, with the top edges level with the top of the last doughnut in the stack; do not press the eyelet flaps against the tongue. Press the candy into the frosting to secure. Add the blue heel piece at the back of the cake, overlapping the 2 side pieces and extending to the bottom of the cake. Use a small knife to cut a clean edge of candy along the base of the cake, removing and discarding any excess. Use a drop of water between the candy pieces to secure to each other, if necessary.

6 Brush the tops of the white toe cap and the 2 rounded heel pieces (1 rounded corner to the left, 1 to the right) with some corn syrup and sprinkle with the decorating sugar. Using a drop of corn syrup to secure, add the toe cap to the toe, sugared side up, and the 2 rounded heel pieces to the back of the sneaker, with the rounded corners facing forward and the 2 vertical straight sides about ¼ inch apart (see photo, opposite page). Attach the white eyelet trim along the edge of each blue eyelet flap, using a drop of corn syrup to secure.

7 Using the wide end of a flat toothpick, mark the stitching along the edges of the candy, down the center at the back, and just above the sugared toe cap and the 2 rounded heel pieces (see photo, opposite page). For the eyelets, use a drop of water to attach 8 of the small candies, evenly spaced, along each white eyelet-trim piece. For the vents, use a drop of water to attach 2 small candies near the base of the sneaker on each side. Use a toothpick to poke a hole through each eyelet.

8 Using some water to secure, wrap the pink bubble-gum tape around the bottom of the sneaker, pressing to attach snugly; trim to fit. Cut the remaining bubble-gum tape, lengthwise, into thirds, about ¼ inch wide. Cut into two 7-inch-long pieces and thirteen 3-inch-long pieces. Pinch both ends of the shorter pieces and, working with one piece at a time, brush the tip of each end with some water, and arrange the pieces in an over/under crisscrossing pattern to look like shoelaces in the eyelets (see photo, page 251). Pinch one end of each of the longer pieces, brush the tip of that end with water, and insert into the second eyelet from the top on each side. Brush a little water on the back of some of the candy hearts and create your own design by attaching them to the cake. Add any extra hearts to the platter. Brush some water on the back of the LOVE rectangle and attach it near the top at the back of the sneaker.

HUGS BOOT CAKE

MAKES 12 SERVINGS

1 Boot Master Cake (page 241) made with 6 glazed
   doughnuts
1 can (16 ounces) vanilla frosting
Neon pink food coloring (McCormick)
9 pink fruit chews (Laffy Taffy, Starburst)
40 soft caramels (Kraft)
2 cups ground pink sugar wafers (about 32 wafers)
1 mini vanilla wafer (Mini Nilla)
1 tube (4.25 ounces) chocolate decorating icing
   (Wilton)
2 bags (2.5 ounces each) pink cotton candy (Charms
   Fluffy Stuff)
1 7-inch piece red licorice lace (Twizzlers Pull 'n' Peel)

Ground pink sugar wafers

1 Tint the vanilla frosting bright pink with the food coloring. Spoon ½ cup of the frosting into a freezer-weight ziplock bag. Press out the excess air and seal the bag. Cover the remaining frosting with plastic wrap until ready to use.

2 Line a cookie sheet with wax paper. As you make the parts, transfer them to the cookie sheet. For the heel piece, soften 5 pink fruit chews in the microwave for 2 to 3 seconds. Press the pieces together and roll out on a piece of wax paper to a 3-x-6-inch rectangle. Cut a 1-inch circle from the scraps, rerolling, if necessary. Soften the remaining 4 pink fruit chews in the microwave for 2 to 3 seconds. Press the pieces together and roll between your hands to make a rope about ¼ inch in diameter and 8 inches long. Roll out 1 caramel on a piece of wax paper to a 1-x-2-inch rectangle. Trim the edges with a knife to straighten. Using the wide end of a flat toothpick, mark the stitching around the edge of the rectangle. (To personalize the boot, you can add a name to the label.)

3 Snip a small (⅛-inch) corner from the bag with the pink frosting. Use the template on page 240 and enlarging to to 200 percent, cut out the sole from a piece of cardboard and place it on a serving platter. Pipe a few dots of frosting on the cardboard, then arrange some of the remaining caramels, side by side, along the inner edge of the sole shape, pressing them together (see photo, page 242). Trim the caramels with a small knife, as necessary, to match the curved shape. Fill the center of the sole with additional caramels, evenly spaced, to make a solid support for the cake.

4 Line a cookie sheet with wax paper. Place the ground pink wafers in a large bowl. Transfer the chilled cake to the cookie sheet. Spread the remaining pink frosting over the cake assembly,

rounding the top of the toe and shaping the top of the boot around the doughnut support pieces. Smooth the frosting. Gently press the ground wafers into the frosting to cover completely. Brush away any excess crumbs.

5 To attach the crumbed cake to the sole, pipe some pink frosting over the caramel sole. Remove the cake from the cardboard using a large spatula and place it on the sole.

6 To make the button, place the vanilla wafer on a work surface, flat side down. Pipe a small X on top of the wafer with the pink frosting. Pipe a dot of chocolate decorating icing at the end of each piped line.

7 Enlarge the snipped corner of the bag with the frosting to ¼ inch. Attach the pink fruit-chew heel piece on the back of the boot, one long side flush with the top of the caramel sole, using some frosting to secure. Pipe a line of pink frosting around the base of the cake, just above the sole. Starting at the top of the sole, in front of the heel piece, press the pink fruit-chew rope into the frosting, wrapping it over the arch of the boot and down the edge of the heel piece on the opposite side. Trim any excess rope. Pipe a dot of pink frosting near the bottom of the heel piece and attach the caramel label.

8 When ready to serve, pipe a vertical line of frosting up one side of the cake, starting at the top corner of the heel piece. Pipe a line of frosting around the top edge of the cake. Press small pieces of cotton candy into the lines of frosting, adding more frosting, as needed, to create the fur along the side and top of the boot.*

* Cotton candy is sensitive to humidity. Once it has been added, do not refrigerate the cake; serve immediately.

9 Fold the red licorice lace in half to form a 3½-inch loop. Place the loop on the back of the wafer button and pipe on some frosting to secure it. Pipe some frosting on one side of the fruit-chew circle and attach the ends of the loop. Press the button and the circle onto the side of the cake, button to the front, with the licorice lace crossing over the cotton-candy strip.

NERDS' DANCE CAKE

MAKES 20 SERVINGS

Let's dance! Get a party started with a no-bake, sugar-smash cake. Colorful frosted dancers inspired by graffiti artist Keith Haring are sugar-smashed on top, while Nerd candies are smashed into the sides. Nerds on the top; Nerds on the sides!

2 family-size (16 ounces each) frozen all-butter pound cakes (Sara Lee), thawed

1 can (16 ounces) vanilla frosting

Neon pink, neon purple, neon blue, yellow, green, and red food coloring (McCormick)

1 can (16 ounces) dark chocolate frosting

½ cup coarse white decorating sugar (Wilton)

3 cups small tart hard candies (Nerds)

1 Spoon 3 tablespoons of the vanilla frosting into each of 6 small bowls. Tint each bowl a different color with the food coloring: neon pink, neon purple, light neon blue, yellow, light green (using the yellow and green food coloring), and orange (using the yellow and red food coloring). Spoon each color frosting into a separate freezer-weight ziplock bag. Spoon ½ cup of the dark chocolate frosting and ½ cup of the remaining vanilla frosting into separate freezer-weight ziplock bags. Press out the excess air and seal the bags.

2 Line a cookie sheet with wax paper. Trim ¼ inch from one short end of each cake. Place the cut ends together, securing with some vanilla frosting, to make one long cake (see photo, following page). Transfer the cakes to a cardboard cut to fit. Place the cake on the cookie sheet and transfer to the refrigerator until ready to decorate.

3 Make a copy of the template on page 261, enlarging it 200 percent. Cut out the figures and arrange them on one half of the chilled cake

(see photo, opposite page, top). Use a toothpick to score the outline of each dancer onto the cake. Rearrange the templates on the other half of the cake, changing the positions as desired, and score the outlines.

4 Snip a small (⅛-inch) corner from the bags with the frostings. Starting with the dark chocolate frosting, pipe frosting on the scored outlines on the cake, (see photo, opposite page, center). Add 2 small curved lines around each figure to suggest motion. Using a different color of frosting for each dancer, pipe an even layer of frosting within the outlines to fill in the figures (see photo, opposite page, bottom). Pipe vanilla frosting in the area around the dancers. Sprinkle the top of the cake with a generous layer of the decorating sugar. Gently press the sugar into the frosting using an offset spatula or your fingertips and level (see Smashed Sugar, page 37). Use a pastry brush to remove any excess sugar from the top of the cake.

5 Spread the sides of the chilled cake with the remaining dark chocolate frosting and smooth. Gently press handfuls of the hard candies into the sides of the frosted cake to cover, (see photo, bottom right), allowing the excess candy to fall onto the cookie sheet (take care not to smudge the top sugared areas).

6 Transfer the cake on the cardboard to a serving platter.

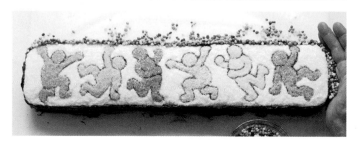

HOOTY AND THE POUND CAKES

MAKES 12 SERVINGS

Give a hoot if you love owls! Carved from no-bake cakes, this colorful foursome is perfect for last-minute nocturnal decorating. And, keeping it really simple, the eyes, ears, and wings are all made from Golden Oreos.

2 family-size (16 ounces each) frozen all-butter pound cakes (Sara Lee), thawed

1 can (16 ounces) plus 1 cup vanilla frosting

Neon blue, green, neon pink, yellow, and red food coloring (McCormick)

8 double-stuffed creme-filled vanilla sandwich cookies (Golden Double Stuf Oreos)

¼ cup each pastel-colored blue, green, pink, and orange teardrop-shaped hard candies (Cry Baby Tears)

2 each red, purple, orange, and green chewy sour candy disks (Spree)

16 thin pretzel sticks (Bachman)

1 each pink, green, blue, and orange licorice twists (Rainbow Twizzlers)

4 each blue, green, red, and orange banana-shaped hard candies (SweetWorks)

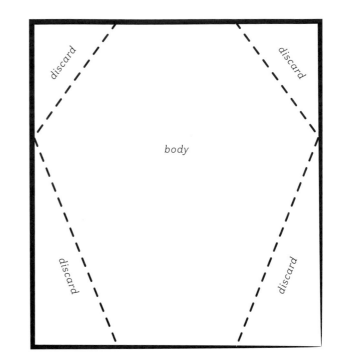

1 Place the pound cakes on a work surface. Trim the short ends of both cakes to straighten. Cut each cake in half crosswise. Position 1 cake half with a short end facing you. Starting at the top left corner, measure 1 inch in at the top and 1 inch down on the left side. Cut between these 2 points to remove a triangle. Measure 1¼ inches in from the bottom left corner and cut from that point to where the previous cut ended on the left side (see illustration, above). Discard the triangles. Starting at the top right corner, repeat the process to remove 2 triangles on the right side. Repeat with the other 3 cake halves. Place each cake on a cardboard cut to fit (see Getting on Base, page 14). Transfer the cakes to the refrigerator.

2 Spoon ½ cup of the vanilla frosting into a freezer-weight ziplock bag. Press out the air and seal the bag. Divide the remaining frosting evenly among 4 bowls. Using the food coloring, tint each bowl a different bright pastel color: blue, green, pink, and orange (using the yellow and red food coloring). Cover the bowls with plastic wrap until ready to use.

3 Line a cookie sheet with wax paper. As you make the parts, transfer them to the cookie sheet. Remove a cookie side from each of the sandwich cookies, reserving the creme side for the eyes. Using a serrated knife, cut the plain cookie sides in half (4 of these halves will be extra in case of breakage). Cut 4 of the cookie halves in half again. The 8 cookie halves are for the wings, and the 8 cookie quarters are for the ears.

4 For the eyes, arrange like-color teardrop-shaped candies on the creme side of 2 cookies, in a matching decorative pattern. Press a chewy candy disk, matching the color of the teardrop candy, in the center of each cookie. Repeat with the remaining teardrop-shaped candies, 6 creme-sided cookies, and 6 chewy candy disks, creating a different pattern for each set of eyes (see photo, previous page).

5 Place a chilled cake on a small serving plate, with the narrow end at the bottom. Spread an even layer of one of the tinted frostings over the cake and smooth. For the eyes, press the matching color of decorated cookies on top, at the wide end. To support the ears and wings, insert 2 pretzel sticks in the top edge of the cake, about 2 inches apart, and 1 pretzel stick on each side, near the middle, leaving about 1 inch exposed.

6 Snip a small (⅛-inch) corner from the bag with the vanilla frosting. Pipe a dot of frosting on top of the exposed pretzels and add the cookie ears, cut sides into the cake and facing out, and the wings in various positions (see photo, previous page). Pipe a decorative pattern on the chest area of the owl (dots, hearts, waves, scallops, etc.). For the beak, attach a teardrop-shaped candy in a complementary color, pointed end down, between the cookie eyes. Repeat with the remaining 3 cakes, creating a different pattern on the chest of each owl.

7 For the perch, place a licorice twist in a matching color on the bottom edge of each plate, trimming to fit. For the feet, add 4 banana-shaped candies in a matching color, curved side up, resting on the perch and pressed into the frosting at the bottom edge of the cake to secure.

Variation with yellow frosting and candy.

ROCKET SHIP CAKE

MAKES 16 SERVINGS

Fly me to the moon! Licorice-lace flames blast our yellow- and red-frosted pound-cake ship into space, while its sugar-coated anisette-toast landing gear ensures a smooth touchdown.

2 family-size (16 ounces each) frozen all-butter pound cakes (Sara Lee), thawed
1 can (16 ounces) plus 1 cup vanilla frosting
Yellow and red food coloring (McCormick)
½ cup each orange and red decorating sugar (Wilton, Cake Mate)
14 orange spice drops
4 anisette toasts (Stella D'oro)
10 red and 8 yellow licorice laces (Rips Whips)
¼ cup small yellow candy-coated chocolates (M&M's Minis)
6 light green chewy sour candy disks (Spree)
2 cups small orange pearlized jelly beans (Jelly Belly)

1 Tint ¾ cup of the vanilla frosting red with the food coloring. Tint the remaining vanilla frosting bright yellow with the food coloring. Spoon 2 tablespoons of the yellow frosting into a freezer-weight ziplock bag. Press out the excess air and seal the bag.

2 Place 1 pound cake on a work surface, bottom side up. Spread some yellow frosting on top. Place the other cake, bottom side down, on the frosting and press the cakes together. To shape the top of the rocket, position the cake assembly with a short end facing you. Starting at the top left corner, measure 1½ inches in at the top and 3 inches down on the left side. Cut between these two points to remove a triangle (see illustration, above). Repeat the process to remove a triangle from the top right corner. Trim ¼ inch from the

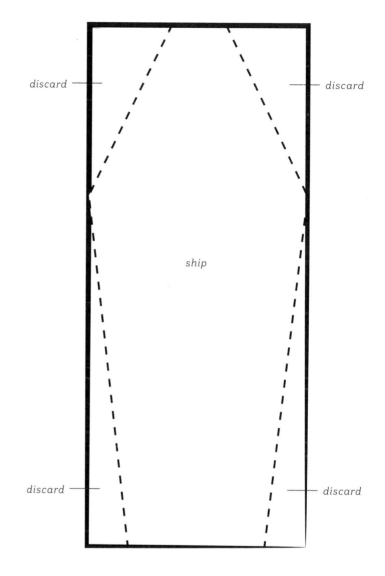

other short end to straighten. Measure ½ inch in from the bottom left corner and 4 inches up on the left side. Cut between these 2 points to remove a triangle. Repeat the process to remove a triangle from the bottom right corner. Discard the triangles. Use a small knife to cut a ½-inch bevel on the 4 long edges of the cake to round the sides slightly.

3 Stand the cake upright. Insert a drinking straw at an angle from the upper end of one side to go through both cakes. Repeat on the other side. Trim the straws flush with the cake.

4 Spread a thin crumb coating of yellow frosting (see Got Crumbs?, page 16) on the cake, filling any gaps, and smooth. Transfer the cake to the freezer for 30 minutes to chill.

5 Line a cookie sheet with wax paper. As you make the parts, transfer them to the cookie sheet. Sprinkle a work surface with some of the orange sugar. Flatten an orange spice drop. Place the candy on the sugared surface, sprinkle with additional sugar, and roll out to a 1¼-inch circle, sprinkling with more sugar, as necessary, to prevent sticking. Cut the rolled candy into a 1-inch circle with a round cookie cutter or the open end of a pastry tip. Repeat to make 5 more orange candy circles. Press the remaining 8 orange spice drops together. Roll out on the sugared surface, adding more sugar, as necessary, to a 1-x-12-inch strip. Trim the long edges to straighten.

6 Place the red sugar in a medium bowl. Spread some red frosting over the 4 anisette toasts and smooth. Sprinkle red sugar over the frosted toasts to coat.

7 Transfer the chilled cake to a cardboard cut to fit (see Getting on Base, page 14) or a small serving plate. Spread the remaining yellow frosting over the cake and smooth. Use an offset spatula to spread the frosting in long strokes, bottom to top, to make it look like panels on the rocket ship.

8 Use a wooden skewer to mark a horizontal line 2 inches from the top of the cake on all 4 sides. Spread red frosting in the area above the mark and smooth. Press a strand of red licorice lace around the bottom edge of the red frosting, trimming to fit.

9 Wrap the orange spice-drop strip around the base of the cake, trimming to fit. Wrap a strand of red licorice lace around the bottom of the cake just above the orange strip, trimming to fit.

10 Press the small yellow candies, about ¾ inch apart, along the 2 long edges at the front and the back of the cake (the flat sides) and down the center of each rounded side of the cake. Place a small bowl or cup that can support the cake and elevate it about 2 inches on a serving platter. Transfer the cake to the serving platter. Press the tapered end of 1 red-sugared anisette toast into the frosting on each side of the cake, resting the other end on the serving platter (see photo, opposite page), and secure with red frosting, as necessary.

11 Press 3 of the orange candy circles into the frosting in a row down the center of the front of the cake. Snip a small (⅛-inch) corner from the bag with the yellow frosting. Pipe a dot of frosting on top of each orange candy and attach a green candy disk. Repeat with the remaining 3 orange candy circles and 3 green candies on the back of the cake.

12 Spread the orange jelly beans on the serving platter to cover. Pick up 1 end of each of the remaining red and yellow licorice laces and press the ends together. Place the gathered ends under the cake to look like the flames coming out of the rocket.

BATTER UP! CAKE

MAKES 20 SERVINGS

This bat doesn't need any batter in the lineup because it's made with store-bought pound cake. The trimmings from carving the stick are used to form a giant baseball. If you're looking for the sweet spot, it's in the flavor-painted wood grain.

2 family-size (16 ounces each) frozen all-butter pound cakes (Sara Lee), thawed
1 can (16 ounces) plus ¾ cup vanilla frosting
¼ cup dark chocolate frosting
1 plain doughnut (Entenmann's)
1 tablespoon vodka or vanilla extract
2 teaspoons unsweetened cocoa powder
1 roll (0.75 ounce) red fruit leather (Fruit by the Foot)
2 red licorice laces, cut into ⅓-inch pieces (Twizzlers Pull 'n' Peel)

1 Set aside ¾ cup of the vanilla frosting, covered with plastic wrap, until ready to use. Spoon the dark chocolate frosting into a freezer-weight ziplock bag. Press out the excess air and seal the bag.

2 As you trim the cake, reserve the trimmings. Trim ¼ inch from one short end of each cake. Place the trimmed ends together on a work surface to make one long cake. To shape the bat from the narrow handle to the wider barrel, start at one short end of the cake assembly, 1¼ inches in from the long side, and cut a long tapered piece from the side of the cake, ending 4 inches from the corner on the same side at the other end (see illustration, below). Repeat on the opposite long side, starting at the same short end. Trim 2 inches from the narrow end. To shape the bat, bevel the edges of the top of the cake and round the corners at the wide end.

3 Transfer the 2 cakes to a long serving platter or a piece of cardboard cut to fit (see Getting on Base, page 14). Spread some vanilla frosting on one trimmed end where the cakes meet and press the cakes together to secure. To make the knob at the base of the bat, trim ¾ inch from one side of the doughnut. Position the doughnut at the narrow end of the cake, trimmed side down, and attach with some vanilla frosting. Spread the remaining vanilla frosting over the cake and doughnut, mounding it slightly on top of the bat, and smooth. Place the cake in the freezer to chill for 30 minutes.

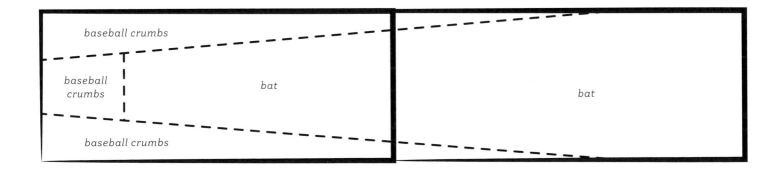

4 Place pieces of wax paper on the serving platter next to the cake to keep the platter clean. Combine the vodka and 1 teaspoon of the cocoa powder in a small bowl. Using a small pastry brush and working in long, smooth, overlapping strokes, paint the vodka mixture down the length of the bat (see Flavor Painting, page 45). Completely glaze the vanilla frosting to make it tan in color, always brushing in one direction and smoothing any ridges or bumps in the frosting. Paint the doughnut knob in crosswise strokes. Add the remaining 1 teaspoon cocoa powder to the mixture and stir until smooth. Use a small craft brush to add the wood grain to the tan-painted frosting. Remove the wax paper and clean the platter.

5 Cut several pieces of fruit leather and wrap them around the grip of the bat in overlapping strips. Trim to fit.

6 Snip a very small (1/16-inch) corner from the bag with the chocolate frosting. Pipe the SLUGGER logo on the cake (see photo, above) or personalize with your own words. Place the cake in the refrigerator to chill.

7 To make the baseball, spray a 10-ounce glass bowl with vegetable cooking spray. Line the bowl with plastic wrap. Crumble the reserved

STEP 7

cake trimmings in a medium bowl. Add ¼ cup of the reserved vanilla frosting and mix until well blended. Press the cake mixture into the prepared bowl and cover with the overhanging plastic wrap (see photo, opposite page). Place in the freezer until slightly firm, about 15 minutes.

8 Remove the chilled cake from the bowl by pulling on the plastic wrap lining the bowl. Remove the plastic wrap and place the cake, flat side down, on a small plate or cardboard cut to fit. Spread the remaining ½ cup of the vanilla frosting on top of the cake and smooth. Let the cake stand for 20 minutes, until the frosting is dry to the touch.

9 Using a kitchen towel or a paper towel, lightly press against the frosting on the baseball cake to create a leather texture (see Toweled Frosting, page 23). Score a semicircle on opposite sides of the cake with a toothpick or by pressing the rim of a drinking glass into the frosting. For the stitches, press the red licorice-lace pieces in a V-shape along the scored lines, with the V stitches in each row pointing in opposite directions.

TIGER LILIES CAKE

MAKES 8 SERVINGS

Here's a project as easy as summer living. The Ball jar is made from pound cake with a smashed-sugar design, while the petals for the lilies are cut from flattened circus peanuts.

1 family-size (16 ounces) frozen all-butter
    pound cake (Sara Lee), thawed
30 orange circus peanuts
5 marshmallows
¾ cup dark cocoa candy melting wafers (Wilton)
1 tablespoon small yellow nonpareils (Wilton)
3 green sour belts (Sour Power)
8 strands uncooked spaghetti
8 green sour straws (Sour Power)
1 can (16 ounces) vanilla frosting
Green, yellow, and neon blue food coloring
    (McCormick)
1 cup coarse white decorating sugar (Wilton)

1 Cut the circus peanuts in half lengthwise. Place 2 circus peanut halves, cut sides down, on a sheet of wax paper and roll out to a scant ⅛-inch thickness. Repeat with the remaining circus peanut halves.

2 Cut each flattened candy into a ¾-x-3-inch petal shape to make 60 petals. Bend each petal into a soft S-shape.

3 Line 10 mini muffin cups with paper liners. Place the candy melts in a freezer-weight ziplock bag; do not seal the bag. Microwave for 10 seconds to soften. Massage the candy in the bag, return to the microwave, and repeat the process until the candy is smooth. Press out the excess air and seal the bag.

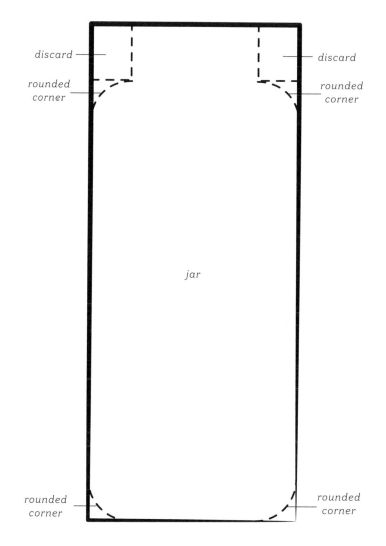

discard — | — discard

rounded corner — | — rounded corner

jar

rounded corner — | — rounded corner

4 Snip a small (⅛-inch) corner from the bag and pipe a dime-size dot of melted candy in the bottom of a prepared muffin cup. Arrange 6 petals on top of the candy, pointed ends out, in the shape of a tiger lily, overlapping the petals slightly (see photo, next page). Repeat with the remaining 54 petals and melted candy to make a total of 10 flowers. Refrigerate until the candy is set, about 5 minutes.

5 Reheat the candy melts in the microwave, keeping the cut tip upright and massaging the candy in the bag, until smooth, about 5 sec-

onds. Working on 1 flower at a time, pipe a small dot of melted candy in the center of the flower. Use a small craft brush or a toothpick to pull the melted candy up the inside of each petal (see photo, above). With the tip of a toothpick, add small dots of melted candy on the petals for the spots. While the candy is still wet, sprinkle the center with some of the yellow nonpareils. Repeat with the remaining 9 flowers. Refrigerate until set, about 5 minutes.

6 Line a cookie sheet with wax paper. Carefully remove the assembled flowers from the paper liners. Cut the marshmallows in half crosswise. Pipe a small dot of melted candy on the sticky side of the marshmallow halves. Attach the base of each assembled flower to a marshmallow, pressing it into the melted candy to secure. Refrigerate until set, about 5 minutes.

7 Line a cookie sheet with wax paper. As you make the parts, transfer them to the cookie sheet. Cut the green sour belts into 6 to 9 leaf shapes 3 to 5 inches long. To make the stems, thread 1 spaghetti strand into the opening of each green sour straw (these will be cut at different lengths when assembling).

8 Place the pound cake on a work surface with one short end facing you. To make the neck of the jar, measure ¾ inch in from the top left corner and 1 inch down on the left side and remove and discard this small rectangle (see illustration, page 273). Repeat the process to remove a small rectangle from the top right corner. To make the shoulders of the jar, use a small knife to round the cut corners from the neck to the sides of the cake. Round the bottom corners slightly. Trim ½ inch from the edge of the shoulders, sides, corners, and bottom of the cake, excluding the neck, to round them.

9 Line a cookie sheet with wax paper. Place the cake on a cardboard cut to fit (see Getting on Base, page 14), then place it on the cookie sheet. Transfer the cake to the freezer for 30 minutes to chill.

10 Tint ¼ cup of the vanilla frosting bright green with the green and yellow food coloring and spoon into a freezer-weight ziplock bag. Spoon ¼ cup of the vanilla frosting into a freezer-weight ziplock bag. Press out the excess air and seal the bags. Tint the remaining vanilla frosting pale blue with the food coloring.

11 Place the decorating sugar in a bowl. Snip a small (⅛-inch) corner from the bags with the green and vanilla frostings. Spread the pale blue frosting over the chilled cake and smooth. For the stems in the jar, pipe 8 lines of green frosting of varying lengths on top of the cake, from the neck angled toward the bottom. Gently press handfuls of the sugar into the frosting, flattening the green lines and smoothing the frosting (see Smashed Sugar, page 37). Brush any excess sugar from the top of the cake.

12 Pipe 4 or 5 horizontal lines of vanilla frosting across the top "lid" area of the cake. Pipe the word BALL in script at an angle across the cake. Sprinkle the decorating sugar over the vanilla frosting, pressing lightly, letting the lines remain raised. Brush any excess sugar from the top of the cake and transfer the cake on the cardboard to a serving platter.

13 Cut the 10 sour-straw stems into different lengths. Carefully remove 1 of the assembled flowers from the cookie sheet. Insert the spaghetti end of 1 stem into the side of the marshmallow. Press the stem end of the flower into the jar open-

ing at the top of the cake (the flower will be horizontal with respect to the serving platter). Repeat with the remaining flowers and stems, overlapping the flowers and arranging them at different heights (1 or 2 of the flowers can also be placed around the platter as decoration, if desired). Arrange the sour-belt leaves among the flowers.

TAXI CAKE

MAKES 16 SERVINGS

Where's a cab when you need it? Make your own with sparkly paint created with sugar and a classic checkerboard design crafted from spice drops.

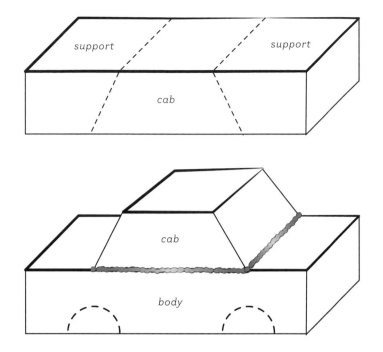

2 family-size (16 ounces each) frozen all-butter pound cakes (Sara Lee), thawed
1 can (16 ounces) vanilla frosting
Yellow food coloring (McCormick)
¼ cup dark chocolate frosting
¼ cup granulated sugar
15 white and 5 black or purple spice drops
3 tablespoons black decorating sugar (Wilton)
1 orange spice drop
12 chocolate-covered wafer bars (Kit Kat)
8 red, 1 yellow, and 2 orange small candy-coated chocolates (M&M's Minis)
1 stick white gum (Extra)
4 mini (2½-inch) chocolate-covered doughnuts
6 white mints (Mentos)
1 cup chocolate cookie crumbs (Oreos)
2 tablespoons light corn syrup
1 cup yellow decorating sugar (Cake Mate)

1 Spoon ¼ cup of the vanilla frosting into a freezer-weight ziplock bag. Tint the remaining vanilla frosting bright yellow with the food coloring. Spoon ¼ cup of the yellow frosting into a freezer-weight ziplock bag. Spoon the dark chocolate frosting into a freezer-weight ziplock bag. Press out the excess air and seal the bags.

2 Line a cookie sheet with wax paper. Place 1 pound cake on a work surface, bottom side down. Measure 3 inches in from one short end of the cake and use toothpicks to mark the top of the cake at the edge on both sides. Repeat to mark the top on both sides of the cake 3 inches in from

the other short end. Measure 2 inches in from one short end along the bottom edge on each side and mark with a toothpick. Repeat to mark the bottom edge on both sides 2 inches in from the other short end. Working on one end at a time, score a diagonal line between the top mark and the bottom-edge mark on both sides. Using a long serrated knife held at an angle, follow the scored lines to cut the cake on a diagonal (see illustration, above top). Cut each end piece into two 2-inch-square pieces, about 1½ inches thick, and reserve to use as the supports under the taxi. Reserve the middle section for the top of the cab.

3 For the taxi body, place the remaining pound cake on a work surface on one of its long sides so that the bottom is facing you. Use a 2½-inch round cookie cutter or a small knife to cut out a 2½-inch wheel well, starting 1 inch in from one short end and ½ inch down from the top of the cake. Make the cut about ¾ inch deep and remove and discard the cake (see illustration, page 276). Repeat to make 2 wheel wells on each long side of

the cake. Place the taxi body, bottom side down, on a cardboard cut to fit (see Getting on Base, page 14). Spread some yellow frosting on top of the cake and attach the reserved cake piece to the center, bottom side down (see illustration, page 276). Transfer the assembled cake and the 4 cake supports on the cookie sheet to the freezer for 30 minutes to chill.

4 Line a cookie sheet with wax paper. As you make the parts, transfer them to the cookie sheet. Sprinkle a work surface with some of the granulated sugar. Press the white spice drops together and place on the work surface. Sprinkle with additional granulated sugar and roll out to a 5-x-8-inch rectangle, about ⅛ inch thick, sprinkling with more granulated sugar, as necessary, to prevent sticking. For the front and back windows, cut out two 1½-x-4-inch rectangles. Cut out two 1½-x-5-inch rectangles and set 1 piece aside. Cut the remaining rectangle in half crosswise to make two 1½-x-2½-inch pieces. For the driver's window, start ½ inch in from the corner of one short end of 1 of the 1½-x-2½-inch pieces and cut on the diagonal to the corner on the same end to remove and discard a small triangular piece. Cut the remaining 1½-x-2½-inch piece in half crosswise and reserve one of the pieces for the rear side window. Cut the remaining

STEP 4

pieces in half on the diagonal; reserve 1 piece for the rear vent window and discard the other piece. Repeat the process with the reserved 1½-x-5-inch rectangle to make the windows for the other side. Sprinkle a work surface with some of the black decorating sugar. Press the black spice drops together and place on the work surface. Sprinkle with additional black sugar and roll out to a 2-x-5-inch rectangle, about ⅛ inch thick, sprinkling with more black sugar, as necessary, to prevent sticking. Cut the rolled black spice drops and the remaining rolled white spice drops into ¼-inch-wide strips. Cut the strips crosswise into ¼-inch pieces to make 40 white squares and 40 black squares (take care not get sugar on the cut edges; they need to be sticky for assembly). Make a checkerboard band by pressing the sticky edges of 20 squares together, side by side, alternating black and white. Repeat to make 4 bands total, starting 2 bands with a white square and 2 bands with a black square. Attach 2 bands, one above the other, horizontally, with white squares above black squares, to make a double band. Repeat to make a second double band. Cut two ¼-x-½-inch pieces from the remaining rolled black candy for the door handles and two ¼-x-1-inch strips for the wipers, tapering them at one end. For the license plate, roll out the orange spice drop in some granulated sugar to a ½-x-1-inch rectangle. Trim the edges to straighten.

5 For the off-duty light, cut each of 2 chocolate-coated wafer bars into a 2-inch length. Snip a very small (1/16-inch) corner from the bags with the dark chocolate and vanilla frostings. Pipe some dark chocolate frosting on the top of 1 trimmed wafer. Place the other trimmed wafer, top side down, on top. Pipe the word TAXI on top with the vanilla frosting. Pipe a dot of vanilla frosting at each end of the assembly and attach a small red candy. For the grille, use a small knife to round the corners of one long side of the stick of gum and pipe ¼-inch vertical lines of dark chocolate frosting on one flat side. Using the dark chocolate frosting, pipe the letters NYC on the orange spice-drop license plate. For the hubcaps, place each doughnut on its side, smooth side up, and pipe some vanilla frosting in the hole. Insert a white mint into each opening, pressing to secure.

6 Mix the chocolate cookie crumbs and the corn syrup in a bowl until sticky. For the pavement, press the cookie crumbs on a serving platter and smooth. For the curb, arrange 4 of the wafer bars, end to end, on each side of the crumbs.

7 Line a cookie sheet with wax paper. Place 2 of the 4 chilled cake supports, about 1 inch apart, on the cookie-crumb pavement near one end of the serving platter. Place the remaining 2 supports, about 1 inch apart, near the other end of the serving platter, about 5 inches from the first two. Spread some yellow frosting on top of the cake supports. Place the yellow sugar in a large bowl. Place the chilled cake on the cookie sheet. Spread the remaining yellow frosting on the cake and smooth. Gently press the yellow sugar into the frosting to cover (see Smashed Sugar, page 37). Remove any excess sugar with a pastry brush. Transfer the cake on the cardboard to the frosted cake supports on the platter, adjusting the supports, as needed. Pipe some dark chocolate frosting into the opening of the wheel wells and insert the doughnut wheels, hubcaps facing out.

8 Snip a small (⅛-inch) corner from the bag with the yellow frosting. For the headlights, pipe a dot of yellow frosting on each side at one end of the cake, near the top edge, and attach the remaining 2 white mints. Pipe some yellow frosting on the back of the gum-strip grille and attach it below the headlights, rounded corners at the top. For the front bumper, pipe some yellow frosting on the bottom of

a chocolate-covered wafer bar and attach it along the lower edge of the grille. For the signal and parking lights, attach a small red candy to the right and to the left of the grille with a dot of yellow frosting and attach a small orange candy directly below the red candy on each side. For the hood ornament, press the small yellow candy, edgewise, into the frosting near the top front edge of the cake. For the back bumper, pipe some yellow frosting on the bottom of the remaining chocolate-covered wafer bar and attach it to the bottom edge at the back of the cake. Use a dot of yellow frosting to attach the orange license plate above the back bumper. For the signal and brake lights, attach 2 small red candies, one above the other, on each side at the back of the cake. Pipe some vanilla frosting on the back of the white spice-drop windows. Press the large front and back windows onto the cake. To each side, attach a driver's window, with the angled side to the front, a rear side window, and a rear vent window, with the angled side to the back. Pipe a line of yellow frosting around each window. Add the wipers to the front window. Using vanilla frosting to secure, attach a checkerboard double band to each side of the cake, centering it above the wheels. Add a black door handle on each side. Place the off-duty light, crosswise, on top of the cake.

TEST TUBE CAKE
Surprise Inside!
MAKES 24 SERVINGS

A Halloween experiment from the Candy Lab! Mix thirteen parts Twinkie, six parts candy, and two parts ice cream with one part fun.

Vegetable cooking spray
1 family-size (16 ounce) frozen all-butter pound cake (Sara Lee), thawed
3 quarts cherry chocolate ice cream, softened
13 vanilla creme-filled snack cakes (Twinkies)
1 bag (12 ounces) neon green candy melting wafers (Wilton)
1 tablespoon vegetable shortening
1 tablespoon white nonpareils (Wilton)
1 cup white candy melting wafers (Wilton)
1 cup vanilla frosting
Red food coloring
1 can (16 ounces) dark chocolate frosting
17 spice drops, mixed colors
17 large white gumballs (SweetWorks)
¾ cup each light green plain and light green pearlized round candy-coated chocolates (Sixlets)
½ cup light green pearlized small candies (Celebrations)
½ cup light green pearlized gumballs (SweetWorks)
17 small brown candy-coated chocolates (M&M's Minis)

1 Line the bottom of a 9-inch springform pan with wax paper and spray with vegetable cooking spray. Cut the pound cakes crosswise into ⅓-inch-thick slices (about 25 slices). Arrange 11 slices side by side, vertically, against the side of the prepared pan to line it. Line the bottom of the prepared pan with 6 of the cake slices, trimming to fit (see photo, next page). Set aside 6 slices of pound cake for the top of the cake. Cut the remaining slices into small cubes.

2 Spoon half of the softened ice cream into the bottom of the cake-lined pan and smooth. Press the cake cubes into the ice cream and top with the remaining softened ice cream. Smooth the top. Arrange the 6 reserved cake slices on top, trimming to fit, to cover the ice cream. Press down on top of the cake to flatten. Cover with plastic wrap and freeze until firm, at least 3 hours (see photos, this page).

3 Line a cookie sheet with wax paper. Spray a wire rack with vegetable cooking spray and place on top of the lined cookie sheet. Place a snack cake bottom side down on a work surface. Cut a ¾-inch piece crosswise from one short end and discard (see photo, above). Transfer to the wire rack. Repeat with the remaining snack cakes. Transfer the cookie sheet to the freezer to chill, about 30 minutes.

4 Place the green candy melting wafers in a microwave-safe bowl with the vegetable shortening. Microwave, stirring every 10 seconds, until smooth. Spoon the melted candy over the tops of the chilled snack cakes to cover completely, allowing the excess candy to drip onto the wax paper. Sprinkle each snack cake with some of the white nonpareils while the green candy is still wet to look like fizz (see photo, above). Refrigerate the coated snack cakes until set, about 5 minutes. Gently remove the snack cakes from the wire rack, trimming any excess candy drips from the edges.

5 Place the white candy melting wafers in a small microwave-safe bowl. Microwave, stirring every 5 seconds, until smooth. Dip the trimmed end of a coated snack cake ½ inch into the white candy melts to create the lip of the test tube. Allow the excess candy to drip back into the bowl. Return the snack cake to the cookie sheet. Repeat with the remaining snack cakes (see photo, above).

6 Tint 3 tablespoons of the vanilla frosting red with the food coloring. Spoon the red frosting into a freezer-weight ziplock bag. Spoon the remaining vanilla frosting into a freezer-weight ziplock bag. Spoon 2 tablespoons of the chocolate frosting into a freezer-weight ziplock bag. Press out the excess air and seal the bags.

7 For the eyes, cut a ¾-inch slice from the flat end of each spice drop, discarding the round end. Press a large white gumball into the sticky side of each slice to attach (see photo, above).

8 Unmold the frozen cake by running a thin knife around the outside edge of the cake and then inverting the pan. Transfer the cake to a serving platter. Working quickly, spread the remaining dark chocolate frosting all over the cake and smooth. Attach the coated snack cakes, white end up and flat edge against the cake, evenly spaced all around the side of the cake, pressing into the

frosting to secure. Return the cake to the freezer until ready to serve.

9 When ready to serve, snip a small (⅛-inch) corner from the bags with the white, red, and dark chocolate frostings. Pipe some of the vanilla frosting on top of the snack cake test tubes, adding some frosting down the sides of the snack cakes to look like overflow. Press some of the green candy-coated chocolates in both colors, the small candy pearls, and the green gumballs into the frosting on top of the test tubes to look like bubbles. Press a few small candy pearls into the drips of frosting on the sides of the test tubes. Sprinkle the remaining green gumballs, candy-coated chocolates, and small candy pearls on top of the cake to cover. Arrange the white gumball eyes, facing the spice drops in different directions, on top of the candy bubbles. Pipe thin lines of red frosting to look like blood vessels on the white gumballs. Pipe a dot of dark chocolate frosting on the spice drops and add the brown candies as the pupils.

tools and basic recipes

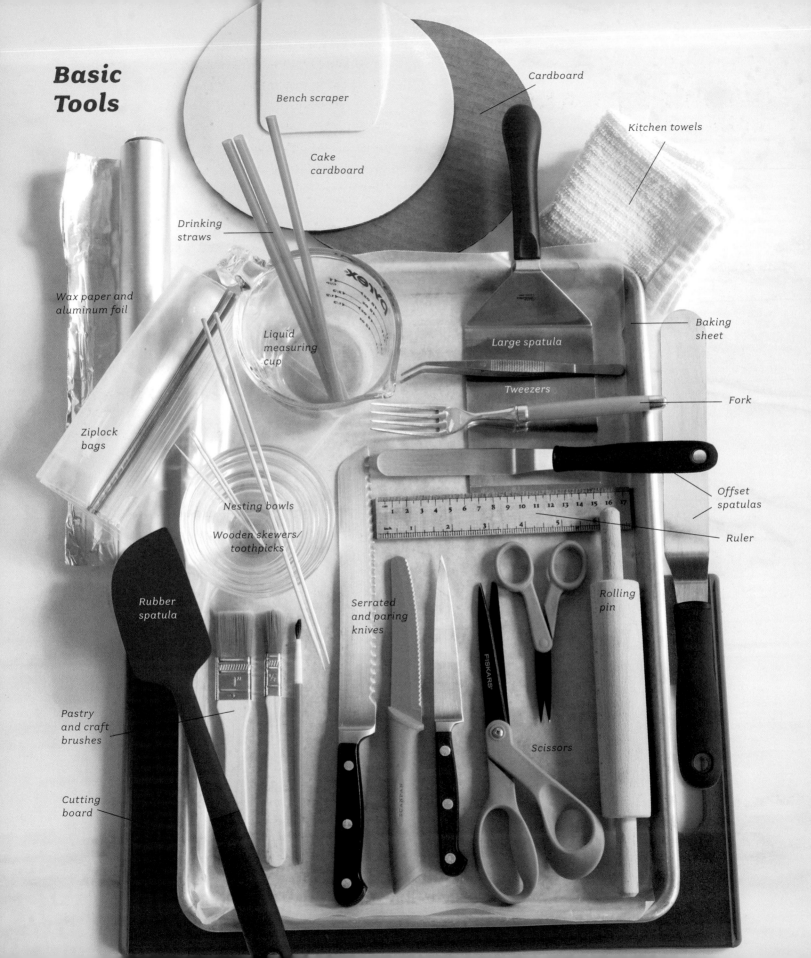

Basic Tools

Bench scraper

Cardboard

Cake cardboard

Kitchen towels

Drinking straws

Wax paper and aluminum foil

Liquid measuring cup

Large spatula

Baking sheet

Tweezers

Ziplock bags

Fork

Nesting bowls

Offset spatulas

Wooden skewers/toothpicks

Ruler

Rubber spatula

Serrated and paring knives

Rolling pin

Pastry and craft brushes

Scissors

Cutting board

Basic Recipes
PERFECT CAKE MIX
MAKES 12 SERVINGS

For projects in this book, you will be stacking cakes on top of cakes, cutting them into shapes, and covering them with frosting and candy. The addition of buttermilk to our Perfect Cake Mix cake creates a firm cake that is the best base for decorating. If you don't have buttermilk on hand, you can make it by adding 1 tablespoon lemon juice to 1 cup whole milk and let stand for 10 minutes to sour.

1 box (16.5 ounces) cake mix, such as yellow, French vanilla, devil's food, red velvet, spice, strawberry, or banana

3 large eggs (or the number of eggs called for on the box)

1 cup buttermilk (in place of the water called for on the box)

⅓ cup vegetable oil (or the amount called for on the box)

1 Preheat the oven to 350°F. Line the bottom of the pans with wax paper cut to fit and spray with vegetable cooking spray (bowls will not be paper lined). (See Please Release Me, page 12.)

2 Following the box's instructions, combine the cake mix, eggs, buttermilk, and oil in a large bowl. Beat with an electric mixer on low speed until moistened, about 30 seconds. Increase the mixer speed to medium-high and beat, scraping down the sides, until thick, 2 minutes longer (it makes about 5 cups batter).

3 Stop at this point for projects calling for Perfect Cake Mix batter and follow the instructions in the project. Otherwise, continue with the next step.

4 Divide the batter between the pans called for in the recipe, spread the batter to the edges, and smooth the tops. (See Even It Out, page 12.) Follow the indicated baking times. Bake until golden brown and a toothpick inserted in the center comes out clean. (See Let's Get Baked, page 13.)

5 Transfer the cakes to a wire rack and cool for 10 minutes. Invert, remove the pan(s) or bowl(s), and cool completely.

6 Cakes that are not used immediately may be wrapped in plastic wrap and frozen for up to 2 weeks.

PERFECT POUND CAKE MIX

MAKES 8 SERVINGS

1 box (16 ounces) pound cake mix
⅔ cup milk
4 tablespoons (½ stick) unsalted butter, softened
2 large eggs

1 Preheat the oven to 350°F. Line the bottom of a 9-x-5-inch loaf pan with wax paper, leaving the paper extending beyond the edge of the pan, and spray with vegetable cooking spray. (See Please Release Me, page 12.)

2 Following the box's instructions, combine the cake mix, milk, butter, and eggs in a large bowl. Beat with an electric mixer on low speed until moistened, about 30 seconds. Increase the mixer speed to medium-high and beat, scraping down the sides, until thick, 2 minutes longer.

3 Spread the batter to the edges of the pan and smooth the top. (See Even It Out, page 12.) Bake until golden brown and a toothpick inserted in the center comes out clean, 50 to 60 minutes. (See Let's Get Baked, page 13.)

4 Transfer the cake to a wire rack and cool for 10 minutes. Invert, remove the pan, and cool completely.

VARIATIONS

PINEAPPLE: Prepare the batter and add ¾ cup drained crushed pineapple. Spoon into the prepared pan and bake for 50 to 60 minutes.

VACUUM CLEANER: Prepare the batter and add 1 cup colored cereal O's (Froot Loops) and 1 cup chopped creme-filled chocolate sandwich cookies (Oreos). Spoon into the prepared pan and bake for 50 to 60 minutes.

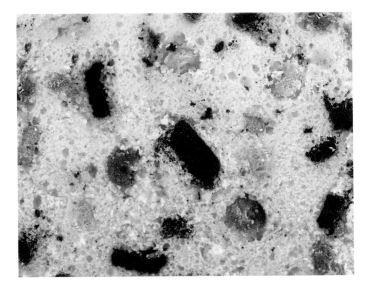

ALMOST-HOMEMADE VANILLA BUTTERCREAM

MAKES ABOUT 3½ CUPS

Starting with Marshmallow Fluff makes it easy to create a silky smooth frosting similar to French buttercream.

3 sticks (¾ pound) unsalted butter, softened and cut into 1-inch pieces
1 container (16 ounces) marshmallow creme (Marshmallow Fluff)
½ cup confectioners' sugar, plus more if desired
1 teaspoon vanilla extract
Food coloring (optional)

1 In a large bowl, beat the butter with an electric mixer on medium speed until light and fluffy. Add the marshmallow creme and beat until smooth, scraping down the sides of the bowl. Add the confectioners' sugar and vanilla extract and beat until light and fluffy. If the mixture seems too stiff, soften in the microwave for no more than 10 seconds and beat again until smooth.

2 Taste and add up to 1 cup more confectioners' sugar, if desired, for sweetness (the frosting maybe be tinted at this time).

ALMOST-HOMEMADE COCOA BUTTERCREAM

MAKES ABOUT 3½ CUPS

1 recipe Almost-Homemade Vanilla Buttercream (opposite)
3 tablespoons unsweetened cocoa powder

Follow the directions for the vanilla buttercream, adding the cocoa powder with the confectioners' sugar and leaving out the food coloring. Beat well to combine.

COOKED FROSTING

MAKES ABOUT 8 CUPS

2 cups sugar
⅓ cup light corn syrup
1 cup water
¼ cup egg white powder (Just Whites)
2 teaspoons vanilla extract

1 Combine the sugar, corn syrup, and ½ cup of the water in a medium saucepan. Bring the mixture to a boil, stirring frequently, until the sugar is dissolved.

2 In a large bowl, beat the egg white powder and the remaining ½ cup water with an electric mixer on low speed until foamy. Increase the speed to high and beat until the mixture forms soft peaks. Continue beating and gradually add the hot syrup and the vanilla extract. Beat until the mixture becomes thick and glossy, about 5 minutes.

3 The frosting should be used immediately once it is made.

CANDY CLAY

1 bag (12–14 ounces) candy melting wafers, any
   color (Wilton)
⅓ cup light corn syrup
Food coloring (optional)
Confectioners' sugar or cornstarch for rolling

1 Place the candy melts in a medium glass bowl.
Microwave on high, stopping to stir every 20
seconds, until the candy is melted and smooth,
about 1 minute (it is important not to overheat).

2 Add the corn syrup and stir with a rubber
spatula until well combined. The mixture will
look grainy. Spoon the mixture onto a sheet of
plastic wrap and cover tightly. Let the candy clay
stand at room temperature for at least 3 hours
to firm up. (The candy clay can be made up to
1 week in advance and stored, covered, at room
temperature.)

3 When ready to use, knead the clay until
smooth. (If the candy clay was made several
days in advance and is too firm, microwave the
clay for 5 to 10 seconds to soften.)

4 Tint white candy clay with the food coloring,
if desired, kneading the clay well to blend the
color. Divide the candy clay into smaller pieces.
Roll out each piece between sheets of wax paper
lightly dusted with confectioners's or cornstarch,
to a ⅛-inch or thinner thickness. Cut the clay into
the desired shapes with a cookie cutter, small
knife, or scissors. To make shapes, work the candy
clay like modeling clay. Place the shapes on a wax-
paper-lined cookie sheet and cover with plastic
wrap to prevent drying. Follow the directions for
use of candy clay in each recipe.

Baking in Glass

Vessels such as glass, stoneware, and ceramic expand the possibilities for creating cake shapes, but you should be sure they are oven-safe before using them. Read and follow the manufacturers' instructions carefully. For best results, we also recommend that you follow these steps.

• Coat the vessel with vegetable cooking spray before adding the batter.

• Place the vessel on a baking sheet before it goes into the oven. This will not only catch any spillovers and make it easier to handle small vessels but also even out the heat under the vessel.

• When removing the vessel from the oven, leave it on the baking sheet and transfer it to a cooling rack. Do not place it directly on the counter, the stovetop, or on a wet surface or cloth because sudden changes in temperature can cause the vessel to crack.

• After it has cooled for at least 10 minutes, remove the cake from the vessel and place it on the rack to continue cooling.

• If a vessel shows signs of wear or cracks, do not bake in it. Small fractures can get bigger with further use. Now is the time to go buy that new one you've been coveting.

Cakes baked in different shapes make decorating more fun.

© Jorge Madrigal

sources

baking supplies

Beryl Loveland
www.beryls.com
5520 Hempstead Way
Springfield, VA 22151
(703) 256-6951
(800) 488-2749
A wide variety of decorating supplies, as well as classes and an informative cake decorating blog.

Cake Mate
www.cakemate.com
A complete list of sugar and sprinkles available at your local grocery store, as well as creative decorating ideas.

Confectionery House
www.confectioneryhouse.com
(518) 279-4250
A wide variety of candy melting wafers, sprinkles, food coloring, and luster dust for decorating.

Costco
www.costco.com
A great source for food-storage containers, and bakeware and cookware, especially heavy duty half- and full-sheet cookie sheets that are useful for cake decorating.

Country Kitchen Sweetart
www.countrykitchensa.com
4621 Speedway Drive
Fort Wayne, IN 46825
(260) 482-4835
(800) 497-3927
Sanding and coarse sugars. A wide variety of candy decors, sprinkles, luster dust, candy melting wafers, food coloring, and paper liners.

Downtown Dough
www.downtowndough.com
W63 N658 Washington Avenue
Cedarburg, WI 53012
(262) 387-0311
A great source for cookie cutters: gingerbread boys and girls, sun, snowflakes, circles, plus a large selection of sprinkles and decorations.

Duncan Hines
www.duncanhines.com
A complete list of cake mixes and frostings available at your local grocery store, as well as creative decorating ideas (including a page from us) and tips for baking.

Fancy Flours
www.fancyflours.com
Beautiful and elegant cupcake supplies, from paper liners to specialty sugars, sprinkles, and decorations.

India Tree Gourmet Spices & Specialties
www.indiatree.com
1435 Elliott Avenue West
Seattle, WA 98119
(206) 286-9988
(800) 596-0885
Beautiful coarse sugars and decorating sugars. India Tree products are also available in some grocery stores.

Kitchen Krafts
www.kitchenkrafts.com
P.O. Box 442
Waukon, IA 52172
(563) 535-8000
(800) 298-5389
A wide variety of decorating supplies.

McCormick
www.mccormick.com
A great source for large-size food coloring and hard-to-find colors like

neons and black and a selection of seasonal decorating ideas. The color wheel on the food-color section of the site makes it easy to create custom colors.

N.Y. Cake and Baking Supplies
www.newyorkcake.com
56 West 22nd Street
New York, NY 10010
(212) 675-2253
(800) 942-2539

Reynolds
www.reynoldskitchens.com
The latest seasonal paper and foil liner selections, as well as foil baking trays.

Sugarcraft
www.sugarcraft.com
3665 Dixie Highway
Hamilton, OH 45015
(513) 896-7089
A wide variety of baking and decorating supplies.

Sur la Table
www.surlatable.com
(800) 243-0852
Crinkle cutters, pastry wheels, bakeware, tiered cake stands. Schedules of decorating classes at stores.

Williams-Sonoma
www.williams-sonoma.com
Cake plates, mini pie plates, platters, sprinkles, and other baking equipment.

Wilton Industries
www.wilton.com
2240 West 75th Street
Woodridge, IL 60517
(630) 963-1818
(800) 794-5866
A wide variety of baking supplies, including candy melting wafers, food coloring, paper liners, assorted sprinkles

and sugars, white candy pearls, and much more. Wilton products are also available in many craft and party stores and some grocery stores.

party and craft supplies

A.C. Moore
www.acmoore.com
Marvy paper punch, plastic eggs, cake decorating supplies and crafts, as well as books. Store locations are listed online.

Beadalon
www.beadalon.com
Offset tweezers. A great source for sorting trays and crafting mats.

Fiskars
www.fiskars.com
Small, regular, and craft scissors, creative craft ideas, seminars, and products.

Michael's Stores
www.michaels.com
(800) 642-4235
Marvy paper punch, plastic eggs, and a wide variety of craft supplies and cake decorating supplies, including Wilton products.

Party City
www.partycity.com
A large variety of colored plastic forks, paper napkins, and plates. Color-coordinated candies in bulk, including foil-covered chocolate coins.

other craft supplies

Hefty
www.hefty.com
Product information on food storage bags as well as promotions and coupons.

OXO
www.oxo.com
(800) 545-4411
Storage containers for sorting candies, spatulas, measuring tools, and mixing bowls in ergonomic designs.

Ziploc
www.ziploc.com
Product information, as well as coupons for Ziploc products.

gourmet candy supplies

Balboa Candy
www.balboacandy.com
301-J Marine Street
Newport Beach, CA 92662
(949) 723-6099
A great candy selection, specializing in retro candies and taffy.

Bulk Candy
www.bulkcandystore.com
(561) 540-1600
Features a wide variety of candy, specializing in candy buffets, kosher candy, and nostalgic candy.

Candyality
www.candyality.com
(312) 527-1010
An outstanding selection of candy, including a tasty licorice brand and an online Candyscope to identify your candy personality.

Candy.com
www.candy.com
(781) 335-2200
A large selection of candies, specializing in favorites of the past.

Candy Warehouse
www.candywarehouse.com
(310) 343-4099
A wide selection of candies categorized to make it easy to shop for candy buffets, colors, flavors and occasions.

Dylan's Candy Bar
www.dylanscandybar.com
1011 Third Avenue
New York, NY 10021
(866) 939-5267
A wide variety of candies, including seasonal offerings.

Economy Candy
www.economycandy.com
108 Rivington Street
New York, NY 10002
(800) 352-4544
A good source for old-fashioned and bulk candies, such as black licorice laces.

Jelly Belly Candy Company
www.jellybelly.com
One Jelly Belly Lane
Fairfield, CA 94533
(800) 522-3267
The largest selection available of gourmet jelly beans, including bulk sizes of individual flavors. The website offers creative decorating ideas.

Old Time Candy Company
www.oldtimecandy.com
(866) 929-5477
An interesting selection of nostalgic and novelty candies; large or small quantities can be purchased.

SweetWorks
www.sweetworks.net
Small decorative candies like Sixlets, Pearls, and Baby Tears. Specializing in fashion-forward colors and shimmer coatings.

index

A

Angora Ombré Cake, *20*, 21
animal motifs:
    Armadillo Cake, *158–59*, 158–61
    Barnyard Master Cake, 52–53
    Bunny Hill Cake, *162*, 163–65, *165*
    Cow Cake, 53, *56*, 57
    Goat Cake, *51*, 53, 58, *59*
    Hippo Cake, *212*, 213–15
    Monkey Cake, 224–27, *225*
    Pat the Poodle Cake, *196*, 197–99
    Pig Cake, 53, *60*, 61
    Piñata Cake, 183, 184–87, *185*
    Reindeer Cake, 183, *188*, 189–91
    Rux the Wonder Dog Cake, *206*, 207–10, *211*
    Sea Turtle Cake, *170–71*, 170–73
    Sheep Cake, 52, 54, *55*
    Siamese Cat Cake, 200–204, *201*, *205*
    Stablemates Master Cake, 182–83
    Teddy Cake, *141*, 143–44, *145*
    24-Carrot Bunny Cake, 154–57, *155*
    Zebra Cake, *181*, 183, 192–95, *193*
    see also bird motifs; insect motifs
appliance and tool motifs:
    Little Clipper Lawn Mower Cake, 118–21, *119*
    Toaster Cake, *110*, 111–12, *113*
    Vacuum Cleaner Cake, *132–33*, 133–35, 290
Argyle Cake, 24–26, *25*, 27
Armadillo Cake, *158–59*, 158–61
assembly techniques, 15

B

baking cakes:
    in glass vessels, safety concerns and, 293
    tips for, 13
baking pans:
    evening out batter in, 12
    prepping, 12
baking supplies, sources for, 294–95

Barnyard Master Cake, 52–53
bases for cakes, 14
basic recipes:
    Cake Mix, Perfect, 289
    Cocoa Buttercream, Almost-Homemade, 291
    Cooked Frosting, 291
    Pound Cake Mix, Perfect, 290
    Vanilla Buttercream, Almost-Homemade, 291
batter:
    adding candy and snacks to, 49
    dolloping, 48
    layering, 48
    piping designs into, 48–49
    tinting, 49
Batter Up! Cake, 268–71, *269*
Bedazzled Christmas Tree Cake, 234–37, *235*, *236*
bird motifs:
    Hooty and the Pound Cakes, 262–64, *263*
    Rooster Cake, 53, 62–63, *63*
Boot Master Cake, 240–41
bowl cakes, 140–79
    Armadillo Cake, *158–59*, 158–61
    Bunny Hill Cake, *162*, 163–65, *165*
    Ladybug Cake, 166–69, *167*, *168*
    Ornament Cake, *174*, 175–76
    Plush Toy Master Cake, 142

T

U

V

W

Z

Bye-bye!
So long!
Cheers!
Toodle-oo!
Later!

Can't bear to go? Then follow Alan and Karen
at hellocupcakebook.com for more decorating fun!

© JORGE MADRIGAL

Karen Tack and Alan Richardson are the authors of the best-selling *Hello, Cupcake!*, *What's New Cupcake?*, and *Cupcakes, Cookies & Pie, Oh, My!*, which have revolutionized cupcake making. www.hellocupcakebook.com

Called the "Cake Whisperer" by *Gourmet* magazine, **Karen Tack** is a cooking teacher and one of the top food stylists in the nation. She has created cupcakes and other desserts for the covers of many of America's top magazines, including *Bon Appetit, Cook's Illustrated, Real Simple, Martha Stewart Living, Good Housekeeping, Ladies' Home Journal, Family Circle, Woman's Day, Every Day with Rachael Ray, Parents, Family Fun, Taste of Home, Parade,* and many more. Karen lives with her family in Connecticut.

Alan Richardson is the coauthor of *The Four Seasons of Italian Cooking* and *The Breath of a Wok*, which won the Best International Cookbook Award and the Jane Grigson Award from the International Association of Culinary Professionals (IACP). His work has appeared in dozens of best-selling cookbooks and leading magazines, including *Esquire, GQ, Newsweek,* the *New York Times Magazine, Food & Wine, Saveur,* and *Washington Post Magazine.* Alan lives with his family in New York.

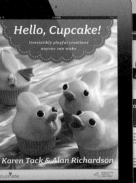

See some of our favorite cupcakes in action
Available at hellocupcakeapp.com